On the Light Path

A Psychic's Journey

On The Light Path,

A Psychic's Journey

by

Peter Lyons

Portland, Oregon, USA

Hervey Bay, Queensland, Australia

Copyright 2010 by Peter Lyons
All Rights Reserved
Printed in USA and Australia

ISBN 978-1-893075-55-9

Library of Congress Control Number:
2009940894

Cover Design by Ethan Firpo
Interior Art: Scott Townsend

Interior design and layout
One Spirit Press, LLC
Portland, Oregon

This book may not be reproduced in whole or in part, by electronic or any other means which exist or may yet be developed, (exceptions are for reviews)
without permission of :

One Spirit Press
Portland, Oregon 97214
OneSpiritpress@gmail.com

Publishers Note

To our American Readers:

Pete lives in Australia and uses Aussie/British English. We have chosen to leave his original spellings such as realise rather than realize, colour rather than color. If you come upon one of these differences between American and British English please enjoy the flavor offered by retaining the author's voice in his work.

Happy reading!

C. Suzanne Deakin

Publisher
One Spirit Press

Table of Contents

Introduction....ix
What Will Tomorrow Bring

Summer Rain....2
Chapter I....3
   Early Years

What Would You Know....32
Chapter II....33
   The Journey Gets Serious

Speak Truth to Me....94
Chapter III....95
   A Psychic Sessions

Yours In Embryo....148
Chapter IV....149
   Revisiting The Past

Children of God Are Butterflies....188
Chapter V....189
   Children of God

Spirit Friends....200
Chapter VI....201
   Guides and Garden Angels

I Had a Dream....216
Chapter VII....217
   Family Members as Guides

Oh God....232
Chapter VIII....233
   Appropriate Meditations

Northern Waters....246
Chapter IX....247
   Reincarnations

The Return of the Wirinum....266

Peppermint Tea....268
Chapter X....269
   The New Age

Fear Not....274
Chapter XI....275
   How To Survive This New Age

Song of Madness....290
Chapter XII....291
   Remote Viewing Experiments

It All Depends on
How You Plan Your Day....300
Chapter XIII....301
   Channeling

Eagle....310
Chapter XIV....311
   In Conclusion

Colophon....319

Acknowledgements

There are many who have helped in the making of this book, some obvious and others not so.

Mike and Sharon: It was Mike and Sharon that basically acted as my sounding board from when I first moved into Queensland. Sharon had seen me work in my early days in NSW, but Mike found it totally alien. Had it not been for our tolerance of each other, I wouldn't have had the confidence to write. Sharon wouldn't have met Mike and developed her Spirit Guide drawings and psychic readings. Mike wouldn't have become the unbelievably gifted psychic he is today. Sadly Queensland's loss had become Victoria's gain. I owe them much.

Dave and Glenda: Not long after moving to Queensland I had a woman visit at a place called Biggenden. So impressed was she with my work that she informed her friend Dave, a mechanic, who had his own business. Dave phoned me and asked if I would like to do psychic readings from his house. We have been very close friends ever since. He married his beautiful lady in October of 2008, and their home had been my parking lot off and on for most of the time I have been writing the book. They, like Mike and Sharon, are my chosen family and closest of friends.

Ian: When I first needed an editor, I went looking at our local library, but without much luck. Then I happened to bump into Ian, who was holidaying in Australia before returning to Thailand, where he teaches English. He did much work in ironing out the grammatical inconsistencies and general editing, and for this I am very grateful.

Then there are the many people who came to me for psychic readings, whose stories, some published in this work, that have given me the knowledge to build the story in the first place. Many will not know I am referring to their stories, simply because I don't wish to embarrass them or to offend them. To each and every person that contributed in some simple way, I thank you sincerely.

Introduction

What Will Tomorrow Bring

What will tomorrow bring slowdowns or sunshine?
Sky's blue a frost is due; tomorrow will be fine.

What will I find to eat the cupboard's almost bear?
Look hard and you will find
Something will be there.

Where is the love I seek, I've waited for so long?
Go out and search awhile, soon she'll be along.

It's been a long and lonely trying time I know.
But isn't that the way you knew
That it was going to be.
Patiently hold on a little longer, don't despair.
All those dreams you wanted
For so long will soon be there.

Who can I speak to when a problem's hard to share?
We'll gladly listen, speak your mind –
We're always there.

1982

From my very first days as a psychic medium, I have had difficulty explaining what makes me different from other psychics. The confusion comes because my advertising sign says Psychic Medium, and it is therefore assumed I am a Jonathan Edwards type medium. I can do that kind of psychic work but my primary function is as a-go-between the person and their guides. I need to be asked the question or query before the session begins.

Now I can hear some of you saying;

"But you're a psychic; you should have known what that person wanted." Of course if a psychic were to know everything, then why aren't psychics the richest people in the world? Surely they'd know this week's, and most weeks, lottery numbers?

Psychics are neither mind readers or have access to all information. This includes not having all the information we need on another or ourselves. I am only allowed to know what a person's guides passes on about genuine need. It is usually the guides of a person who gets them to the psychic in the first place.

Very few people know much about psychics, how they operate, or how they know that which they couldn't possibly have gained from normal sources. Luckily, my experience is that most people are willing to listen with out preconception to what a good psychic has to pass onto them. There are those that have no idea how a psychic works and don't want to know. They just want a magical answer to their problems. If they don't get that magic wand solution to their problems they expect their money back.

There are those that assume all psychics have the same understandings, systems, source and principles. They assume we psychics all have a standard understanding or code in common. This is not the case, we are all different, and a client is likely to get different answers from different psychics.

The psychic church is as diverse as the Christian one, with as many disagreements as there are agreements amongst its members, followers, and supporters. Sadly there are too many psychics who know very little of the workings of their gift, other than what they have read or of what others have told them. It would seem genuine psychics are few and far between.

The enjoyable area for me is when people ask me how they can develop their psychic skills as well as how I developed mine. Particularly questions relating to how to discern when information was coming from my guides, wayward spirits and lost souls, or my own thoughts.. For these enquirers at least I am able to explain briefly what I believe and how my guides work. I encourage those who ask to get to know their own highest guides. For those willing to accept they have guides, or at least are willing to try and interact with them, they are shown a specific meditation to do regularly. This then allows that person's guides to lead them in the right direction for their particular soul's journey.

Of course the limited time in each sessions doesn't permit me to address the different needs each individual person has in relation to their spiritual journey, nor does it allow me to pass on to the wider community this vital spiritual message.

I have always known that a wider audience of searchers was waiting for what spirit had to give. And somehow this information had to be passed on to those searchers looking for direction for their own spiritual path. The question was who could do this confidently? I certainly didn't see that confident person as being me.

I should have known spirit wouldn't just let me brush off their intentions. When I visited a psychic in the beginning of 1994, she told me my guides wanted me to write a very detailed book as a teaching aid for psychic development. As early as the mid 80's I had already started to write up some thoughts under the heading An Interesting Life and it was from this the psychic said I would start to write this new and important work for spirit.

It wasn't till after I had moved to Koumala in Queensland in 2003 that my good friends Mike and Sharon confirmed what I had been denying. Spirit wanted me to get serious and to write this book. Initially I had trouble getting started and kept blaming my procrastination on writer's block. I then decided to look at what I had written under An Interesting Life and use that as a base. The more I read it, the more I felt it had no bearing whatsoever on what was supposed to be a work of major spiritual significance.

Each Friday I would travel to Mackay in my very battered 1980 Nissan Urvan mobile home, where I would do psychic sessions at a local alternative gift shop. Then I would travel another hour and a half to a caravan park a little south of Proserpine. There I would stay overnight, before travelling onto Airlie Beach the next day to do sessions at a book shop.

One particular weekend around July, while staying at the caravan park, I had a woman ask me about what I did, as a psychic, and how she could find out more. Though I had spend almost two hours with her, I felt what she had wanted was not what I had given her. Not that I wasn't giving her plenty of information. It was the fact that she needed to have something in writing she could read. I felt frustrated because what she needed was a book, or something similar. I had not been able to find in any bookshops. I felt driven to do something, even if it was just to get a pamphlet together, to briefly explain what my spiritual beliefs were all about.

Over the next few weekends I began writing the pamphlet. I realized a lot more than a few pages of information had been written. Spirit had started me on the new book, whether I liked it or not.

I had been writing with pen and pad at this time and it was very difficult to keep up with what they (spirit) were passing on. So I started to write questions that most people asked, as the heading, and then they would write the reply. However, because the answers came faster than I could write, I had to devise a shorthand method I could decipher later on. It wasn't long before I found myself staring at my scribbled hieroglyphic shorthand, without a clue as to what it meant. I came very close to throwing the whole project aside.

I had a main computer, but that wasn't practical when on the road. I needed a laptop, but couldn't afford a new one. I had been thinking about a second hand laptop. But as I believe everything I have is owned by spirit, I felt it wrong to buy one unless I was absolutely sure it was they who wanted me to have one. Each trip up to Mackay I would ask, "Should I go and at least have a look at one," and each time I kept getting "No, not yet."

One day in September 2004, after finishing work in Mackay, my Nissan Urvan home wouldn't start. I called my road maintenance club. After looking over the electrical wiring, they said it would have to be taken back to the depot for a further inspection. I phoned to cancel my appointments at Airlie Beach for the following day and was surprised to hear there weren't any. I had been booked out the week before.

On returning to pick up the bus on Monday, they informed me they could find nothing wrong, but that there could be a loose wire or a shorting in the steering column. As they didn't do electrical work, I would have to visit an appropriate auto electrician.

I drove home slowly, keeping to the left side of the road, just in case a shorting out should stop the motor. At a certain point I got stuck behind a parked car and a heavy stream of traffic to my right, which meant I would have to wait awhile for the traffic to clear, so that I could pull out and pass the parked car.

It was then I realized I was right out front of a second hand computer shop. The traffic was getting thicker and I knew I was going to be stuck there for a while, so I decided I'd park the bus where it was and go visit the shop. I didn't bother checking with my guides; after all I wasn't going to buy anything, I would just look.

On entering the shop the owner asked what specifically the laptop would be used for. When I told him for writing, he said a particular unit had just come in. The suggested price was far less than I had expected to pay. I was certain a good bargain would be lost if it was not bought right away. I was in a quandary. Do I go home, have a quiet time with my guides, and if they approve, come back and buy the laptop, knowing in the meantime it could be sold, or buy it now? Also on my mind was the thought of how much the repairs to the bus electrical system might cost. The difficulty with making a psychic decision on the spot is what is called front end loading.

Would I get a clear signal to buy from my guides, or could I have already contaminated the answer by having strong feeling towards wanting to buy it in the first place? Could I have front end loaded their decision? I made an excuse to the owner and went out to the bus. I sat quietly for a short time meditating. After becoming deeply at one-with-them, and apologising for not having sought their guidance first. I stated that it wasn't something I was happy having to decide on and asked did they want me to leave it till another time? I assumed that if I was to have a laptop, no matter what the circumstance, they would get me one. I honestly expected them to say "leave it for now, it isn't the right time". Instead I felt a very strong message of buy, buy, buy.

What to do? Could this be me overriding what spirit wanted for me? Could I afford it? What if there is a better option waiting around the corner? My strong attitude was, if it is your decision for me to buy, I will. If it is not your decision for me to buy, please give me a sign. I returned to the shop and went through the motions. Nothing stood out to prevent me buying the laptop, so I bought it.

On returning to Koumala, I visited my psychic friends Mike and Sharon, and in a psychic circle, using the Yes-No process spirit had shown us. We asked if spirit had wanted me to make this purchase. They both got a resounding yes. I believe it was spirit who had set up the whole matter in the first place, including giving me a day off from my psychic sessions at Airlie Beach.

A footnote to this story was that when I slowly and finally got my bus home, I took a look in the steering cover that housed the starter key area and found a loose, bare wire had been earthing out intermittently when I went to start the motor. I snipped off the exposed wire, covered the end with electricians tape and the bus ran smoothly to the time I replaced it with my current Toyota Coaster mobile home.

What I offer you within the pages of this book are points of view that I hope will cause you to review, and if necessary, adjust your life so that you are on your Light Path. I hope you enjoy the work.

The Summer Rain

The summer rain is falling on the rusty iron roofed shack
And I feel it's trying to call me back

But nothings going to stop me now: I've waited far too long

For this change in circumstance
I'm just happy to be floating down river,
Watching lights shimmer,
As the leaves quiver. And
It don't matter where the streams takes me,
I'm content to be,
Floating far and free to the Ones that waits for me

And there I see them smiling in a full moon light
And I know that what I've done is right.
Their smiles invite me as they wait there at the door
I'm glad I'm in Their Golden Light.
I'm just happy to be floating down river,

Watching lights shimmer,
As the leaves quiver.
And it don't matter where the streams takes me,
I'm content to be,
Floating far and free to the Ones that wait for me

2002

Chapter I

The Early Years

It is so hard to recall all of the events that have lead me to the path I am now happily travelling. Time has erased most of the memories. There were some memorable events that intrigued my parents about me. I remember at the ripe old age of three I somehow broke out of the barricade my father and grandfather had built around our newly constructed house. Mum had gone to hospital to have her third child, John, and I decided I would look for her. Dad having looked everywhere for me and fearful something dreadful had happened to me, rode his posties (postman's) push bike to the local police station. This happened in nineteen fifty, when very few people had phones or motorcars in Australia. He arrived at the police station to find me sitting on the front desk, wearing a policeman's cap and eating an ice cream. A policeman had found me sitting in the middle of the road and crying. Thankfully there were very few cars around in those days and they moved a lot slower.

Another story that shows my friendliness with people at a young age was when I was about three or four. I used to stand at the newly constructed picket gate or stand on the railing of the picket fence and talk to passer byes. As I got older and under mum's watchful eye, I would go outside the gate, where I would help little old ladies carry their shopping bags from the fence perimeter on one side to the fence perimeter on the other.

One lovely old lady would always reward me with a boiled lolly (sweets) wrapped in cellophane; something considered a sweet of the wealthy by those of us that couldn't afford any sweets. It wasn't long before my brother Mick realised I was on a winner, and started to compete with me for this woman's rewards. The obvious fights put an end to my charitable intentions.

From a spiritual perspective, I can vaguely remember having flashback incidents when I was sitting in Mass, in my roll as a Catholic alter-boy, but can remember very little of the contents. I recall, as a boy, being awe-struck and inspired on more than one occasion, as if I had a very special calling and that I was going to fulfil some kind of special purpose. I was particularly drawn to the life of St. Tarcisius, the alter-boy's Saint. This young lad apparently carried the Sacred Sacrament from community to community in the days of Christian persecution by the Romans. At that time in my life, I was living in the aftermath of our local church's one and only proven miracle, a very public affair that still leaves me with questions I can't answer.

A child, a year or so younger than myself, had been born with some physical illness, which may have been Cerebral Palsy. She needed callipers to support herself.

At the Church, as was the tradition, a week had been held aside for devotion and prayers to the mother of Jesus in one of her many Catholic titles. I can't recall which particular one at this time, but I have a strong feeling it may have been Our Lady of Lourdes. As was the fashion in those days, a statue of Our Lady in her particular apparition, would stand on a side alter, adorned in flowers and candles. The flowers were mostly lilies that grew wild in the creek-ways behind our family

Chapter I

home. These were regularly gathered by the local faithful for various denominations.

On certain nights a Novena to Our Lady was held, which consisted of a public recital of the Rosary and the Litany of the Blessed Virgin. Also customary at these sessions, were the pilgrimages to the statue by the many sick of the parish. They would come to the priest at the side altar, who would pray over them. They would then return to their respective places to join in the rest of the Rosary and Litany. On one such night the young girl's parents brought her to the Statue. The priest, as usual, blessed her and they returned to their seat. Weeks later the rumours went through the church that the child had started to improve and that the doctors were claiming a miracle. The claims were kept within the congregation; after all, most of the doctors in our area at that time were Protestants. We couldn't have a protestant declaring a catholic miracle now could we? To the best of my knowledge Bernadette never went back to wearing callipers and went on to live a normal life.

As for my psychic development, it certainly didn't come from any family, school or friend's influence, although it was common for family members to say, at the time of the passing of an elderly relative, they could feel that person around them, or that they knew a certain deceased member of the family was looking over them. For reasons I have long since forgotten, I can remember getting into serious trouble with my father and constantly being called a liar by him. How many of the things I said that upset him were from my psychic knowledge?

I have always been a person to question all things of importance, not just those of psychic and spiritual significance. I instinctively know the other point of view or argument, even if I have not read or heard of the subject before. It comes from a natural discernment. To some I may appear as bloody-minded and strongly opinionated, but on closer observation, it shows my natural devil's advocacy. My poor mum got more than her fair share of these debating skills of mine, and dad, who hated any argument at all, would leave the room when I started a conversation with her.

The knowledge I gained from these experiences was immense. The information I was espousing was not coming from the failed school student that I knew I was. Somehow I was different, and I needed to find out what that difference was. Though unaware of it at the time, I was being directed or guided towards a particular road, a road I could easily have missed but for this tenacity.

From a very early age I can recall being a great storyteller. This got me into terrible trouble with my dad, because I would be telling my brothers stories when we were supposed to be going to sleep. I can further recall, when asked to do something, I found it hard to refuse. I would have made a perfect slave or servant. This was definitely the case with my brothers and their requests for my night-time stories. I think this was the early form of my psychic ability coming through. Even as an adult, I often go to sleep with the outlines of a story floating through my mind. I couldn't possibly have made it up from my own knowledge. So where did these stories come from?

I am not one to visualise, as a clairvoyant would, although I can recall seeing faces in the old willow that grew next door as it moved gently in the night breeze. I was frightened by certain feelings at different times in my younger life, but these are very vague memories now. It was feelings more than from seeing or hearing that my gift grew. I recall feeling very high at times when attending Mass or Benediction, and feeling very light, as if I was floating above myself.

I can remember having fearful events as well, especially when going to the movie, where I spent two thirds of my time with my fingers in my ears and my head behind the seat in front of me. It was like I was reliving a real past experience. The most vivid recall during such a movie, or pictures as we knew them back then, was a British Tarzan movie where, in the opening scenes, a person is lying in his thatched hut in Africa, and the baddie, a native person naturally, comes in and kills the person in their bed. That particular scene gave me nightmares for months afterwards and caused my parents to stop me from going to the movies for a while.

Another fearful event was when my Aunt Anne gave me an LP of the Pier Gynt Suite by Grieg. The shipwreck theme for some reason had me petrified and I eventually gave it away as a swap for a whole bunch of old 78's. Had I been aware of reincarnation, I may have had a better understanding of how to deal with this overwhelming fear. Then again, by not having that knowledge I have gained much from the experiences. A particular theme in Bambi also had a profound effect on me. The bushfire scene apparently was one of those cases where I blocked my ears and covered my eyes, so my aunties have told me. I was around five or six at the time and don't remember all that much about the movie.

To this day numerous songs by various artists have had continued effects on me, some good, some not so good. For example Len Paul and Mary Ford's multi tracked songs of the 50's, for some reason, get me emotionally high and I start crying. I can remember from a very early age, loving the sound of a harp, and later, remember being enthralled with Harpo Marx's brilliant playing. Later, I bought my most treasured instrument, an acoustic 12-string guitar, possibly the closest I'll ever get to play a harp. I also become quite emotional when I hear Irish music, especially the Irish harp and pipes.

As the reader will no doubt have ascertained, I was raised a Catholic and attended Catholic schools. In a sense I still consider myself Catholic, although I'm not sure the Church would feel the same about me. It is the theological side of the

Church, the actual spiritual base of their teachings that I find my own beliefs closest to of any of the Christian Churches. It is the human structure and fear based rules that have me in disagreement with them. Too much importance is placed on ceremony, such as the Mass, the clergy's holiness and of course the power of the Pope; none of which were a part of the originally church.

I can always remember feeling that I would have no need to worry about failing at school; because I was convinced I would be a priest. Of all the subjects I failed at school, religious education was the exception. I would get over 60% repeatedly, often the highest marks in the class.

I was always drawn to Christian matters of a Spiritual nature, especially the lives of the Saints and was particularly drawn to John Boscoe and Dominic Saveo, two Saints associated with children. Later, I was drawn to the Benedictine Order, and in fact took its founder's name, Benedict, as my confirmation name. I also became interested in the Columban fathers after a Columban student, an older brother of a boy in our class, visited our school.

There was one very distinct memory of a bizarre nature I can recall occurring when I was about 13. My aunty Claire and I used to go to confession every Saturday afternoon. We would walk the mile or so from my Nursery Street home up the lane way to Pretoria Parade, over the rail bridge where I would love waiting for the steam trains to go thundering underneath. Then onto the stone mason's fence at the corner of Pretoria Parade and the Pacific Highway, where I would run on top of its raised surface. From there we would pass Barker College Boys School on the Pacific Highway. Past the St. James woollen mills that burnt down under suspicious circumstances a few years later; past the Blue Gum hotel, where the horse trough remained until well into the seventies.

Chapter I

Then we went onto the Waitara Catholic Church that was then on the Pacific Highway. This particular day, for reasons I can't remember, and a subject I wish I had forgotten, I dressed myself with whatever was at hand, as closely as possible to resemble Superman under my ordinary clothes. As soon as we got over the bridge and close to the stone mason's wall, I whipped off my outer clothes to expose my semi naked body, red undies and yellow T-shirt. I ran along the wall calling out "up, up, and away". My Aunt was horrified. I coped a thrashing and a half from my father for that outburst. Though I felt I had unduly humiliated myself, I knew there was something significantly special about my strange actions that day, but I didn't have a clue then as to what that significance was.

In another instance, while watching the Walt Disney cartoon Lambert the Sheepish Lion, I can recall feeling like that was my life story. I was somehow in the wrong environment.

It wasn't till much later in my life that spirit told me this was a subconscious awareness of who I was going to be. Not an X-ray visioned, flying super hero, or a cowardly lion becoming the superior protector, but a very special teacher in the making. However, before I could be that teacher, I needed to get my ego in check. This meant I needed to sustain humility and learn to ride both the good and bad tides to fully appreciate God's sense of purpose for me.

The first seriously unsettling event in my life was when, at fourteen years and ten months, my doctor told my parents it was in my best interest, health wise, that I leave school. The shock came with the realisation that I didn't have the education to be the priest I was convinced I was going to be. At that time in 1961/62 the unemployment level in Australia was quite high, and it was obvious I would be lucky to get any kind of a job. It must be remembered that at that time there were no unemployment benefits for youth who left school at that age, even with a medical certificate.

On the Light Path Peter Lyons

I can recall my mum taking me to a Vocational Guidance interview to be told the best available jobs for me were to learn French polishing, where I would have to finish schooling to current Year 10 level, warehouse gofer or road labourer. My health stopped me getting the latter job and my education the former. My aunty got me a job sorting holy medals in the warehouse of the company she worked for. Thinking back, it was no doubt spirit's early lesson for me to trust and not worry about my future.

Back then I had no idea of occult practices, such as Astrology and Numerology or anything to do with matters psychic, other than all good Christians should shun them. To put this into perspective, I was sixteen or seventeen when the Catholic Church was still operating in the pre Vatican II days, long before I had any awareness of my psychic journey ahead. In fact it would be another ten years before I became aware of this part of my life.

My first interest in the occult was back in the early 70's, when I remember buying books and reading magazine articles on palmistry and astrology. Something caused me to go looking into this forbidden psychic realm, though what specifically, I can't recall. Though the books were interesting, they still didn't quench my thirst. In fact, that devil's advocate aspect I mentioned earlier, kicked in with a vengeance. So much so, I used the arguments against what I had read in these works as a means of searching for alternative material that supported Christian teaching.

Being the good Catholic I can recall checking out the different literature that was on sale at the back of our local Church, particularly the material pertaining to matters psychic. What I read indicated how evil and wicked psychic phenomena could be, and how involvement in such was tantamount to devil worship. However, for all of the negative posturing, there was no real base for the Churches objection to this phenomenon. From memory, I think the Redemptorist Fathers, a Catholic Order well known for their fearful fire and brimstone sermons at the time, printed these books and pamphlets.

Even with this very strong anti-psychic mentality amongst the teachings within the Catholics Church, there still remained a certain honour for those Saints who exhibited similar psychic traits. This seemed to be the case amongst certain Celtic or European Catholics, particularly the Irish, Gypsies and Poles. The likes of Martin de Porres, Joan of Arc, Theresa the Little Flower, Frances Of Assisi, the events and happenings of the Children of Fatima and the Miracles of Lourdes, are just a few that come to mind. I can recall my dad telling us as children the story of John Vianney, the Curate of Arles in France, well known, he informed us, for telling the people their sins in confession before they had even uttered them. Catholic objection to psychics therefore didn't make sense to me.

My Long and Winding Road

It was during the 1970's that I started to buy books of an alternative nature, particularly books on palmistry and astrology. The most regular magazine I purchased each month was the Australian Astrological magazine, and though the predictions didn't seem to relate to me, I found the articles fascinating. I had one of the first computer-generated Astrology charts done, but it was very stilted and vague in its interpretation. This led me in the late seventies to visiting an Astrologer who did my very first full scale Astrological chart. Again the chart was full of information, but I found the predictions were more miss than hit, and I must say the predictions were not all that accurate. Astrology still remains a subject that I find fascinating and which I feel deserves ongoing scientific research.

It was this astrologer who recommended me to my first psychic reading. I can't recall where she lived or her name, but I can recall her as being a lovely old British lady with a beautiful English cottage – like home inside and out. As she was a psychometrist she asked me for an article to hold. I gave her my watch. She said lots of flattering things about me, including that I had a beautiful blue aura, but not much else. I left her $2 on the plate near the card that said, "Your donation of $10 is gratefully accepted", and hoped she didn't put a curse on me when she discovered how miserly I had been. Had there been any meaningful information, I would have gladly left her the $10 or more. In hindsight, I did the very thing I now criticise some people of doing when they come to me or other psychics for a session. I determined her value, and therefore payment, based on the information I had received, not on the time the dear old soul had spent trying to assist me.

Do we pay a psychic for information or for their time? If the information is not pleasing to us and indicates no coming changes, this is still information. What should determine whether we pay or not? Do weather forecasters get paid on their accuracy or for their time?

I guess we are entitled to expectations with a psychic, but if we live reasonably predictable lives, and don't change the way we live, but rather wait for other people or circumstances to bring changes, then we are going to get very little from our psychic reading. Too high an expectation can also bring disappointment when we visit a psychic, as it can block our guide from giving us what they need us to hear, as opposed to what we want to hear.

I was privileged to see Doris Stokes, the brilliant British platform reader, when she performed at the Sydney Opera House in the 1970's. I can recall having mixed feelings at the time. Like everyone else, I hoped she would have some psychic information for me. And at the same time wondering how many of the audience, who she seemingly gave accurate messages to, weren't supporters, deliberately planted amongst the rest of us.

Chapter I

In hindsight I realize it was an excellent performance and that my not getting a personal message meant that there was nothing that spirit had to give me at that time. I also now know that she was every bit as good as she claimed, having met her in spirit a couple of times at some of the psychic circle, or spiritual gatherings, I have attended. Around this time, the American sceptic James Randy was in Australia claiming that psychic phenomena, such as the work done by the likes of Doris and Uri Geller were nothing more than magician's tricks. From memory Uri Geller is an Israeli psychic whose claim to fame was his ability to psychically overpower the physical, such as bending spoons and stopping clocks by sheer psychic power.

James offered a very large sum of money for any psychic that could prove their abilities, and I believe that sum still stands. He demonstrated the simple test that he claimed was a failsafe way to determine if someone was truly psychic. In a specially prepared room, he had six large cardboard sheets, each with a different symbol on one side, and blank on the other, placed up against a glass wall with the blank side against the glass. He then invited a number of well-known Australian psychics, one at a time, to sit in front of the blank sides of the cardboard sheets. He got each one to pick which card coincided with a set of cards of the same symbols, laid out in front of the psychic. I can't recall one of the psychics getting all of the cards right and nor has anyone claimed the sceptic's money.
It wasn't till much later that I realized the sceptic's test was not set up to test a psychic's sixth sense ability, or their ability to commune with spirit, but to prove Randy's belief that psychics weren't mind readers.

If James and the Sceptic society had genuinely wanted to test a psychic's skill, and not to prove their straw-man argument which, psychics believe they were mind readers, he would have set up a genuine test. To do this he would have selected a number of renowned psychics to interact with the same spirit, but not with each other, at the same time. If each psychic had got the same or similar information independently of the others then there would be cause to believe there is something genuine about communing with the spirit world. A system best used for such a test could be the one set up and used by the Stanford Research Institute and later by the CIA for their psychics in their Remote Viewing Stargate project. One would wonder why the Sceptics society, if genuine in their search for truth, and not as a means of dismissing psychics out of hand, wouldn't have at least consulted the Stanford Research group for pointers on how best to test psychic claimants.

Today it is hard to believe, that back in the 70's, especially here in Australia, all matters psychic were very much frowned upon. Even though there was a slackening of attitudes, especially after Woodstock and the hippy - new age movement, the world, especially the establishment, took its time accepting this newness.

Prior to this new attitude, psychics were grouped along with gypsies, snake oil sellers, get rich quick schemers, and the generally undesirable. Even car salesmen, real estate agents, politicians, lawyers and insurance sellers had a better reputation than psychics. Under the vagrancy act of most states in Australia, it was illegal to charge for a psychic reading, but they could accept donations if it could be proved it was a genuine donation and not a pseudo fee. Hence why, "Your donation of $10 is gratefully accepted", though a common little note placed strategically amongst the Tarot cards, candles and crystals of a decent psychic, was not enforceable by the psychic. After all, a donation is what ever the giver gives. Most states have long since abandoned the vagrancy act and those that haven't, no longer act on them. There are still people today, even amongst those who support psychics, who believe psychic readings should be by donation only. My suggestion to these people is if their particular job, service or occupation

Chapter I

is offered with a donation being their wages, then I will support them.

From what I have learned from other psychics, there are very tight restrictions on what a psychic can or can't say in Europe, especially Britain, and it has to be stated from the outset by practitioners that psychic readings are entertainment and not to be taken seriously. It is important for anyone outside of Europe, visiting a European psychic either in Europe or in the enquirer's own country, to understand the psychic's reading will be coloured by the laws and policies governing that reader's country.

Even when that European psychic particularly from Britain, has immigrated to another country, unless they are conscious of the differences, will stick to their old country's rules. This particularly applies in Australia and New Zealand where there are many British psychics who assume the rules in these countries are the same as in Britain.

America became the hub of the new age market, blending all sorts of beliefs, including Native American, Eastern mysticism and humanist philosophies, often with minimal knowledge of the origins of some of those beliefs. Psychics and mediums sprang up all over the country, some blending snake-charming Christianity with middle-ages witchery.

After September 2001, there was a noticeable change in psychic New Age development. New Age and New Thought ideas that were at odds with Judeo-Christianity especially fundamental Christianity had a very difficult time. It goes without saying that if Christian fundamentalism continues to expand, many aspects of the New Age will be challenged in areas of parapsychology, pseudo-scientific fields as well as in all areas of alternative spirituality. It is almost like we returned to an earlier conservative time when it was evil to involve ourselves in any form of occult practice, no matter how innocent it may have seemed.

It was in the 1970's that I had my first memorable psychic experience. At a hardware store on Sydney's north shore, in my capacity as a cleaner, I came across a rather expensive looking ring lying under one of the display cabinets. I was concerned that if I were to put it in my pocket, chances were I might accidentally take it home, or be possibly charged with stealing, so I decided to hold it.

The cashier arrived around 8.30am and commented on the way I was standing and moving. I didn't feel I was standing any differently to normal, but she disagreed saying I looked far more self confident, chest more pronounced, my walking steps slower and more deliberate. As I was talking to her she also noted that I was rubbing my chest and taking sharp breaths. It was when I looked at my hand on my chest that I realized I was carrying the ring, which I handed over to her. She smiled and said "Boy, aren't you gifted. This ring belonged to my late husband. He had been a very proud and arrogant man. He was always sure of himself and always walked with a slow deliberate pace, his chest out like a peacock. He died of a heart attack after being told that the pains in his chest needed to be looked at. He never did have his heart seen to."

She said she was convinced that I had a psychic gift, having been an active spiritualist and having belonged to a particular psychic circle a couple of years earlier. She had lost contact with her group, but said she would try and get me a contact number and put me in contact with them. In the meantime she suggested I look around for a development group. A few days later she said her old group had disbanded, but that she had found a parapsychology group. They were operating out of a building in York Street Sydney one day a week and she suggested I look them up in the phone book to see if they still operated. I was frightened at the very thought of such a thing,

Chapter I

after all I was more than a regular Sunday Mass going Catholic, often going to Mass during the week if I wasn't working. As I have said the Church teaching and society generally had me believe this so called gift I had was a tool of the devil.

My confusion wasn't helped much when this woman offered me a prayer called -- I Am the God of Circumstance – These Things Are from Me. It was my first insight into the realization that maybe being psychic was not against God's will, but part of it.

You will notice, as you read through the book, that I reference to God as both a singular and a plural person. It took me quite awhile to accept their explanation that God is neither male nor female but instead a non-sexual conglomerate of all that is perfect. The core we call God is the core from where we have come, and both our spirit and physical beings are manifestations of that Love. God is therefore it, not he or she. It was Jesus who first used the term; I am the I Am, an indication that God was, and is inclusive and not exclusive to those that are at one with God's Power. Those who are in this category rarely refer to themselves in this manner because of the respect and humility of Jesus. We all can espouse to this position, assuming we follow the right path and not that of self-assuming and humanist elitism.

In continuing my journey, at this early time in my life, I wondered if I was in some way responsible directly or indirectly, for the destruction of certain structures, businesses, and establishments. Places seemed to get pulled down, burnt down, or destroyed in some way after I had moved on from using them.

I was baptised and spent most of the first 30 years of my life involved one way or another with the Waitara Catholic Church, Our Lady of the Rosary primary school, and later the Mercy Nun's Foundling Home. The army barracks that ended up become Peacefields, the holiday centre my family and I built in the Mudgee district in the 1980's, came from this Foundling Home. The Church, the school and the Foundling Home were all pulled down and the land sold off to developers within a few years of my moving to the Central West of NSW. This gave the Church the necessary money to build the new Church and school, further down the road.

Many can make similar claims of such endings happening to them as I have. For me, following a very unsure path in a direction opposed to what many claimed was God's road; this was a very unsettling history.

Back in the 1970's, to say I was totally confused at that point in my life is an understatement. On the one hand I was a practicing my Catholic faith with probably a lot more dedication than most of my age. Yet it seemed that I was also dabbling in the ways of Satan. My very deep rooted feelings of guilt from these new developments weren't helped by my family. They couldn't understand why I just couldn't follow the Catholic doctrine and just stop this ridiculous new interest.

I had to find some guidance, someone who knew what they were talking about and someone who wouldn't hammer more negative energies into my already guilt-ridden soul. Many questions came to mind: Who to turn to? Where do you look for a Christian psychic teacher? Who do you trust? How do you differentiate between God given Gifts, cited in the many books I had read on the lives of certain Saints, and the works of Satan? Did I have to wait till I died, when a team of priests would run through my life with a fine toothcomb before knowing once and for all whether I was a Saint or a Satanist? Most importantly, would God wait that long? Who in the Catholic Church knew of such things? Who could be my mentor?

Chapter I

While all this was going on, I was fast beginning to believe I had an ego problem. The old feelings that I was someone very special returned. Feeling of being unique, almost Superman-like purpose to fulfil or complete reoccurred as it did in my teenage years. I remember wrestling seriously with thoughts that kept telling me I was God-like, a new Jesus, a commencer of God's work in this New Age.

How dare Satan put such thoughts in my mind, but more importantly, how did I get rid of these imposed thoughts? Were they mine, or someone else's? Had the devil possessed my thoughts and how many showers would it take to remove the satanic spell?

The belief system of the Catholic Church at least had some similarities expressed in the form of their saints; the Protestants belief however didn't even come close. I had to search outside of my safety net and the only way I could do that, it seemed, was to go to the least of the devil's worshippers. Though I had heard of the Spiritualist Church, I was reluctant to visit them, as I had heard they were into witchery and paganism, and that wasn't quiet the devil I was ready for. I needed somewhere softer to start. I needed a middle ground.

There had been some stories on TV about groups in America that researched the paranormal and so I decided to see if such a similar scientific based organization existed here in Australia. I called a number of university campuses to see if they knew of anything relating to matters psychic. Many assumed me to be a crank and didn't even bother to give me the time of day, let alone courtesy.

One kind old woman (at least she sounded old) suggested I try the Psychic Research Centre in the city. It was then I realised the similarity of this information to what the woman at the BBC Hardware had told me. I checked the address the old lady had given me with the address the BBC lady had given me and they were the same; York Street Wynyard in Sydney. I thanked the old lady and immediately phoned the Centre, but there was no answer. I tried most of the day, till finally around 4.00pm, someone answered to say they only met one specific day a week. As I was working that particular day, they suggested I come to a spiritual awareness evening held every Tuesday at the Enmore Spiritualist Church.

Arriving at the Enmore address I made my way into the old house that had been converted into a large, one-room meeting hall. A lovely old lady, with a noticeable hunched back, welcomed me and asked had I brought anything for the psychometry session. I had no idea what she was talking about, because although I had done a psychometry reading for the woman at the BBC Hardware store, I didn't know what it was called. My vacant stare caused her to direct me back outside, and with the aid of a brown paper bag she supplied, got me to pick a branch off one of the shrubs growing there, hold it in my hands for a short while, and then place it inside the bag. No wonder the shrubs and trees looked so unhealthy with so many people coming each week, stripping them of their branches and leaves for the psychometry session. "Now remember which bag is yours." she said, "otherwise you may select your own bag, and that will never do." I nodded in my ignorance, wondering what would happen to me if I chose my own bag.

Inside the very large room was a circle of chairs. To the left of the front door was a slightly raised area that I was told was where the spiritualists performed their platform readings on Sunday. These were terms that meant nothing to me. In the right back corner was a small kitchen area and opening out from that was a small alcove where I could see a number of people chatting. There was also a scattering of people around the chairs, while the many smokers had gathered outside in the chilly night air.

Chapter I

At 7.00 pm a gentleman in a dark shiny green sloppy Joe with light coloured green bands on the sleeves, called us all to attention. I remember it well because I was wearing a similar one in blue. There must have been 50 of us in all. We were all asked to take a seat in the circle, and as the chatter quietened down the lights were dimmed. At first it seemed the lights had been extinguished completely, but as my eyes grew accustomed to it, I realised there was a small blue bulb hanging from the ceiling where the gentleman was standing. He introduced himself as Ian and he got us all to introduce ourselves to the room. He had an accent that I didn't at first recognise, but later found was French.

We were asked to close our eyes and to relax ourselves by breathing slowly and deeply, while at the same time concentrating on certain colours that he introduced to us one at a time. He suggested that we should now be in a deep state of meditation. He then got us to draw to mind any visualisations, no matter how weak or how insignificant they may be. I wasn't seeing anything. The entire time, my mind was whirling around in almost total panic. What was I doing here with this devil group? What if a ghost starts to appear in the middle of the circle? What were we supposed to do? Questions, more questions and no answers.

After what seemed to be an eternity, I heard people moving or rustling. I slowly opened my eyes to see most had returned from wherever they had gone. One old dear had gone to sleep and was snoring happily in the corner nearest the kitchen. Ian and the others took no notice. It seemed this was a normal occurrence. Ian then went around the room to each of us, asking us what we saw, felt, or had received that was appropriate. One woman said she had received a rose quartz crystal from some heavenly being, and was told to pass it onto another woman sitting opposite, to which the receiving woman offered her thanks. Another woman said she had seen her mother in spirit and started to weep. Ian told her not to be upset, and queried as to whether this had happened to her the previous week, and the week before that, and the week before that. She replied yes.

The next woman said she just went away and was still having difficulties coming back. One of the other women immediately told her she needed grounding. If she didn't, she was warned, she would leave half her spirit behind in the room when she left, or worse, she could easily be taken over by walk-ins. The first woman thanked the second woman, and excused herself as she wandered off into the kitchen area to do a grounding exercise. I was petrified at the thought of a walk-in taking me over, what ever a walk-in was. Then it became my turn. Ian asked me what had happened, and I said nothing, other than feeling very peaceful and sleepy.

That was true; I was feeling that way, mixed with apprehension and concern about what would happen if a ghost appeared. One old dear said that as I was not yet initiated, I would probably not receive anything of significant value for at least 12 months, as it has taken her that long from when she had first started coming. I was both disappointed and elated. I would have liked to have some psychic things happening, but apprehensive as to what harm they might cause me.

We broke for a short while and the smokers went outside again to pollute the crisp night air. Most of the group were women, and most of them smoked. As I have never smoked in my life, I took a toilet break.

Smoke break over, we were called back to the circle. The old lady, who had introduced herself to me outside when I had first arrived, collected a tray from a side table and started moving from chair to chair. On the tray was a stack of brown bags like the one I had put the branch in when I had first arrived. Each person took a bag, checking first that the bag was not their own, before the tray was passed onto the next person. I

Chapter I

took a bag off the tray when the tray was offered to me and waited to see what magic trick we were about to try next.

We were asked to remove the contents of the bag we were holding, and to concentrate on what we were feeling. I was feeling an almost dead, withered flower. Ian then asked each person to comment on what they were feeling, starting with a woman three or four seats up from me. She was the one that had passed on the crystal to the other woman who was now sitting next to her. She said that she was getting a very warm, fussy feeling connected to the small cameo piece she was holding and that she felt this person was looking for a warm hug and some unconditional love. She was very theatrical in her description, and I thought what a wanker, an Australian expression for what an idiot. It was all I could do not to smirk. Ian then asked who owned the cameo. A young, attractive, lass said it had belonged to her grandmother, who had passed over two weeks before.

Ian asked did the information she received make any sense to her. She hesitated before saying, "it didn't." She then said she was the grand daughter of someone they all knew as having been a regular to the circle. Apparently the theatrical person got it terribly wrong, but it didn't seem to worry her one bit.

The next person Ian asked said she was happy not to try this time, as she was new and wanted just to observe. Ian seemed contented with her wish. Next was a rather large woman, who most knew to be a practising psychic from Kings Cross in the heart of Sydney. She spoke very confidently about the feelings she was receiving from the flower she had chosen, and was very informative with what she was saying. I thought I'd never ever be able to do a similar psychometry.

Ian asked who owned the particular flower and the little old lady who had introduced me to the bag and branch raised her hand. Ian asked if what she heard made any sense, and the woman replied most certainly. She then confirmed each comment the large lady had made, right down to a small detail concerning her husband's lost medication. I couldn't help but be impressed. Ian thanked both the ladies and continued on the session by asking the woman next to me what she had received. She said she was just getting a cold and sad feeling coming from the ring she was holding, and nothing more. Ian asked for the owner, and a quiet man, who I hadn't noticed before, stood up and said it belonged to his wife. She had Alzheimer's' disease. He thanked the woman and she said she would talk privately to the man, as she felt she might have more information for him.

Then Ian came to me. I had no intention of saying anything other than I felt nothing, because I really didn't feel anything at all. I went to say what I had planned, but stumbled. Ian asked what I had said, and I tried again, but again I had trouble getting words together. Ian asked me to take a long slow breath and then to count slowly to five, which I did. He asked, "If the flower had a heart or soul, what would be the feelings you would use to describe it?"

Before I had a chance to speak, a voice said, "The person is like this flower, broken and in pain. They feel they are useless, of no use to anything or anyone."

The speaker stopped, and I realized it had been me. I was stunned. Ian said how good I was, and did I have any more info, again my mouth spoke for me, "Yes, I feel the person has no idea how very special they are and how beautiful they are, deep inside. I feel they let others put them down, and that they are unable to defend themselves. I feel whoever this other person is, the one putting this person down, is very jealous. I feel this person the flower relates to will be making a very big decision soon that will release them from this other person's dominance."

Chapter I

Oh my God, what have I done? You can't just blurt out stuff like this, I scolded myself. What if you're wrong? What if this person goes and does something silly because of what you've said? What if…?

"Very good," Ian interrupted my self-scolding, "and who owns this?" I cringed in anticipation of a severe reprimand.
"It's mine," a sweet middle-aged woman said. There was an audible gasp in the room as the woman stood up. God, here it comes, I thought as I prepared for the worst.

"And did this make sense to you?" Ian asked, his smile seeming to say, "I know it did."

"Absolutely," the woman replied, "I have been coming to this group now for eighteen months and this is the first time anyone has given me anything that makes sense." Realising how that could be misinterpreted she went on to apologise but was stopped by the big psychic woman from the Cross.

"If you don't mind dear," she started, "I feel it is important to say this to the young man," She pointed in my direction, "Needed to know he has a gift, and his guide has shown him, with this reading, exactly that." Thank you so much," the woman said to me.

I was busy catching flies with my open mouth. "Well done," smiled Ian, "not bad for your first attempt." The room started to quietly clap. I was shocked. What was going on?

After the session, the large woman psychic from the cross called me aside and congratulated me on the information I had given the other woman. She told me she was one of the regular overhead readers that came to the Spiritualist Church on Sundays, and the one designated to observe on behalf of the Church this night. She said she could see a very special guide around me, a woman of great spiritual experience, who I had know when she was in the physical world, and that this guide didn't want me to be concerned with what was happening. She said this guide would give me a sign soon to show that what I was doing was not bad. I thanked her and wandered into the smallest, most inconspicuous corner I could find, still feeling every eye in the place was watching me.

Ian came over and congratulated me, as did a few others. Then the woman, who had given the rose quarts to the other woman, came over and warned me not to do any more readings till I had learned to ground myself. She said she could tell I was mixing with negative energies, from the dark colours she could see in my aura, and I immediately knew she was as psychic as my shoe, which was probably more psychic than she could ever be. I thanked her and moved into the kitchen, where I made myself a nerve-settling cup of Peppermint tea.

I came back the following week, and a couple of times after that, and was starting to feel quite confident with what I was able to do with psychometry. However, as I was not able to visualise anything, and most of the group said you aren't psychic unless you can, I just assumed I was at the beginning of my psychic journey and had to be patient a while longer.

I can only recall one occasion at this place where I had a visualisation and that was while I was trying the transfigure exercise. In this exercise, we had to stare, without blinking, into the face of another person across the other side of the room. Their face would go blank and another face, usually a spirit who had recently passed over, would superimpose over the person's face. I had no luck at all with the transfiguring exercise, but instead could see a vision slightly to the left of the person I was staring at. I could clearly see a beautiful wicker chair sitting in moonlight up on the platform stage. It was painted white and had a very large circular back. There was no one sitting in it and to this day, I don't know the significance of that visualisation.

Chapter I

It is interesting to note that of all these sessions I went to, no one actually got anything of importance for me from the psychometry exercises. Because of my Catholic background I decided to share this newfound information with my friend, a Catholic Priest from my parish. He was horrified to hear where I had gone and of the claim that I was psychic, suggesting I visit a certain Catholic family who were in the throws of starting up a Pentecostal style community within our parish. The father of the family had developed either a cancer in the eye or was going blind some years earlier, and so put his life into God's hands, saying if he were to be cured, he would serve God in whatever capacity he could. He gained his sight and true to his promise, he and his wife started a Charismatic Spiritual Community in the Waitara area, a community dedicated to improving Catholic Christian Spirituality.

I agreed to go and visited them the following weekend. On arrival I was treated with respect and courtesy, after all our families were regulars to the Church and my younger brother and one of their sons were good mates. They had no idea why I had visited them, so after formalities, and a cup of tea, I informed them of why I was there and immediately sensed their fear as if I were about to give birth to the devil himself. I told them that if what I had done was wrong, if I had any anti Christian entities around or in me, then they had my full permission to exorcise it from me. And I meant it. They said what I had done was very wrong, without specifying where, how or why, and I later realised it was more fear of the unknown that was driving them, rather than a proven malevolence.

They laid their hands on me and prayed openly and loudly, his hands getting heavier on my head and hers getting heavier on my shoulders, as the prayer volume increased. The pressure was so uncomfortable, that I literally slipped out of the chair. Finally they told me I had been exorcised and was to keep away from the Spiritualist Church, as it was a satanic centre and to forget about such dangerous practices. There was no discussion as to what was happening to me, other than I had somehow created or caused this silliness to happen, and I had to stop entertaining it immediately.

There was no improvement; in fact I started getting stronger feelings as more events occurred. I was getting quite worried that the seeds now sown were permanent, and no amount of praying would remove them. And pray I did, every afternoon after work at the local Catholic Church. I returned to my friend the priest who had sent me to this Charismatic family, to say that I was having troubles getting rid of this evil and needed a stronger exorcism, preferably a priest that was aware of such things. He suggested I visit a particularly good Franciscan priest at Wahroonga who had made a study of the occult. I made an appointment to meet this man a couple of days later.

It is important to mention that the secular priests, the ones that most people know and who reside in most towns, have a different understanding and certainly less training, than those in certain Orders. The Franciscans are such an Order.

Father Rob was a very big man, in both build and nature. I was immediately impressed by him, and told him my story. From the incident at the North Shore hardware store, the happenings at the psychic phenomena evenings at the Enmore Church and some other incidents that have been lost to time. He didn't seem at all perplexed and in fact listened to me with a very understanding and open-minded attitude. He made reference to different beliefs, philosophies and ideologies and it was then I noticed the books on his shelves of his very small cell. There were the entire works of Edgar Cayce, The Aquarian Gospels of Jesus the Christ, the Predictions of Malachi and Mother Shipton and numerous other occult books. When we had finished chatting he asked if he too could come to the next night at the Spiritualist Church. I was initially shocked that a priest should want to visit such a place, but organised with

Ian to bring Rob along for the next session Rob was available for. I didn't tell Ian that Rob was a priest, but an interested friend.

On the particular Tuesday night that Rob and I were to go to Enmore, a fellow priest at the Franciscan Priory at Mt. Alverna, who had previously been diagnosed as having cancer and who had been receiving chemotherapy, had been informed that his cancer had stopped and that there was every reason to believe the cancer had been cured. After a special mass of thanks, the priests had celebrated with a few glasses of some alcoholic beverage, so that when I came to pick up Rob, he was running late.

We arrived almost a half-hour late at Enmore and quietly joined the circle. Rob was dressed in civilian clothes and no one, other than me, knew him to be a priest. Ian seemed a little pre-occupied on our arrival and I wondered if he might have sensed that Rob was a priest. At the break half way through the proceedings, Ian called me aside and asked how well I knew Rob. I explained that he was a Catholic Priest and that he had come as an observer. Ian said that if I vouched for him he would let him stay, otherwise Ian would ask him to leave.

Ian had sensed that Rob had been drinking and as alcohol was a banned substance during these meetings, I could understand Ian's concern. I further explained to Ian about the reason for the priest's celebration, our being late and Rob's reason for the alcohol. Ian agreed it was OK for Rob to stay. As the night progressed Ian and Rob became quite talkative and I had hoped for a hand across the waters scenario to come out of this encounter, but sadly it never happened. I think Ian's Protestant past prevented this from happening.

During the second half of the evening, where again the light was dimmed to just a very low light blue, we did the transfiguration exercise where we were again encouraged to concentrate on the face of someone opposite us. Ian said we might see the face of someone from spirit that may have a special message for us personally or someone near to us. Rob seemed to be trying with unusual enthusiasm.

It was during this exercise that Rob described to the group the face of a woman he saw who seemed to be dark or scarred on one side of her face. She seemed to be framed in an oval formation with white on the top and white on the bottom. No one in the room could connect with this person, and it wasn't until we were on our way home, after Rob described more of what he had seen and sensed, that I realised it was one of my great aunts, now in spirit, who had been a nun. The white on the top and bottom that the priest had seen was part of her religious habit and not a part of a picture frame. She had suffered a stroke that had paralysed one side of her face some years before she finally passed into Gods Kingdom.

Rob's message to me from aunty Regis was,
"You're doing very well and are on track. You are very special, with a very special calling, and you are very, very safe. Remember God is with you as I am with you."
It was then I remembered the message I got from the big psychic lady on my first night at the centre.

"I can see a very special guide around me, a woman of great spiritual experience. You knew this woman when she was in the physical world. She doesn't want you to be concerned and she will give you a sign soon to show that what you are doing is right."

Now this was a sanction that I couldn't deny. A Catholic priest, with a message from a Catholic nun, and a family member I trusted, telling me I was on track. If they were getting it wrong, what chance did I have? I visited Rob at Mt. Alverna a couple of times before he was transferred interstate. I have never heard from him since, but have heard recently that he had been working somewhere back in NSW.

It wasn't long after that I moved to Wollar in the Mudgee district to set up a holiday camp for disabled and disadvantage city kids with the aid of the priest who had first suggested my visiting the Pentecostal family and the Franciscan priest. Years later I found that my ex wife's sister was married to Ian's son. Ian had apparently returned to New Caledonia. In hindsight, the Pentecostal Christian I mentioned actually got it right. Their praying over me had worked; it was their expectations that were wrong.

On the Light Path   Peter Lyons

What Would You Know

You say I'm living in a world of make believe,
Living in a world that I perceive to be perfect.
What would you know?

You say I'm living in my own reality,
I'm living in my own modality like a blind man.
Well how could you know?

That my real world has let me down,
I'm like a king without a crown.
And you have the hide to say I'm down because of my be-
lief.
Well what would you know?

You say you're fearful of the people that I see,
Fearful that they're undermining me and my values.
Well how would you know?

You say I've stepped over the edge of sanity,
I'm drawing down by the New Age and it's evils.
Well what do you know?

Hocus-pocus you're out of focus, nothing is as it seems.
Hocus-pocus the evils that scare you aren't from your bad
dreams,
They come from your dark fears deep down inside you.

1999

Chapter II

The Journey Gets Serious

It was around this time I met and fell madly in love twice at the same time. My first love was a twenty-five acre property at Wollar, north of Mudgee in Central Western NSW, and the second was my first real girlfriend I'll call Libby. I bought the property at Wollar and for a time she and I went out to the farm and stayed in a tent, till the autumn cold made it impossible to continue doing so.

I had a neighbour in Wollar, who claimed to be a builder, and I got him to build me a 12' by 20' shed where we stayed when it got colder. It was an incident at the property in 1977, just before I moved there permanently, that added another notch to my list of psychic skills.

Libby, her friend, two of my brothers and my youngest sister, had gone abseiling at a place called the Bluff, not far from my property. As Libby was a very experienced abseiler I had no thoughts of her being in any danger. It would have been more likely to be a problem if I had gone. I stayed behind in the shed and had an afternoon nap.

At 4.05 pm, one of the ropes came loose and she fell. Luckily she was able to grab onto something that slowed her fall. She wasn't seriously injured; in fact she only had a few scratches, bruising, and a dented pride. Had she not slowed down her descent, she would have been seriously injured, possibly killed. At the exact moment she fell, she smashed her watch against a rock face. This was the exact moment I had woken up from a very vivid and frightening nightmare, convinced I had been falling.

At the end of 1977 at the ripe old age of 30, I decided to leave home and camp out in the bush in my newly built shed. Three teenage lads, who had been getting into serious trouble in Sydney, had already moved into the shed, where I had hoped they would assist me to built the intended holiday hostel planned for the site. I had also hoped Libby would join me after I had got the basic hostel built, but she had other ideas and decided to find someone else.

Just before I was to move up to the property, a severe windstorm took the roof off the shed, so I arrived to a very soggy and exposed shell of a building with three unruly teenagers and no alternative accommodation. I found out on inspection of the crumpled roof that the so-called builder neighbour had used shoddy materials. The walls were equal height so that there was no runoff when it rained and he hadn't sealed the eaves so the wind easily got up under the roof and lifted it off. I made many visits to the builder only to have him tell me he'd fix it the following week, which he never did. At least his wife gave us accommodation till we could get the shed liveable.

The three lads had befriended a family that lived further up the valley, and they asked the father if he could help us put up a roof. His son Len, who had just separated from his girlfriend, convinced his father it was in the best interest of all if they helped get the shed liveable. At first I couldn't understand his reason for such support, till he asked me, repeatedly, if there would be many young girls coming to stay at the hostel once it was built. It took a few weeks, and an expense

Chapter II

I hadn't budgeted for, to finally get a decent roof to cover us. Because I could only afford second hand roofing iron and it was hard to get a good slope for the water to run of, it still leaked when we had a decent downpour.

Once we had the shed weather proofed, it was time to set some basic rules for the lads. Though these were just commonsense living skills, two of the young men objected and ran away to Len's, claiming I was expecting them to work long days without pay. The third lad had joined them in protest, but returned a week later.

The first night of the week that I was alone, I sat out the front of my poorly constructed 12' X 20' shed on my 25 acres of rock and noxious weeds, looking at the sunset, feeling devastated and lonely for the first time since leaving home, wondered what the hell I'd got myself into.

Three weeks after leaving me the two wayward youth called to say they had been asked to leave Len's and wanted to come back to my place. I had planned a trip down to Sydney to organise a meeting with the newly formed hostel committee. I suggested all three boys come with me. I explained it would give them a chance to see if they wanted to stay down there or return with me. They took up the offer and travelled to Sydney with me, only Slim returned. We got back to find a rumour had spread amongst the locals that I was a defrocked priest. The running rumours stated I was a priest on leave, possibly in trouble or something similar. I had been painted as a shady character.

Slim would often visit Len's parents, particularly going shooting with Len. Slim became concerned at Len's anger when he'd been drinking heavily. He cut back his visits to Len's and Len read this as me preventing Slim from visiting. This particular night Slim and Len had gone to the Ulan Pub where Len had become quite drunk. On their return Len had asked if Slim could go with him the next day to do some shooting. I replied that Slim would be needed more than ever because we were getting close to starting the building of the hostel and I was in the early stages of Glandular fever.

Len, who was obviously drunk, left. On his way out the front gate he told Slim that he was going to do something once and for all about me. To say the least this frightened me. I could see no alternative but to stay calm and hope that when Len got home he would change his mind or at least go to sleep. He didn't. About a half hour later he was back. I had told Slim not to leave me as the Glandular fever had made me unable to defend myself. My hope was that with Slim there Len would back off. Len arrived with a large hunting knife. I was sitting on my bed aware that only the grace of God could save me now. Len was talking gibberish and it was later that I realised the hatred he could never say to his father, he was letting out at me. A voice inside my head kept saying be calm, be calm, but that only seemed to make things worse. Suddenly, when I was sure Len was about to lunge at me, I remember taking a deep breath and the rest is a complete blank.

Slim later told me that after I took the deep breath, I seemed to somehow grow taller and to develop a fatherly superiority. It wasn't me. Slim didn't remember much of what was said, except for two noticeable things. One was if Len were to take my life, millions upon millions of 'Pete's' would be sent to replace me. The second, and the one Slim said brought the biggest change over Len, was when I said Len would have a tormented, unhappy and painfully short life if he killed me. Slim said later he hadn't realised Len had an intention of killing me, only threatening me.

When I came too I saw Len stabbing the mattress we had stored against the wall. He was repeating saying I'm sorry, I'm sorry, to no one in particular. I staggered over to him and gave him a hug, went out side, sobbed my eyes out and col-

Chapter II

lapsed. I have never felt an emotion like it. I think part of the emotion was my being sick, but also the awareness that something special had 'overtaken' me, and thought I was very confused, I knew it wasn't a bad thing. It was the first time in my life I had fully tranced.

A slightly amusing event arising from this encounter happened a few weeks later. Slim and I had been discussing what had happened with the Len incident and I explained it was probably a psychic thing. I explained that I had probably gone into trance and that some peaceful power had calmed down the situation. Unbeknown to me, I had scared the living daylights out of him. He thought that at any time a power could take him over and do dreadful things.

He had gone into town to do some personal shopping. The original plan was for some friends to drive him home and that would have got him directly to the shed, but they had a change of plans so he had returned on the school bus. It arrived at the Wollar post office around 5.00 pm, and he then had to walk the remaining distance, which took him another half hour. It was quite dark by the time he had started his walk home. The creek crossing at the bottom of our property was always colder than most other places, and this combined with the few beers he had had in Mudgee, had him needing to walk over to the fence to urinate.

At that exact time he heard a rustling sound, looked up, and was staring into the eyes of some horrendous monster. At least that was what he thought. He let out a cry, tried pulling up his pants, and ran back towards the roadway. Tripping over on his half hitched pants allowed him to hear and see what the monster truly was. He had had an encounter with an emu. It must have been grazing on the other side of the fence when Slim spooked it. He arrived back at the shed, white as a ghost, and panting from exhaustion. Slim returned to his fam-

On the Light Path — Peter Lyons

ily in Sydney towards the end of 1979, Len having moved into Mudgee some months earlier.

Though he had not done the right thing by me, I still remained good friends with my neighbour Grant, the builder, and his wife Coral. This feeling of love for my enemy seemed to override my normal human nature of wanting to physically make amends, or as we Aussie's say, "punch his lights out." Not that I would have had much chance of that, he being twice my size and possibly four times more powerful. I would wander down to their place around 10.00am to gather my food from a freezer that I kept at their place, because I had no electricity at the shed. I would also collect my regular quota of fresh milk, for which I would take my turn in milking their cow when required.

Up in the hills at the back of our properties, about an hour or so drive into the scrub on a very, very rough road, was a hippy community. One memorable character from this community was a camel trader I'll call Unison, who rarely wore clothes. One day he came visiting my neighbour's wife Coral, looking for his camels that had wandered off from the community's property. I was gathering my day's milk and supply, when I heard her let out an expletive. She had been standing at the door, looking out towards the hills when she saw someone coming through the paddocks. At first she thought he was wearing very brief under-pants, as he made his way towards her open paddock, full of Saffron and Scotch thistles, till the awareness hit her. He was totally naked. It was funny to watch them talking, him with normal eye contact, and her with eyes everywhere but on him.

We spent much of the time after he left, discussing the leather like qualities of his scrotum, and the resilience of his testicles, considering what we had seen him putting them through. It was painful to watch him mount the cantankerous camel's

Chapter II

back and ride off into the scrub. It brings tears to my eyes just thinking about it.

There were a number of people who either lived at the hippy commune, or passed through on their way down the Hunter Valley, who were involved with camels. One such person was the younger brother of the original owner. Danny was a teenager and not long out of school when I first met him. He was an easygoing young man with dreadlocks and skin like leather. He had inherited his brother's camel interest after his brother had died of leukaemia a few years before. Danny, like other camel traders, would walk over to Central Australia to catch and break in wild camels. They then walked them back to the commune before either selling them or using them in camel races or circus performances.

One particular camel that stood out as a story worth telling was Ginger. Ginger had been seriously injured, possibly from an accident in the wild, before Danny had captured him. Most traders would have put the animal out of its misery, but Danny took a liking to it and so undertook its training. By the time Danny had got Ginger to Wollar, it was obvious it would have to be castrated, as its sexual interest, coupled with its blindness, made it a very dangerous animal to itself, the other camels and Danny.

On a sunny Sunday afternoon in the middle of winter, Danny brought Ginger down to Coral and Grant's place to perform the necessary operation. There were a number of reasons why Danny chose their place. Firstly, the paddock he intended to use, across from the house, was clear of trees and quite flat. This meant that in the event Ginger should get loose while the operation was being performed, there were fewer obstacles for him to run into. The paddock was small enough for us to be able to recapture Ginger, and the fences were high enough to keep him from jumping out. The second reason was the farmhouse had electricity and fresh water. As far as

On the Light Path   Peter Lyons

Danny was concered the sterilization of instruments was just as important to the operation of an animal as to a human. The farmhouse was only a three quarter hour drive into Mudgee, on a reasonably decent road. In the event something should go wrong, Ginger could be either taken to a vet, or a vet could easily get to Ginger.

We all got the camel down on the ground, legs hog tied, and genitals exposed for the operation. Grant and Coral were sitting on the hindquarters, their three kids were sitting on the front legs and I was stuck with the head. Being an ex city boy, I had never experienced anything like this in my life. I was grateful I was at the front end and not the rear, as I hate watching operations of any kind. All was ready and prepared, and Danny yelled, "OK here goes."

The next thing I know I was flat out on my back, the kids had been thrown about two feet away uninjured. Their parents and Danny were in hot pursuit of Ginger who had bolted towards the only tree in the paddock. He hit the tree and knocked it clean out of the ground. He also knocked himself out. The operation went without a hitch. Other than a small gash over his eye, Ginger recovered to trek many a mile with Danny.

Originally the 25-acre block I owned had no name. It was when my then teenage brother arrived with his mates they dropped off a creek crossing sign they claim they rescued from a swollen river somewhere in Victoria. This gave the place its first sign of identity. It was called Seldom Seen, which they thought adequately described my new lifestyle and me. It became the original unofficial name of the property.

For the next five years, with the help of my family and some dedicated supporters, I concentrated on building a hostel for disabled and disadvantaged persons that became known as Peacefields. The planning, building and running of the hostel

Chapter II

gave me very little time to spend in pursuit of my psychic gifts. This time allowed me to develop my sense of humanity and people skills. Spirit on the other hand, constantly filled my head and thoughts with matters spiritual. Looking back I realize that this and all my time at Peacefields were full of instances where spirit downloaded huge quantities of spiritual understanding into my subconscious.

It had been my understanding from the very outset that Peacefields would be a free or low cost holiday hostel for disabled and disadvantage kids run by a community of volunteers. This community would include people with disabilities and restless but still good hearted city teenagers. Included would be members of different religious organizations looking for a break from their routines. I felt that particularly those young men and women studying to become priests and nuns who were questioning their vocation would be involved.

The building, establishing and promoting of the hostel became the priority for the first few years. As the years progressed it became obvious there wasn't going to be enough income to sustain the community. On a particular afternoon, after consuming too much alter wine, the only wine kept at the hostel for religious purposes, I decided to confront my maker. After all this was supposed to be his project, not mine. With bottle and glass in hand, I made my way to the top of the rise and sat down on a large boulder.

The hostel was build just off the top of a very rocky basalt ridge, where it was quite common for lightening to strike when the frequent dry electrical storms came through. To the west a storm was gathering strength, a reflection of what was going on inside me, and I didn't care. I put out in no uncertain terms EXACTLY how I was feeling with what God was doing and had done to me. I dared Him to strike me down, to take me so that I could have it out with him once and for all. Nothing happened. I cooled off enough to feel quite silly at what I had done and returned to the hostel kitchen to have a much-needed strong cup of coffee. No sooner had I walked into the room than a lightening strike hit the very spot I had been standing shortly before. I sat very quiet and still except for involuntary shakes and spasms, for most of the afternoon.

There were some very strange events with a spiritual leaning that happened to me throughout my time at Peacefields. One such incident was when a white witch, who called herself Maitreya, visited the hostel with the intention of making it her new spiritual centre.

I had received a phone call from a couple in Sydney wanting to come to Peacefields to check it out as a place for spiritual retreats. They mentioned that they were associated with the Wayside Chapel in Sydney. They said there was a holy spiritual person, who had been directed by an intuitive voice to look west of the Blue Mountains for a special place and person. They had already spent previous weekends looking around Rylstone and Kandos and had heard of Peacefields. I explained they would have to pay the usual fee, which was $4 per person per night and provide their own food, which they said they would happily pay.

Their car arrived Friday night about 5.00 pm and the couple disembarked from the two front seats and approached me. After small talk and introductions, I offered them a cup of tea or coffee and pointed towards the dining area. It was at this point that the husband went back to the car, and the wife informed me that the holy woman Maitreya, had come with them. I looked back to see her husband opening the back door of the car and literally bowing as this woman gracefully, almost royal like, emerged from the back seat. She was in her mid to late fifties with an air of superiority. Not a good air to be emanating around me, as I believe all are equal until proven otherwise.

Chapter II

After introductions, cups of tea and coffee and the mandatory inspection of the hostel, something I did with all visitors, I showed them the bunkrooms. Maitreya didn't seem too impressed with the very basic structure of the place, and was less impressed when I explained that it was primarily a holiday centre for children. I had the distinct impression she disliked children.

The Saturday started well with the couple and myself having a solid breakfast of bacon and eggs as the female Christ reincarnate (which is what this woman claimed "Maitreya" meant) slept till late in the morning. They spent most of the day visiting the local sites, checking out the property and generally relaxing. At about five that evening, it had become obvious this Maitreya was ready to talk business. She explained about her reincarnated status and how she had been sent by Mother God to restart a new feminist-based spirituality that would eventually overtake the world.

While her interests were broad and all encompassing, and rather wafty, mine were immediate and centred on the matter at hand. I ask for payment. The couple were quite willing to pay for the three of them, but Maitreya stated that as she was someone of importance, bordering on royalty, her stay at my humble abode should be free. As if the matter had been decided, she left the room without further discussion. While she retired to the showers, to prepare for a ritualistic task that had to be done before sun set, the couple quietly explained that they would pay me what was due for all three on Sunday night before they left.

She returned approximately a half hour later wearing a see-through cheesecloth-like caftan, and nothing underneath. The couple quickly left and headed for their bedroom. Maitreya informed me that she had chosen Peacefields as her new temple. In order to consummate its dedication, I would have to make love with her before the sunlight had left the sky that evening. She informed me that after this ritual I was to hand over to her the deed to Peacefields. This was a command from the Goddess and it had to be obeyed. This was the last straw for me.

I explained that I totally disagreed with her belief that she was the Christ reincarnate. Telling her I believed that we were all potentially the Christ. And that the word simply meant anointed and we were all capable of being anointed. I explained that Jesus, to my mind, was the first to bring the concept of God/man to the Jewish people, and since his death and resurrection, we are all capable of achieving this status if we follow his teachings. I also highlighted the differences between her and Jesus. For example, He liked children; she didn't. He was non-imposing; she wasn't. His life style drew people to him; hers was repulsive. He was humble; she didn't know what the word meant.

I said that Jesus was not known to have had a sexual union with anyone and certainly not as a means of bringing God's world into this one. I concluded by stating this was not my property but that of a charitable organization. As the governing Committee of the organization had set the condition of people staying it would be appreciated if she would pay me the fee owing, for which I would gladly give her a receipt.
She stared at me in a frightening way and headed out the door. The couple must have overheard some of the conversation and when Maitreya left the room they entered. They warned me to be careful what I said to her. They said she was a very powerful person with a very powerful knowledge in sorcery. I explained that I too was a very powerful person and that I believed the real power of Christ protected those that stood for what was right - no matter what the consequences.

Our conversation was interrupted by the sound of something being slopped against the hostel walls and Maitreya chanting in a very loud and aggressive voice. The couple paled out

Chapter II

white claiming she was putting a curse on the place. They implored me to leave as soon as possible as nothing good would come out of this place again. They immediately left for their bedroom and within the hour they and their weird friend had packed their belongings and had returned to Sydney. The couple had left me the due payment for all three under one of the pillows, I assume so that Maitreya didn't find out they had paid.

Peacefields took a down hill curve after that. We had hoped the planned State Government Sandy Hollow Rail line system from Ulan to Newcastle, initially constructed as a coal line, would include passenger services at a later time, but the Government never followed up the idea. This would have allowed our guests to join the train at Newcastle and arrive at Wollar. Every attempt to improve bookings, which included me visiting countless schools, charities, and organizations all over NSW, failed. The lack of bookings plus the worst drought ever recorded in the region sounded the death knoll for Peacefields.

The committee took a long serious look at possible options and found neither my dreams or a holiday program would sustain Peacefields. So in July 1986 the committee closed the hostel down. I moved with much disappointment to Mudgee and after I got back some money owing to me from my loan to the Hostel project, I bought a comfortable little cottage in Gulgong. I stayed there till I moved into Queensland in 1997. My time in Wollar from 1977 to 1986 was the most memorable time in my life. Jesus had 40 days and 40 nights in the wilderness, I had 9 years, and I loved every emotional up and down moment of it.

It was from my contact with the people of the hippy commune that I first heard of a purposely-built meditation, retreat and spiritually enhancing development centre about twenty minutes north of Mudgee on the Ulan Road. I visited the centre not long before it first opened, looking for answers concerning my psychic experiences. The biggest mistake I made was to mention the indirect support to Peacefields from the Catholic Church and its followers. After that I was never invited by the owners to any of their activities except the first two or three open seminars. I only heard about activities from people who were regulars to the centre and who could see the gift I had. Eventually, because I dared to show my abilities when asked by one of the performers to do some platform healing work, I was banned. Had I declared myself a psychic, there is a good chance I would have been accepted with open arms, but at that stage I was still battling to reconcile my Catholic beliefs.

Since declaring myself a psychic I have found that people treat me differently. In my early days the information I passed on to people was either dismissed or ignored. After I declared myself, it was like I had suddenly gained a huge power or a diploma, which allowed me to say things that had no credibility with the same folks before. In the case of my own family I am still remembered as the talkative young man, especially with one particular aunty. Pity she couldn't have remembered some of what I had said maybe she wouldn't have had to endure such sadness most of her life. I probably would have been taken more seriously had I studied in the areas of psychology or spoken from that perspective. It is sad but true that people want an opinion from a credentialed individual.

I believe we are all fluid. There is no conclusion because the journey is ongoing. We are all travelling on different paths with no particular handbook or map directing us to our particular destination. Therefore we have to give more credit to ourselves as individuals and our personal guides. In no way should we assume we or our beliefs are better then others. Nor should others consider themselves or their beliefs, better than ours. None of us have a right, no matter how justified it may feel, to override other individual's beliefs. We certainly have a right to speak our mind when we have a difference of

Chapter II

opinion with someone else's journey and point of view. But we should not assume our journey is right, and theirs is not. No one is right or wrong, just different.

At some time in our journey, some people will have to take the hard, rough and untried road as part of their particular learning, while others seemingly travel the often trodden travelled other-road. Spiritually we all travel on hard, as well as, smooth surfaces in our soul's journey.

When we hit a particularly hard and difficult bit it may seem very easy for them. For example, if you have had major difficulties in a personal relationship, and the other person finds relationships a breeze, then there is no way that other person is going to understand your predicament. Conversely when someone says something concerning our belief, spirituality, or religion often our first reaction to this person's comments is indignation. If in our thoughts we strongly feel the questions, "How dare that person question me? Who do they think they are?" When we couldn't answer their simple questions concerning our basic belief, then we need to look seriously at why we are indignant. Could it be that we are hiding a weakness in our spiritual base? Are we following our highest Guidance, or are we merrily drifting along, blindly assuming we are OK?

Others have a right to discuss their beliefs with us or even question our standing on a matter. This works as long as we don't come across as taking a stance that is superior. We must not assume our beliefs are necessarily under attack. Instead we would be far better off assuming this person is assisting us.

For those that believe their source is pure, especially those that believe they have a strong link to God or God's message, remember Jesus said you will be known by your fruit. You may think you are producing good spiritual shoots, but others are the mirrors that allow us to know if our belief is truth-based or if we are fooling ourselves.

I definitely encourage a person to be choosy and strongly discerning when it comes to the source of the information they are receive. This is especially important for those persons doing psychic readings or sessions, psychic teachers, healers, and particularly those persons who are channelling.

There have been too many New Age gurus and television-evangelists saying the right words and making the right claims, but whose life and personal weaknesses have seriously tripped them up. I have also seen many a TV personality claiming to be a medium, allowing all sorts of spirit entities to enter them in trance state and I have had to turn the show off because I can sense the low level energy using that person. Many are not what they claim to be. Or put better in a once often-used phrase, 'All that glitters is not necessarily gold'.

Then there are those who claim psychics can see into every secret a person has. They think psychics can use this psychic power to negatively affect this person in some way as if to hex that person. Of course it is pure lunacy even to imagine a psychic has such power. But there is still a very wrong misconception as to what a psychic is, can do, and know. Remember to be discerning in your choices of input, be that input spiritual or physical.

I continue on my long and winding road. After the closure of Peacefields and my moving to Mudgee I had a number of different jobs. The one I liked the best was working with disabled people. This job was as the leader of a life skills team for people with intellectual and developmental disabilities. One memorable case was working with a young severely disabled autistic woman. She was in her early twenties and lived with her mother and father on an isolated farm in the backwoods

Chapter II

of Mudgee. It was impossible to communicate with her or even to show her the most basic of living skills.

During my many visits to ascertain how our service could best help her and her parents, I noted that she would, from time to time, start to quietly sing a very pretty song without intelligible words. Her mother said she had sung this same song for as long as she could remember, and would often sing it, over and over. It wasn't a song anyone recognised and her parents couldn't understand how she could have learned it. The daughter was their only child and never interacted with other people outside of them. There was no way she could have mimicked the tune or heard it from the radio or TV as they had neither.

During one of my visits she started to sing this song and in my psychically developing mind I could see a Native American woman, quietly rocking a baby in her arms and singing this same song. I freaked. I had never had such an experience before. I had had previous psychic events happen to me, but never had it been someone else doing the weird stuff.

Around the late 90's when Mike and Sharon were expecting their first daughter the three of us were getting various bits of information concerning a Native American and a very young child. Over the time of the pregnancy we kept getting more and more information connecting Mike to his unborn child in a previous past life. Mike kept getting a lullaby and the presence of a Native American woman singing to him. I felt Mike had been a baby in that life and his unborn daughter had either been his mother or an older sibling or aunty.

When we all moved to Koumala in late 2003, we noted the child would do a particular dance and sing a particular song. This didn't seem to have any relevance to any of us at the time. As she danced, she would do some very unusual hand motions and gestures we didn't see anything significant in this. The day I started to write the basic story of the autistic girl and her song I started to put together the autistic girl's song and Mike's experiences with his first daughter. The autistic girl had sung a lullaby she had been taught by a Native American woman in spirit, from the late 1880's, or possibly earlier. This was now related in the 90's to my friend and his yet unborn daughter.

A part of my life that affected me the most and the one I wish to dwell on the least had a major bearing on my psychic expansion. It was when I met and married my only wife. Back in 1984, I visited a lot of Sydney schools, church groups and organizations promoting Peacefields. One of the places I visited was a children's playgroup at Wahroonga. I left brochures and a phone number with the organiser and expected nothing to come of it.

Some weeks later I received a phone call from a woman saying she had a disabled daughter and was in a stressed state because of this daughter's condition. I arranged for her to visit with her daughter for a week's rest. It became pretty obvious from first meeting her that though her four year old daughter was seriously disabled. The condition of the mother was also of concern.

This woman Jean and I became close friends, then lovers and then later married. Her mental stature was very much up and down and eventually I learned that she had bi polar disorder. Her condition was seriously inflamed by fundamentalist Christians who were very quick to support whatever image Jean would conjure up, without checking out the facts. On at least five occasions Jean left me, convinced by her so-called Christian friends, that I was a Satanist. Each time she returned we became that bit closer till finally, after leaving Peacefields, and moving to Gulgong and after a time in Mudgee, I asked her to marry me.

Chapter II

After the engagement at her mother's home in Sydney, Jean took a serious turn and went absolutely crazy. It was evening and she had stormed off down the road through the bush calling out crazy things. She said, she wasn't going to marry Satan and that she was not going to be controlled by some evil wizard. I was sauntering behind and when she finally sat on a rock at the end of the street I strolled over and sat next to her. I went to say something soothing to her, but instead got that familiar tingling sensation at the back of my neck and the next thing I knew I'm in trance. When I returned to normality I was aware Jean was half way up the road, running at full speed and screaming at the top of her voice.

It was two days later that she was finally sane enough for me to talk to her and understand needed to be shared. She told me I had started to talk strangely, much calmer and slower than normal. She said I was smiling but that I looked different in some way. She said I told her that she had been badly affected by confusing thoughts that were playing games with her mind so that what was good was appearing as bad and visa versa. I had strongly advised her to come with me and visit a psychiatrist to see if there was any treatment for the mood swings. The Power within me asked her if she would give permission for a release. She said yes and almost immediately I felt the energy building up within. A very strong voice said "Be gone Satan and do not tempt that which does not belong to you."

Jean took it that she was the Satan being sent away, hence why she ran screaming. At this point I had very little to no experience with mental illness. Had I know then what I know now I most certainly wouldn't have become involved with her. With the support of her family, she and I went to visit a psychiatrist who diagnosed her condition as bi polar and suggested a course of medication. However, under mental health rules, she didn't have to share with me, either as her fiancé or as her husband, what she was or wasn't taking.

On the Light Path — Peter Lyons

Telling her fundamentalist Christian friends that a psychiatrist was now treating her was like red to a bull. They told her medications were chemicals that played games with her mind and were unsafe. They told her all she needed was to declare Jesus as her lord and saviour and all would be well. The fact that Jean had been declaring Jesus as her lord and saviour for at least the four or five years I had known her, and possibly longer, with little to no effect, didn't seem to matter to their extremely naive minds. She reluctantly took the medication and continued her visits to the psychiatrists.

I spent most of my time reassuring her that the medication was the best option, and that the fundamentalist Christians had never been there when she had had a breakdown and was rushed off to the mental health ward of various hospitals.

We married in 1991 and lived in my humble cottage in Gulgong. She became an active member of both my Catholic church and her adopted Anglican Church. But deep down the devil that plagued her mind refused to remain still. And in the same way that I have a voice or a power that speaks or acts out through me for the good, she had a power that acted and spoke the opposite. It was much later that I found she had accused me of having done some horrendous things, all baseless, and had convinced some very important people in the town, including the Anglican minister and his wife that I should be shunned.

Towards the end of 1993 it was pretty obvious that Jean was no longer taking her medication, and under NSW state law I could do nothing. Her temper tantrums, violent outbursts, and screaming terror episodes had me scared. Not so much that she was a danger to herself or me physically, though she definitely was, but that she was so convincing when she made accusations concerning me.

Chapter II

At a Catholic Church function in the November that year, she informed the priest she was leaving and going to visit a friend in Sydney. Assuming I was aware of the arrangements the priest suggested I come visit him in her absence. When I questioned her as to her intentions, she raged at how a priest should keep confessional matters to himself and should not have told me.

She did leave for Sydney, but instead of visiting her friend as originally planned, stayed with my family instead. Her friend, concerned that she hadn't arrived, phone me and I in turned phoned her family. They hadn't heard from her. I phoned my family to ask if she had turned up there, and they quietly said yes. She had told them not to tell me where she was. She indicated she was fearful of me and that she needed time to get her head together. My mum didn't bite she knew me well enough to know that what Jean was saying was nowhere near the truth. Dad on the other hand, being a simple man and though supportive of me as a son, had his concerns at the level of accusations she was making about me. He assumed there must have been some basis in fact for her to make such convincing claims.

It was my sister, having had dealings with mental illness, who strongly suggested Jean contact the Mental Health Emergency Team, or MHETs, or she would. Jean contacted the MHETs team under protest and they admitted her to the local mental health ward of Hornsby hospital where she stayed for two weeks.

Our adopted son and I travelled to Sydney as planned for the Christmas celebrations and headed to my wife's mother's place as arranged. Every aspect of my life, beliefs, integrity, and moral conscience base was tested. I even believed that as a true Christian I should lay down my life for my friend, and took that actual stance. It was Jean who made the final choice.

On the Light Path

Peter Lyons

Early Christmas morning at about 6.30 am I awoke to banging and bashing as she packed her car and in a manic rush raced out of the driveway in reverse. Her family had no idea where she was going, or why. We were totally in the dark. I contacted the mental health team but the staff who had dealt with Jean earlier were on holiday break. They repeated the oft-heard mantra that is commonly stated by mental health workers in such a situation: "Unless the person is a serious danger to themselves or others, there is nothing the METs team can do."

Jean's sister Debbie, seeing my total state of despair, suggested I contact a psychic she knew. This psychic had helped Debbie when she and her ex were going through some serious troubles. I phoned the number Debbie gave me and was greeted with a youngish voice, with lots of noise and music going on in the back ground. I explained why I had phoned, apologising for doing so on such an auspicious day. The young woman said that her mother wasn't doing any sessions till the New Year. My heart dropped a couple of thousand floors. I was so hoping I might get some reassurance that things would turn out better between Jean and me. A muffled sound from a hand across the mouthpiece, a lot of fidgeting and a new voice came on the line.

"Hello I'm Joan."
I started to repeat what I had just said, but she cut me off.
"You are in an awful mess, aren't you?" She said sympathetically.
"Confused" was all I could think to say.
"Spirit told me I'd be hearing from you." She said, which blew me away.
She organised a time and day for me to visit, and gave me the address.
The meeting with her was a major challenge concerning my understanding of psychics. She had pictures of a number of saints, including well know icons, on the wall, and made a

point of telling me that what she did was a God given gift as far as she was concerned. Whether she said this to all clients, or it came from my guides to reassure me, I don't know, but it sure was needed. I gave her no advanced knowledge of why I had come.

She gave a very unflattering description of Jean, saying a very evil force had possessed Jean and had tested us both. She said I had passed with flying colours. She told me that the relationship was dead in the water and that I was not to try redeem it as this would just cause me to loose more power, and for the evil to gain. She further said "I can see you moving to Queensland, where the whales birth their young. I think its Maryborough, or at least Maryborough will play a very important part in your future up there."

She said I had to wait awhile longer before the move was meant to happen, but after I moved, I would be living a new life, almost like I would be reborn. I panicked a bit when I heard this. To me it sounded as if she were gentle trying to tell me I was going to die. As it transpired what she had said was spot on.

As Joan predicted, Jean's mental condition grew steadily more severe after she had left me at Christmas and returned to Gulgong. By mid 1996, I was still living in Gulgong in a very fragile state. Jean made it impossible for me to trust anyone or to find anyone to talk to. Learning from her past mistake, Jean had gone to the Catholic Priest and invoked the confessional rite when discussing any matter with him concerning me. This virtually made it impossible for me to talk to him on the same matter, as he would have been technically breaking the confessional rite with her.

Our adopted son had chosen to stay with me, so this meant I was unable to make any real moves in my life till after he had finished his schooling. Through necessity and with the confirmation that came from the psychic woman's reading I turned back to my psychic roots with a vengeance. I was starting to feel spirit was well and truly working through me. I would meditate on a daily basis. I wasn't getting much information, but the serene feelings and a knowing that something was about to happen for me gave me a new lease of life.

I lived a hermit's existence during this period, afraid to go out for fear Jean would verbally or physically attack me. Without cause she had taken a domestic violence order out against me, which severely limited my movements around the town. She used every opportunity to find a reason to bring the police to my door, claiming I had broken the orders. The police were totally powerless to stop this. There were no support services for men, in such a situation, in regional Australia. I would get up in the morning, get my son off to school, do basic house cleaning and then go back to bed. I would go for a walk around three in the afternoon, knowing my ex had to collect her daughter from school, and would arrive back home at four as my son arrived off the school bus.

One evening I was woken to the sound of air rushing around the room. I sat up in bed in the dark, listening for the source of this strange phenomenon. The windows were all shut, as were the two doors, and the slow combustion log heater was slowly smouldering; yet I felt extremely cold. Vapour came out of my mouth as I breathed, so I went over to the fire and put in a few more logs. The moment I left the bed, I felt like someone was standing behind me, and I didn't like the feeling at all. I was still quite green in my new spirituality. Had this happened to me now, I would have immediately drawn on my guides' energy to protect me. I could feel the hairs on my neck prickling. I put the logs in the fire and opened up the damper to increase the burning process.

I returned to my bed, shivering both inside and out. I had this overwhelming feeling of despair and panic surging through me, with thoughts and abusive comments from my ex bom-

Chapter II

barding my mind. It was then I called on my guides. It took a very long time for me to block out the psychic attack. Eventually, thanks to my guides' help, I could feel sanity returning to me. I raised my hands, in a similar manner to the way I did when spirit moved through me and released the energy from an old house in Mudgee. I could feel an overwhelming feeling of peace streaming out from deep within, as the cold fear began to dissipate. A voice in my mind was peacefully chanting, "Have no fear, have no fear," as the positive energy spread out into the room.

Suddenly I heard an aggressive voice in my mind, as if it were coming from the doorway, yelling, "You can never get rid of me. You will never get rid of me. You will pay. You will pay." The source of the peaceful chanting seemed to smile as it gently but firmly closed the door against this hate. It was within a few weeks of this occurring that my ex was forced to change her daytime activities, due to her daughter's commitments. This left me much more freedom to get out and about in the wider community.

One morning, not long after this event, while meditating, I got a very strong feeling to contact a naturopath I knew well. She worked out of her own clinic in Dubbo in Central Western NSW. Spirit told me that I was to phone her to make an appointment, and to visit her as soon as possible to deliver a message to her from them. I felt such a fool as I phoned and make an appointment for the next day.

I arrived at her clinic around 10.00am as planned, but she was not there. Her mother was at the desk and she told me her daughter had got a number of extra bookings and that she may not be able to see me today. She asked me if I'd like to wait just in case she got a spare moment, and though my humanness said "no" they said "yes."

After about a half hour, her mother asked why I had visited. I said that I was a psychic and that I had met her daughter in

Mudgee some time earlier and that I had a message for her from spirit. Her mother asked me about the contents of the message, so that she could pass it on. I felt very strange and totally inadequate, because though I knew there was a reason for my coming over, I couldn't for the life of me think what it was. I opened my mouth and it started to speak independent of me.

"Well your daughter has been thinking about setting up some kind of meditation groups for people that are ill or suffering in some way," I started, quite to my surprise. "I feel she is uncertain as to how to start, if to start at all, and I have been sent to tell her it is very necessary that she do this work."

I went silent, and tried removing my foot from my mouth.

"Interesting," her mother started, "when did you get this information?" To which I replied I was in a state of meditation and it came to me that I was to come over especially to see her daughter and pass on the message. Her mother took a gasp of air and smiled.

"Well," she started, "I recently went to the cancer clinic, just up the road here, to have a check up. When you go to the clinic, you have tests done, and then you return some weeks later for the test results. You sit in the waiting room and wait to hear whether you get thumbs up or thumbs down. I got thumbs up thankfully, but many don't. I had said to my daughter, wouldn't it be a great idea if there could be a meditation group formed in a place like that, so that whoever was waiting in the surgery waiting rooms, could be helped with a de-stressing type of support group. I have been thinking about it for a while, but I need support from someone of authority to help me with this, like a doctor or a nurse. I've been waiting for a sign. I think it was me you were supposed to see, not my daughter, and I think you've just given me my answer. Thank you."

I never got to see her daughter.

Chapter II

A couple of years ago, while doing some psychic sessions in Adelaide, I heard that some hospitals and cancer clinics down there were now running regular meditation groups. I was told the idea had come from up in country NSW, around Dubbo, where the same idea had started some years earlier. I often wonder the outcome had I not gone over to Dubbo that day and made a complete fool of myself. I wonder how many times you, the reader, have passed up similar opportunities for fear you too, may have deemed such an action as foolish? Not that I could blame you.

After this stunning and out of the blue experience came more unusual and unexpected ones, the first being an encounter with a full trance medium. She had come to stay a few days with my friends Mark and Joyce who lived about a kilometre away from my home in Gulgong. This medium was the first person I had met who actually went into a full trance. This particular night, after some gentle coaxing, she gradually went into a tranced state and changed from a very quiet and sombre, middle aged woman, into a very youthful and almost hyperactive young man.

In trance state, she took on this teenager's personality, scratching and itching constantly, moving about in the seat, distracted when the questions didn't suit him, and generally a good sign that this was a definite trance. I was very uncomfortable with the whole show. Though I knew very little about full trance then, in fact I was hoping this woman may give me a few pointers, I kept getting this very deep feeling that this youth was a lost soul and needed releasing, not a four and twenty questions session.

Joyce asked this youth questions that gleaned for us he was from either France or England at the time of the Black Plague and it was obvious from the questions he was dodging that he wasn't as innocent as he was claiming. The scratching was from his flea infestation, which we assumed was how he died, because he was constantly trying to rid himself of his infestation, as if he knew they were some how responsible for the deaths around him.

When the medium came out of her trance, I asked her how she felt, and she said she was very drained and tired. She said she hadn't been doing much trance work anymore because of the after effects from some of the ordeals she had to go through. I asked in my innocence, should she still feel tired and drained if her highest guides sanctioned the source she was channeling? I asked if she shouldn't be protected by this highest guidance and therefore not be tired or drained?

She didn't answer but her "I think she is just wonderful" supporter, who had come with her, admonished me for even doubting this medium's abilities. Quoting many instances where she had helped many lost souls, and had passed on much needed information to grieving relatives of those who had passed over.

The next day, the medium called me aside and asked me what else I knew of trance work and I embarrassingly said very little, other that what came into my head. It was she who told me she could see a huge positive energy around me when I spoke the way I spoke to her the night before. She said she felt more than heard what I was saying and knew it was right. That is she felt it was coming from an acceptable and honourable source. She said she had been having difficulties, though she hadn't been telling anyone. She said she was certain it was as a result of her particular trance style. The last I heard was she had stopped doing trance work completely, which is quite sad, as she was a very good medium.

In another encounter, while visiting Mark and Joyce I psychically sensed there was a spiritual presence in the house, particularly around Joyce. With her permission I checked her aura. I found she had angry and aggressive male spirit energy around her. Joyce was shocked when she realised from my

Chapter II

description this young man was her brother's son who had been killed some years earlier in a bike accident. Joyce had heard that both he and his girl friend had been decapitated in a motorbike accident in New Zealand.

Through me my guides asked Joyce to address her nephew in spirit as if he were physically there. They instructed her to ask him to go to the White Light, but he became more aggressive. Through me my guides started to talk to him. A sudden jolt made me aware something dramatic had happening. Joyce, being very gifted psychically, looked at me with shock and said, "He just punched you." Though I was aware something dramatic had happened, there were no serious effects.

My guides I told him they were happy to help him, but if he wasn't interested in getting their help that they would have him removed till such time as he was willing to behave properly. They added that he would have to wait till another time, and by then both Joyce and myself may have moved on. This seemed to settle him and again my guides asked him if he would like to be released, he said he didn't want to go to the Light till he had found his girl friend. At this point I heard his girl friend from somewhere in the Light calling to him. My guides asked him if he could hear her calling, to which he replied, "Of course I can, and her voice had been driving me mad, because I can't find her." My guides said look up and you will see her. He said "don't you think I've already tried that? Don't you think I would already have looked up there for her? It was the first place I looked."

"And did you see her there when you looked up?" They queried.
"Well of course not," He replied angrily, "Or I'd have gone to her."
"Then why is it she can see you, and you can hear her, but you can't see her?"

"How do I bloody well know," his anger increasing, "You're the one with the answers, you tell me."
"It is your anger," They replied quietly. "Her guides won't let you anywhere near her while you are in a state of anger."
He went quiet, and then replied, "Well I have every right to be angry. One minute she is there with me, the next thing I know, I have lost my bike and she has gone."
"Are you aware you and she were killed in a biking accident?" They asked. "What? Bullshit," he replied. "If I'm dead, how come there are no angels around me, just this pitch black night."

"It is because you won't accept the obvious. Your aunty and her friend, through whom we are speaking, aren't there in the dark with you. They are back in Australia and it is now five years since you lost your bike and your girlfriend."
"Is this true?" He asked Joyce.

"Yes it is." She replied with tears in her eyes. "You both died in a tragic bike accident in New Zealand."
He went silent.

"OK, then what am I supposed to do?" He said finally.
"Close your eyes and take some long, deep, peaceful breaths." My guides instructed. "Let all your fears, hurts, and sadness lift away from you. Then, slowly open your eyes and look upwards."
After a number of weak attempts, basically going through the motions, followed by my guides' admonishments, he made a more serious attempt to meditate as instructed. Both Joyce and I could feel he was doing as he was asked. Suddenly, we felt a tingling and an emotional feeling as he began to open his eyes.

Tearfully Joyce said, "He can see her, he has found her."
Slowly we felt him ascending towards her in the light, till he had finally gone. Joyce and I were both in tears by now, as

Chapter II

was her husband Mark, and so we all had ourselves a cuppa (cup of tea) while we composed ourselves.

I called back to their place about a week later. During the discussion, Joyce sensed something happening in spirit and we both tuned in. Her nephew was back holding the hand of his girlfriend, who was nursing a baby. They were both dressed in white and we were told they had just been married. Joyce hadn't known that the girl had been pregnant when she had passed over. Joyce later phoned this young man's father, who didn't believe in anything of a psychic nature, and told him what had happened. He hung up. About two weeks later her brother's wife wrote to say her phone call to her brother two weeks earlier, had shocked him so much that he couldn't talk to anyone about it. She had written that it wasn't common knowledge the girlfriend had been pregnant when she had died. She further said that two days after Joyce and I had encountered him he visited his father to say all was well. The son's visit had been the day before Joyce phoned to confirm what the son had said to us. As a result of this encounter with his now departed son, the father, who had been a very heavy drinker, never touched another drop.

While I am on the subject of strange encounters, my meeting Mark and Joyce was one of them. I had been visiting Steve and Linda, a couple with Aboriginal heritage, for quite a few months and we had been discussing the similarities of psychic events with those of Aboriginal secret ways. On one occasion, I arrived to be greeted by a very excited Linda, who said her Aboriginal friends, living north of Gulgong, had just met their new neighbours. Not only were these new neighbours Aboriginal, they were also very knowledgeable about the Wirradjuri people that once inherited the area.

In a separate incident, Linda's eldest son and his mates had gone out on the northern road and down to the creek where they found a circle of stones on the northern side of the road crossing. Intrigued by this, Linda and I went out for a look. When we arrived we realised the creek was a part of the property of this new aboriginal family Linda's friends had told her about. We took it upon ourselves to call on these people, to ask what the stone circle represented, and that was when I first met Mark and Joyce.

Mark said aboriginal ancestors in spirit had instructed him to make the Bora ring as a calling card to a psychic they had wanted him to meet. At first I thought it may have been other aboriginal people, but we discovered over a short period of time that they had been calling me. It was from this encounter that I learned the secret ways of the aboriginal knowing. There were field trips to known and up till then unknown areas where aboriginal people had been slaughtered. The four of us regularly held psychic sessions at their place for a few years.

In another unusual encounter, Linda and Steve had invited my son and I to visit and stay with her sister Sue for a few days in Bellingen on the NSW north coast. They were convinced that I would be moving to that area after I had received that extraordinary psychic reading in '94 from the psychic woman. Though this psychic had told me I would be moving to Queensland, I found it hard to believe; in fact I thought she was totally wrong because I had no connections in Queensland, especially in Maryborough. We were convinced I would be moving to northern NSW.

My son and I packed up our things and went for our first decent holiday since my wife had left. Bellingen is a very pretty place, nothing like I had expected and I could easily have settled down there. We arrived at Sue's place, which was way out on a dirt road in the middle of nowhere. The house was built with the back cut into the side of a hill. The front was up on stilts and faced into the valley and road below. It was constructed in three levels out of second hand materials, and

Chapter II

sat beautifully in its bush setting. I loved it so much I would have moved in immediately if it had been possible.

I slept like a log in a cute room, which was more like a loft than a room in its own right. During the night, as I am prone to do, I got up and went to the toilet. The place was pitch black, and I didn't turn on a light concerned I would wake everyone. As I made my way to the toilet located across the hall from the bedroom I had been allocated, I heard this strange scraping sound, like someone dragging a sheet of plastic softly across the floor. I reached for the toilet light and switched it on. There on the floor, where I had just been, was a carpet python. It was making its way up the stairs and out into the hill behind the house. It goes without saying I turned the light on ever time I went to the toilet after that especially because Sue told me death adders sometimes came in through the back door to cool off in the summer months.

The next day we all went to the Bellingen markets. The intention was to see if a market site might have been a means by which I would do psychic readings if I moved to the area. Country market days had become quite widespread from around the late 70's and varied from area to area. The New Agers and alternative believers were fast infiltrating most of them, so this of course meant the markets were now drawing the kind of people who would be interested in psychic readings.

The markets at Bellingen were definitely under the spell of these New Agers. There were fruits and vegetables of a tropical nature and homemade wares, mixed with tarot-reading psychics. Dream catchers and crystals could be had at almost every store, as could young maidens who look like they knew more about sex at 13 than I did at 40. The dress style was anything but modest, unless you class G-string panties and a see through mosquito shawl as overly dressed. And as for one young male, one didn't need to look hard to ascertain his pubic hair had been coloured. It was an interesting market to say the least.

That evening back at Sue's place, as we were about to go to bed, Sue mentioned she no longer slept in their bedroom while her husband was away. She said she was convinced it was haunted. Sue's husband Rob, who had built the mud-brick, alternative house, worked away for a week or more at a time building similar houses.

Linda and Mike also said they had felt uncomfortable when they and the kids had slept in this room on previous occasions. Sue said that when her husband was home, she would have doubts about his fidelity, yet when he was away, she had no doubts about him at all. Sue mentioned that the main bearer timbers used for the house, had come from the demolition of what had originally been a brothel in the Kings Cross area of Sydney.

Knowing of my psychic skills, Linda asked if I could sense anything. Though I had done psychometry and sensed areas of land where aboriginal people had been massacred, I had never done anything relating to a house before. I decided to give it a try and see what could be sense.

Using my outstretched hands as antenna, I slowly walked into the room, and immediately felt like I was back in 1920's Sydney. I couldn't see anything, but I could feel the presence of some very nasty women and men. The women had no respect for men, and the men were extremely cruel towards the women, which indicated to me that this had been a very different kind of brothel. By getting me to raise my hands and slowly move around the room, as if I were ushering an unseen force to the door, my guides released the spirit energy. I assumed the timbers had locked in and carried the energy of these persons from the brothel. Later I was told that the feeling was the energy of the souls, who were indirectly linked

Chapter II

to the materials, but not actually there. That night Linda and Steve said they had the best sleep they had ever had in that room.

My son and I returned to Gulgong from our holiday a week before they did, and on their return they told us Sue had slept in the room the night we left. Later I heard she had been sleeping there every night since, with no disturbances or concerns.

Though I'd been able to do some wonderful work for Sue and her husband, I was no closer to finding my new home as the psychic had predicted. I was back to where I'd started. I had long been without work and knew that if I didn't get something soon I'd be heading for the soup kitchen.

I headed to Mudgee where I registered for unemployment benefits and work at the local unemployment office and then headed to the local shops. On my way to the supermarket, a woman approached me asking if I was the person who had worked with a mentally ill woman in Wollar some years before.

I had indeed been drawn into a serious situation by a mentally ill woman who had trudged her way from Mudgee to the Peacefields hostel. It was an event I remembered most vividly. It had been mid week and winter and I had a group of 10 year old school children and their teachers staying at the hostel. As was the case with this age group there were mostly women schoolteachers. This meant I usually got supervision duties in the boys' showers while the women supervised the girls. This was to ensure that showers happened as quickly and as safely as was possible and to conserve our very limited water supply.

It was during one of these showering nights I noticed an unusual quietness outside in the courtyard, where I would have expected to hear bedlam, as young, freshly cleaned children chased each other around the hostel veranda. A knock on the bathroom door soon told me why. A schoolteacher informed me I had a visitor, and it was obvious from her expression that this visitor was unusual to say the least.

I went outside to find a young woman in her mid to late twenties in very light clothing, no socks and poor footwear standing in the courtyard; two small ports by her side. She looked vague and at first I thought she might have been on some kind of drug. I asked her name and she said it was Maria, and that she was looking for the Townsend family. I explained that she had taken a wrong turn after leaving the Wollar/Ulan road and should have gone left instead of right.

It was not unusual for people to take the wrong road. One of my aunts and her husband has spent a night in freezing conditions on the Mogo Road after taking the left turn instead of a right. The Mogo Road led to the hippy commune where the camel traders were based. I asked where she had come from and she said she had caught a train from Orange to Mudgee and then she had walked. As it would have taken her most of the day to walk that distance, I suggested she have a 'cuppa' and I would phone Elise Townsend to come and get her. While the schoolteachers took her into the dining room, I phoned Elise and told her the story. Elise was horrified. Her son had just spent a couple of months in Bloomfield, the mental health extension of the Orange Base Hospital where Maria, a seriously ill mental patient, had become infatuated with him. She had asked Elise's son if she could visit him once she had been discharged and he had said yes.

Considering the seriousness of her mental illness he had assumed that she would never be permitted to leave the hospital. However, under the new mental health act, which had not long been implemented, no one could be held against their will in such centres unless they posed a physical danger to

Chapter II

themselves or to others. Because she wasn't considered dangerous, she was able to discharged herself and visit her "boyfriend."

Elise wanted nothing to do with her and when I asked her for a suggestion, she said I should phone Bloomfield. Bloomfield suggested a phone call to the police, but only if she refused to leave. They explained that she was to be treated the same as if anyone else had landed unannounced on the doorstep. I returned to the dining room to be told by some very concerned teachers, she had found herself a bunk in one of the girls' bedrooms and had gone to sleep. This was causing a major problem with the school children, to say nothing of school protocol and policy. I had no choice but to try to remove her. One of the teachers suggested it would be better if a woman approached her instead of a man, especially in view of the fact that there was mental illness involved. I agreed and so they went to her. Suddenly I heard screaming and yelling followed by a door slamming and heavy banging coming from the bedroom. I looked in the direction of the fracas to see the schoolteacher leaning against the veranda post as though she had been pushed there.

Maria was swearing at some unseen person or persons in the bedroom swinging one of her bags around in a very dangerous manner. One blow caught the fibro wall and cracked it. I immediately phoned Mudgee Police and explained the situation, asking that they get here as soon as they could. In the mean time, with the children fed the teachers moved them over to the lounge room where they started some creative activities. I phoned Elise Townsend and told her of what had happened and what was planned. She was horrified and very angry. She said I had no right to bring in the police. She said, this was a health matter and Mudgee Hospital should have been contacted. We hung up agreeing to disagree.

In the meantime, Maria was aware that the children had moved from the courtyard and were now singing happily in the lounge room. With her suitcases she had made her way toward the music. As she got to a certain spot she started to argue violently with some unseen force and returned to the other side of the veranda. From there she swore at the top of her voice at the unseen obstacle, getting more emotional and hysterical as the time dragged on.

At about 9.00 pm, and still no sign of the police, Elise Townsend had arrived. Obviously still angry at me for involving the police, she offered to take Maria to her place with a view to taking her to Mudgee Hospital the next day. She said she had no faith in Bloomfield after they had allowed such a sick person to leave. Maria was more than happy to go with Elise and they headed up the driveway just as the police arrived. I believe the police allowed Maria to go with Elise, but I heard a few days later that Elise had to call the police herself the next day, as she couldn't get Maria out of her house and Mudgee Hospital refused to take her.

This woman, who had approached me in Mudgee some years later, had been one of the schoolteachers at that time. She said her daughter was a serious schizophrenic and wondered if I could help her. I explained that she would be better off contacting someone in the special mental health team based at Mudgee hospital. She said she had, but that they could only act if the daughter was physically doing damage to her self or others. Although I had no qualifications I said, as a friendly gesture, I would visit simply to give an opinion. Upon arriving it was clear this was not a case for me and with the mother's permission, immediately phoned the local mental health nurse. It was while we were waiting that I started to commune with this very sick young woman in a way that actually had her attention and me totally stunned. Normally when people are in such a serious state, they have trouble comprehending what someone else is saying, but she seemed to understand

Chapter II

and interact with me as if we were having a normal sensible conversation.

It was while we were deeply interacting with this very strange gibberish that the mental health nurse arrived. Normally in such a circumstance, the mental health worker would expect to be confronted with an agitated and sometimes aggressive client, whom they have to calm down before administering medication. This client didn't need stabilising medicating to get her to the hospital in fact she was quite happy to go off with the nurse for treatment.

Later this mental health nurse asked me where I had learned such a skill, and I said it just happened. I mentioned how psychic matters had been fazing in and out of my life, especially recently, and that I assumed it had something to do with that. So impressed was this nurse with what she had seen me do that she had passed it on to Judy Tandy, another nurse who lived in a nearby town.

About two weeks after this particular encounter in Mudgee, I received a phone call from Judy. She had heard of my psychic work from the psyche nurse and wanted to know if I would like to visit her home sometime soon as there had been some strange things happening there.

The following weekend I called in to visit the family, who live in a very historic house on the main street. After pleasantries, Judy showed me around the beautiful old guesthouse style place. At the back of the house I had the strangest feeling that there was trouble at the back door or out in the yard. As I was about to ask about my feelings, the phone rang. Judy excused herself and went off into an adjoining room. I approached the door and in my mind asked if there was anyone there. I felt a strange sense of rage and anger coming from out in the yard and felt very much out of my depth.

In my mind I asked my guides for assistance, particularly if they could give me a sign as to whether I should stay or go. Immediately there was the sound of something scratching twice at the back door. I was quite surprised at this as it was a physical sound, not a sound in my mind. I had been lead to believe, by my guides, that it was unusual to hear a physical sound unless it was coming from very, very low-level energy. I asked if what I had just heard was the sign of yes, and I got two scratches. I asked; what is the sign for no? And this time I heard one scratch. I found this whole matter quite concerning. I didn't like the idea that I had to deal with something of such a low level this early in my psychic development.

Judy returned, apologizing profusely for the racket her Rottweiler dog was making out in the back yard.

"She always scratches on the back door when she hears strangers in the house," she said. I felt more than a little foolish at what I had assumed to be a poltergeist, but very grateful I hadn't verbalized my thoughts. Though I still felt there was something strange happening at the back of the house, I put it down to my overreaction to the dog's actions and joined Judy for cake and pleasantries. Wondering what I was meant to do next, when Judy told me the phone call was from her work. She had been called on to replace the other nurse, who had phoned in sick, and would I mind coming back another time.

A few weekends later I was invited back to the house for lunch. I knocked on the door and could hear the Rottweiler pounding up the hallway, followed by footsteps, the sound of a struggle, and finally the door opened. Roy, the husband, introduced himself while struggling to hold the dog by the collar. He invited me in, and as I passed the dog, a sense of apprehension overpowered me. Sensing what he must have thought was my fear; Roy took the dog through to the back yard.

Chapter II

Judy met me taking me into the huge dining room, where her family was watching TV. For some particular and unexplainable reason, I was attracted to their 14 year old daughter. Not in any physical or romantic way, just something about her that held in my mind. We had a beautiful baked lunch, followed by cake and cream, and talked of many things, including my developing spiritual gifts and unusual beliefs. As the afternoon moved on, I kept getting increasing strange and disturbing feelings. The first was to do with the dog, but not the dog itself. Then there was the daughter, who was dressed more like Morticia from the Adam's Family TV show, rather than a girl her age would be expected to dress.

During lunch, I had a strong feeling of pretentiousness, as if the family were keeping deep, dark secrets. I kept feeling there were far more people in the house than the family members I had met, almost as if souls were held prisoners within secret rooms of the old house. The discomfort associated with the back yard from the last time I had visited seemed much stronger and much angrier now. It was as if a male, who I assumed had owned the house, had been locked outside, while his wife and child, who seemed keen to be united with him, had somehow been locked inside. What would be preventing the couple and their child from uniting with him, and who or what was keeping them apart? Logic told me these entities had to be in spirit, rather than physical beings, and the answer to the perplexity would most likely have to do with how they passed over, and in what time frame.

The conversation moved on to why I was there. I asked if they knew the history of the house, and particularly, when it was built, who built it, and for what purpose. They said it was one of the oldest buildings in this town, even predating the gold discoveries of the late eighteen hundreds, and was originally built and paid for by a founding father of the area as a private hospital.

It was during this conversation, that the fourteen-year-old daughter mentioned she had the ghost of a young woman staying in her room. She wasn't perturbed by this spirit and asked if I could get any information on whom the ghost was. The father asked if the presence of the spirit woman was the reason the daughter had become reclusive and reluctant to leave the house or her room. She didn't answer her father directly, saying instead that the world was a bad place. She said she had nothing to live for outside of her room, away from her thoughts and her ghost friend. Their 13 year old son left the table and disappeared obviously disinterested in the conversation and disappeared out the back. A few moments later I heard him return followed by the sound of pounding paws. The father called out not to let the dog run free, and the son and the dog both disappeared into the son's bedroom.

The meal over, it was time for me to do a psychic search. Judy and Roy first led me up the hallway towards their front bedroom. There was no particular concern with that main room however, the little closed in porch area, which jutted out at the front, was a bit disturbing. I sensed that there had been at least one small child buried below the flooring of this room, and I was certain it wasn't alone. I felt like stillborn babies had been buried here.

The bedroom itself would have been where the mothers delivered their babies, and the front extension would have been the crib room. As the mothers recovered, they and their babies would have been moved to other rooms in the house. I showed Judy and Roy how to do a release, and on completion, moved back towards the hallway. I entered the hallway to see the son emerging from his bedroom, followed close behind by the massive dog. It growled a little at first, before coming over to do a sniff test on me. Then we made eye contact. Its action was swift. It leapt at me, aiming its jaws at my throat and would have killed me for sure, had the husband not been positioned between the dog and myself. He grabbed its col-

Chapter II

lar and, with the aid of his son, dragged the very angry and aggressive animal out the back. Judy exclaimed, "Well she's never attacked anyone before. I wonder what got into her." I was so shaken and disoriented that there was no choice but to call it a day, saying I'd return later in the month.

It was while I was away from the house that I started to get more information. This led me to look more closely at what I was dealing with. I felt my mental status and spiritual protection was such that I was more in control than I had been on previous occasions. With what I gained from my guides, historical things the family knew, research at the local library and information gleaned from an old friend at a local museum, I began to piece together the full extent of the history of the many lost souls linked to this very evil house.

Originally built as a private hospital and a gift to the local community, its use was far more sinister. The son of this so-called pillar of society was anything but a decent lad. He and other pastoralist's sons of the district thought nothing of having sex with the under aged daughters of the poor employees, which included aboriginal workers, who worked on their fathers' huge pastoral properties. How could these poor people object without loosing their jobs and homes? If the girls fell pregnant, they were offered hospice at this private hospital, where the worried parents were promised good care would be taken of their daughter and the new arrival.

Most of the parents, with little other choice, took the offer in trust, especially when it was offered freely. The story for the young pregnant lass was anything but what was promised. Many died at the hands of butchers masquerading as nurses, midwives and doctors. The survival rate for mother and child was next to nil. It was caused by an attempt to abort the foetus, breech births, or just poor hygiene.

The worst treated were the young aboriginal girls, regularly rounded up from camping grounds and pack raped by these same animals. If any of them complained, they were offered help, but never heard of again.

When I returned to the house, spirit got me to work from the front to the back, working each room separately, and releasing the souls of the many mums and babies that had been tragically linked there for so many years. It was quite exhausting, both physically and psychically. They got me to go to the closed back door of the house and ask the male spirit in the back yard to turn away from the door and to walk slowly out into the back yard. Once he had done this, they got him to turn back and face the closed door, asking him to relax and remove all feelings of anger. They then had him call out to the spirit of his wife and child, still locked in the house, to come to him. He did as he was asked, and immediately I felt the presence of a woman carrying a child, making her way from where I was standing inside the house to the man waiting in the yard.

Spirit told me she had been raped by a son of one of the pastoralists and had come to the hospice to have the child. As her husband spent most of the time away cattle droving, she was able to keep the matter secret. Her hope was to have the baby, and then have it adopted by a caring and affluent family. Sadly with small towns, rumours are often the means of news, and when the husband returned home, he heard very quickly an adaptation of what had happened to his wife. Outraged and with very little planning, he had confronted the pastoralist's son and threatened him.

Some weeks later he was found with a bullet in the head, fired at close range. The baby had been very sick and taken from its mother. It had been killed by the butchers masquerading as doctors and nurses. The mother died from complications a few days after giving birth, and her spirit, wracked with re-

Chapter II

morse refused to leave the house until she had been reunited with her child. The spirit of the outraged husband had refused to leave the grounds of the hospice until he could speak to his wife; he had assumed she no longer loved him. The guilt of what she had done prevented her from going to him, as did her fear of his anger.

Guides first released the spirit of the baby, which had been buried under the floorboards in the front room, allowing it to go to the mother. The father's change in attitude allowed the mother to feel safe enough to take the baby to him, and the reunited couple allowed all the other lost souls, linked directly and indirectly to them and the house, to be set free. Each member of the current family, as well as my self, experienced very strong emotional feelings as this spirit family, along with the other lost souls, were led by their individual guides to their particular Peace of Heaven.

The young fourteen-year-old daughter, to whose aura the young mother had been attached, felt the release very strongly. Though she was happy for what was happening for the young mum and her daughter, she was still very tearful and sad. The dog had been acting as a guard dog for not only the daughter, but also the spirit of the young mother. When it had made contact with my eyes, it sensed the fear of the spirit girl, who feared any unknown man, and it reacted accordingly.

Two weeks after the release, I came back to the family and with the dog well and truly in the care of the owner, I tentatively looked into its eyes. It growled at first, but I kept speaking gently and calmly, while at the same time, asking the woman in spirit to speak to the dog on my behalf. After a while, the dog relaxed, and from then on I could come and go around the dog without fear or concern.

The daughter's recovery was miraculous. She changed her dark makeup for a lighter and socially accepted one. Her dress style became trendy for that time, and her days of staying away from school, and spending hours in her room in a morbid, introverted state, were gone. She started mixing with her own kind, and even started dating with a local lad, something her parents said they never thought she would do. Last time I heard from the family, they were contemplating painting up the old place and putting it on the market.

My psychic skills were developing faster than I could comprehend. I still hadn't found anyone who could help me decipher it all. At that stage I was still looking for answers in astrology. After all it had been an astrologer who had told many years earlier that I would be a much sought after psychic in my later years. Mark and Joyce's son Michael, who was also an astrologer, confirmed this for me not long before I left for Queensland.

I had been putting out feelers looking for a teacher of astrology from my days at Peacefields, but was fast beginning to believe no such person existed in the area. Then the contacts who had helped me with my healing abilities at the New Age centre, north of Mudgee mentioned a woman in town who dabbled in astrology. I made contact with this person, Sue and I started to visit her regularly at her Mudgee home. She often mentioned how she felt it would be good if her friend Sharon could meet me. She felt Sharon and she could help me with my searching. One day I received a phone call from Sue to say she had gone down to visit Sharon who now lived in Wollongong. She asked me if I could pick up anything concerning the house in which Sharon was living.

I was walking down the hallway of my Gulgong home, just like I was walking down Sharon's hallway. I described a bedroom where a young boy slept and I was concerned at the spiritual energy that seemed to be in that room. I showed Sharon how to bring down the White Light to protect her son, and got her to pass it throughout his room. I then went to the

Chapter II

back of the house and into the kitchen area. I could sense a doorway or entrance close to the stove on the right side. There was no door, Sharon informed me. But I can see it, clear as day. To this day I don't know if there wasn't a door way there sometime in the house's past. I suggested Sharon do a similar exercise here to what I had suggested in the boy's bedroom and we ended the conversation.

Sharon phoned me a few times after Sue had returned to Mudgee, and I was able to pass on some more information concerning psychic matters. I encouraged her to expand her own psychic gifts. I told her I felt she would be moving to Mudgee. Sharon was pretty sure I had got that wrong, because, she had already lived in Mudgee and couldn't see herself moving back there. I thought I had got that wrong as well. About 6 months later, Sharon moved back to Mudgee and stayed in a caravan at Sue's place.

As my friendship with Sue began to wane, my friendship with Sharon grew. On one of the visits Sharon asked me for a psychic reading. I could see her going to her father, or being called to her father for a reason that was not necessarily the truth, or as a result of a misunderstanding. I could see her meeting up with a man that would be older than her or who had lived a pretty hard life to that point. I could see her living near the water, with a summery feeling, and I could see me being in some way connected to her. This disturbed me a little, because I was much older than her, and I didn't like the idea of spirit match making.

In the October of 1996, Sharon moved to her fathers place in Queensland, to live in an extension he had built onto his existing house. She wasn't overly pleased with this arrangement, and had reservations as to whether she would stay there long term. At the end of 1996 she went to the local hotel, to celebrate New Years. While there a strapping young lad approached her and asked if she played pool. She replied that she did, and so this young lad Andrew, asked another lad Tony, to join them. They needed a fourth player so they asked Mike, another slightly built young man sitting alone in the corner if he wanted to join in. Tony, Mike and Andrew are brothers. Once Sharon saw Michael she knew she had found her partner.

They both moved into a shed that Mike had been living in, and in the January of 1997, they asked Sue and I if we would like to come up for a visit. After spending a few weeks with them, Sue and I returned to Mudgee. In the April of that year, I packed up my possessions and travelled alone to Mike and Sharon's new home in Bundaberg Port and never went back to the central west.

Most of my early sessions were psychometry readings, where I would hold a person's article, and get pretty accurate feelings that would relate to that person. There were instances where I had consciously trance, and in two noticeable cases, full trance, I didn't feel all that comfortable doing sessions this way. It was when I moved to Queensland that the gift began to grow away from psychometry and towards the full trance sessions I do now.

In January 1997, when Sue and I had visited Mike and Sharon in Bundaberg, I got directed by spirit to take a trip down to Hervey Bay. In the event that I should move to Queensland I would need an outlet to do psychic sessions. At that point it didn't seem likely that I would get much work in Bundaberg as neither Mike nor Sharon knew any outlets that would be adequate for my particular skill. I had come across the Hervey Bay Spiritualist Church and its minister in an alternative magazine that listed all the Spiritualist Churches at that time.

Imagine my shock when I arrived in Hervey Bay to find it referred to as the Whale Watching Capitol of Queensland, and that the humpback whales regularly travel north to the Bay to raise their young. I had previously made an appointment to

Chapter II

meet this minister, whom I assumed was a psychic, to confirm the previous message I had received from the extraordinary psychic woman in 1994. Contrary to my assumptions, most Spiritualist ministers are not necessarily psychics. This particular one most certainly was not, but said her way of doing private sessions was hypnosis, to which I cautiously submitted myself.

This is a transcript of what I said while in the hypnosis state. The woman graciously recorded it for me:

Peter,

You are living in a time of change, the change that has been predicted. The masses are confused with the messages of the false prophets. They are looking for reliable spiritual information. They are looking for the truth. It is time now for you to know what you have to do and who you are.

You are a messenger representing the Council of the Greater Good, a worker of the White Light, God's own. You will be on call for us when we need you and will work primarily alone. You will be a wildcat going where we want you to go, doing what we want you to do. Circumstance will be how we call you, because it will be hard for you to pick the false individuals from the genuine. This is the time Jesus spoke of when he said there would be those that would say, "Here, I am the Messiah. No, here I am the true Messiah."

Be aware and discerning so that we can prepare you for the subtle changes in people that you would not normally pick up on. Let Us help you look between the lines in other people's predictions, perspectives and spirituality. This is for your ears Pete. This will make more sense to you later. We will organise the contacts and prepare them for your arrival. A main part of your work will involve travelling to different towns from a home base. You will not be involved with the Spiritualist Church here in the Bay, or any of the Spiritualist Family, though you will keep in contact with those that you have met through the Church, meditation groups and healing groups, till We can be of no further assistance, through you, to them.

Many of the psychics that are active here in the Bay and other centres you visit, will be moved on, or will be stopped from doing readings and we, working through you, will be the cause of this.

You will not be the one to make these changes happen. We will make the changes so that it will seem as if they are leaving you, and that way, you will not be blamed for breaking up friendships.

The Spiritualist Church in Hervey Bay will move from where it is currently to a different centre before you leave and there will be other Churches, meditation groups and alternative other bodies directly in competition with this original group.

At around this time you will be called on to another location to re-start our work with other groups. We will call others to you or you to them, who are like-minded. Those who are similar to you in their searching for Truth will interact with you, as you will with them. This linking up will create a very loose spiritual connection that we will explain to you as time progresses.

Some will stay with you for a long time and some will have other paths to follow. And sadly others will find it easier to accuse you of being off track as a means to justify why they will prefer going back to their old ways. Always remember that they are our children, and they can run as far as they like, but they can never hide from what is meant for them in this life. Remember to think well of them at this, and all times.

Chapter II

You may meet a future potential partner, but not before you do our work. You will be operating alone because what we want of you cannot be interrupted by any emotional attachments as we, through you, serve humanity. Any future potential partner must put their self-needs, and their hopes and wishes for you in second place for what we have for you to do, and we must say sadly there are very few women who are capable of this challenge. It will be the choice of the women in your life as to whether they become your partner.

It is not time yet for you to move to Queensland, as we still have some matters for you to clean up in Gulgong. You will leave Gulgong permanently within the next few months, and will stay with your friends in Bundaberg for a short time, before moving and working permanently in the Maryborough/Hervey Bay area.

Shalom my boy and we promise you, you will never be alone again, and you will never have to go through what you have had to go through these past twenty years.

There seemed very little difference to me from this session to what I now do as a trance medium. In other words, I was in trance. I haven't as yet had the opportunity to meet anyone who actually does hypnotherapy sessions, but it seems to me the principle is the same. Either someone else leads the participant into a trance, or they do it to themselves.

I returned to Gulgong and three months later, with my little yellow Lite Ace van packed beyond the ceiling, started my trek northwards. I had old roof racks loaded with a lounge and two arm chairs, and inside I had a double bed and TV amongst the other articles stuffed into whatever corners I could find.

Some twelve months earlier I had the Lite Ace converted to LP gas by a supposed professional, though it still could run on petrol if I chose. It goes without saying that I made the long two-day journey from Central Western NSW to Bundaberg in Queensland, but only just it seems. I had been having trouble with the little van well before leaving Gulgong, almost impossible to start it on gas, and even when started on petrol it took quite a few turns of the motor before it would kick over.

On arriving at Bundaberg, and after a few days of settling in, I took the van to a local mechanic who swore his disbelief the moment he looked under the bonnet. When the gas switch was turned on, the petrol pump, because it can't send any petrol past the off tap, is supposed to stops pumping. The petrol fuel line in my van had developed a split so that the petrol fuel pump had been spraying petrol all over the motor. As if that wasn't bad enough, the gas-petrol switch hadn't been properly installed. It was shorting out, sending sparks that could well have ignited either fuel. The mechanic further let out expletives when he discovered the gas tank had been installed under the body of the car, which is totally illegal, and a number of stones had pierced the outer tank. Had they pierced the inner tank the gas would have sprayed over the exhaust pipe and my van would have been a bomb. Suffice to say, from then on, I openly called the little van the Yellow Peril, but under my breath, Little Miracle.

After I had returned to Gulgong in the early months of 1997, Mike and Sharon began to look for a place for me to do psychic readings. They arranged for me to work out of a crystal shop in Bundaberg. This was also the main motivation for me moving permanently back to Queensland.

After unpacking and settling in with Mike and Sharon, I organised to meet Matt, the owner of the crystal shop. He was away at the time of my first visit, but his sister said he wanted me getting myself established in his shop and when he returned, he would decide if I was to be a regular or not.

Chapter II

The day I was to meet Matt he was late. His sister said I had a woman booked for a reading and that after I was finished with her session, Matt should have arrived. The client arrived and I started giving her a lot of information about her family and general personal matters. I noticed whenever I looked up to check that what I was saying was relevant to her, she would be looking around the room like she wasn't interested. Then a question time came.

Normally, after giving as much information to someone as I did with her, I would have expected her to state that I had answered all her questions and I would have expected to give her a little prompt. You can imagine my surprise when she pulled a long list of questions from somewhere inside her bra and started asking me detailed questions. After the session I had expected her to give me a very poor performance rating in the feed back book I keep, and again I was surprised when she declared she would give me 100%.

I was about to leave the woman to write her comments as I do with all customers, when the owner popped his head in and introduced himself. Before I had a chance to comment, he smiled at the woman and said, "Well, what do you think mum? Did he pass the test?"

The reason she had been so distracted was that her son had, with her permission, listened in to the reading from behind the curtain that was at the back of me. She kept looking away for fear she would start smiling or laughing. They both had worked out the questions at great length the night before. It was a wonderfully reassuring session for me, especially as it was my first real outlet in Queensland.

Not long after arriving in Bundaberg, in fact only two months later, my family contacted me to say my dad's health was slowly deteriorating and to be prepared for the worst.

On the Light Path — Peter Lyons

One morning, around 7.00 am, I was sitting in the toilet, or the Tardus as Mike, Sharon and I call it, so named after the British Dr. Who TV Show and because, just like that Tardus, we seemed to enter a different world whenever we went there. It was quite common for us to return back to the other after a visit there, with a lot of psychic information.

I had this feeling that dad was around me in a spiritual way. I spoke to him in my mind and asked him what the matter was. He said he couldn't raise the flaming nurses, a common expression of dad's. I could visualise him walking up the corridor of the hospital where he was staying, using a support frame, looking lost. I said, "Dad go back to bed and I'll send a nurse to you." He said OK but that I'd better hurry up, as he was busting to go to the toilet. He seemed to slowly fade away from me.

When I had finished my business in the Tardus, I went out to Mike and Sharon, without giving them any details asked if they could get any information relating to what had just happened. They both became emotional and shivery and said they felt my dad had just passed over, or was in the process of passing over. I hadn't told either of them what I had experienced in the Tardus. Around 10.00 am I got a phone call from my family to say dad had passed over peacefully around the time I had encountered him.

After returning from dad's funeral, I began working full time at the crystal shop in Bundaberg. My psychometry readings were becoming much stronger, far more accurate and with lots more information. It wasn't long before I found I was having difficulty holding articles. At times my hand became so hot and energised that I was unable to continue with my readings. Matt, the owner gave me certain gemstones to hold, saying they would release any energy build up. It was the first time I had experienced an energy transfer. It wasn't long

Chapter II

after that I found I no longer needed to hold onto articles to give a decent and accurate reading.

This then created a slight problem for me. To this point when doing readings, I would concentrate by looking at the article handed to me. I had originally done this because I'd heard from some sceptics that psychics pick up on the person's body language. Now that I couldn't look at the article, I started staring at a point on the wall above the client's head.

One day at around this time, a sceptical woman, nudged by her friend to visit me for a session, made a booking and had it quite clear in her head that she was not going to be fooled by some psychic trickster. The early part of her session was difficult for me, because while I was looking at the spot above her head, with my peripheral vision, I could see she was restless and distracted. When we got to question time she asked was there any information relating to her father who had passed over some years before. As a means of concentrating, I closed my eyes. Immediately I could feel the difference. It was like I had been fooling around before, and was now doing my job.

"I see a man with short grey hair, standing quite erect and wearing an army uniform. I think he's smoking a pipe, or at least he's holding one, and occasionally he taps it against the palm of his hand. I'm a little confused here because I don't think he's a smoker, and I'm further confused because, though I feel he's army, he looks like he's at an airfield. I can see a hanger in the background and he's saying that he wants to thank the family for giving him this beautiful view. Does this make sense to you?"

I opened my eyes to fine her sobbing. Her father, who I had described perfectly, had been an army man and had asked that he be buried at that particular spot near an airfield. Though he had given up smoking many years before, he still liked to take the pipe out of his vest pocket and stick it in his mouth, occasionally tapping it on his hand. She later told the owner of the shop that she had serious doubts about my psychic ability, till I had mentioned her father's story.

From that time on I started to close my eyes when doing a session. This intensified the concentration, so that by the time I had started to work at a Health Foods store at Hervey Bay, I had progressed to doing a form of trance. As I became more comfortable trusting what was coming out of my mouth, and allowed the words to have their own power, I became more at ease and natural, and so the trances became stronger. Finally, as if it was the most natural thing in the world, I did my sessions in a full non-conscious trance state. The less I listened and comprehended what was being said through me, the stronger the message became, and the more I felt like I wasn't even there. This method is now my standard practice when doing psychic sessions.

To give some idea what happens within me, it is like opening your mouth to talk, with no idea of the subject matter, or what you are going to say, with no discerning, no control whatsoever, just a flow of meaningless words. The words are meaningless to me, but obviously meaningful to the person receiving the message. I have little to no memory or recall of any of what I've said afterwards.
If you remember when I first started to give information at the spiritual development group at the Enmore church, it was as though someone else was talking, but it was coming out of my mouth. One of the most difficult aspects of psychic work is knowing if the information you are receiving is from that highest source, lower level entities or from yourself.

 I have no idea how accurate sessions are, because I don't always get feedback at the time of the sessions. Even on the odd occasions when I would ask the client if I was on track or making sense, I'd usually get a "go on" or "keep going," which told me nothing, other than the person didn't want to

Chapter II

end the session at that point. From my perspective, I have no way of knowing if I'm on track, or just recording a whole hour of irrelevance, to be used against me later at the next sceptic society or fundamentalist Christian's gathering.

It is usually much later that I get some feedback that indicates how well I did for certain clients. This can be when a person recommends their friends to come and see me, or from confirmation letters, emails or phone messages. I still have a young woman who rings me periodically from England for an up date on certain aspects of her life. I also get good feedback from the staff of the shops and outlets I work from. On the other hand if I were off track, the number of complaints would be very high, the bookings would be down. The shop owners would no doubt be suggesting I change my day job, while encouraging other psychics to take my place. Luckily so far that hasn't happened. In the early days, I was slow to trust that I was actually a genuine psychic and not a well-meaning fraud.

Not long after having done my first reading without psychometry, Matt asked Sharon, Mike and I if we would be interested in doing mini readings at a psychic fair to be held in a few weeks time at a beautiful reception centre in Bundaberg. Sharon, Mike, Matt, and my self set up our respective displays and tables for what was to be a two day gathering. We weren't the only ones. A number of well-known big-name psychics had been invited to participate.

One such person had gained his reputation by reading tea-leaves and coffee grounds. He was the main attraction of the weekend. We were informed that we would get a percentage of the doors takings, while he would be paid a set fee. It was a very high fee indeed. Many other psychics complained, but we just left it up to Spirit. After all, as far as we were concerned, it had been they who had set up the weekend. Because it was meant as a sample day, and we weren't expected to do full sessions, I chose to do psychometry readings.

During the late morning, we were visited by three women, all dressed in blue-grey capes with hoods. They walked among the many visitors, and didn't seem to be particularly interested in any one psychic. A few moments after they left, in the middle of a session, I stopped dead. I couldn't get anything. I tried to restart, but again the flow had stopped. Directly behind me sat a psychic artist who was known for her beautiful angel drawings. At the same time my intuitive flow stopped she started to draw hideous images on what had been a beautiful angel image. Mike had been sitting and enjoying sending Peaceful energy to the room. Suddenly he felt physically sick, with pains in places he hadn't had pain before. Sharon, who had been doing some psychic artwork for a client, also stopped.

Excusing myself from the client I went to the booking woman and asked for a time out. This caused some difficulties because people had been lining up to see the coffee-tea reading guru. Once they realize how expensive he was, they had decided to try me. I had a huge queue waiting for me. While talking to the booking woman, psychics started coming over to say they too needed to have a break. As we started to share how this strange occurrence had affected us, we all looked over to the guru to see if he had been affected. He was working away merrily, with no hint of interference.

It was some time later I found out that the three women were from a witch's coven that did not like the guru. It was claimed they had put a spell on the fair in the hope it would stop his activities. At first we thought he may have been somehow better than us and therefore had some special protection. Later when we started getting clients of his coming to us for readings, we realised he would have been better off as a conjurer at a circus. And as for the spell the three women cast all it did was to disrupt genuine psychics. It certainly showed the guru up for the fraud he was and that their spells really worked.

In my early psychometry days I was not completely certain my skills were at their best for that time. Something seemed to be missing. I constantly asked my guides, in my daily attuning mediations, for a sign that it was they and not I or other entities doing the channelling. There wasn't any specific answer either way from them. It didn't help that while doing some Sunday sessions at a community hall at Bargara, near Bundaberg, I noticed that there was a problem with some of the sessions. In particular I was getting strong feeling from the previous sessions interfering in the current one.

I had a very difficult time clearing my mind of the thoughts that had gone before. Was I doing something wrong, and if so, why weren't my guides helping me? On one of these Sundays John Appletree, a wonderful man who had helped set me up at Bargara, quietly pulled me aside and said; "Pete, I know very little about what you do, and how you do it, but I keep getting a strong feeling that I have to tell that you are doing something wrong with your readings."

I asked him to pass on what he felt I needed to hear. He started by saying he had no idea, then he stopped and said. "It has something to do with closing off, or closing down after each reading. Does that make any sense to you?"

John had no idea I was having difficulties with the sessions, because I asked if he had he heard anything from people who had been to see me and he said no. I knew immediately that this was spirit getting through to me via someone else. I thanked John, went off to a small quiet corner and went to my guides for clarity on what John had given me. I didn't get anything that day, nor did I have any further sessions, but when I went home I kept getting this flow of information.

The imagery I received was like a flow of milk going through a pipe, followed by beer, then by some other fluid. At the end was a mess of all three, and pretty much useless. The next imagery had me seeing each fluid being stopped, and the pipe being cleaned, before the next fluid flowed. A common sense thing when I saw the imagery, but not so when I was doing the sessions. I had been intermixing client's readings like blending milk with beer. Thanks to John, I have learned we psychics can often get a specific answer to question from the least likely of people, acting as mediums on our guides' behalf. Wasn't it Jesus who said, in a slightly fractured interpretation, it can come from "the least of my brethren", but it still "comes from me?" I heard a few years ago that John had passed away peacefully, and I know he knows how special and important he was for me back then.

It was also at this time I first started my daily affirmation statement or prayer, which I said and still say, every morning and every night. This is said to remind myself who I am and what I represent and the seriousness of my commitment to this power. It isn't said as a ritual, or something I need to say like a Mantra. It changes slightly but this is the basic format:

I affirm and confirm my oneness with you, the Greatest good, God, the Creator Force, not of my will or power, but of and for the will and power of the light, peace, and Truth. May I do the will of this power for its purpose and intentions, in whatever capacity that maybe. With no interest in personal gains other than what you may give that you feel I need to do your will, which I warmly and humbly accept. We are one because you are God within me and I am your humble servant.

Speak Truth to Me

I guess I'm wondering why.
Why I never seem to leave here.
Why I hang around, I need something to believe in.
Knowing life's a flame, it burns you over and over again.
When you seek a special friend, you get let down again.

So my question to you is
Are you here to take advantage of me?
Just to take my money. I'd prefer if you'd just let me be.
Though I've got lots on my mind,
And I know I'm not the only one.
I'd prefer to stay at home, than have you tell stories to me.

Sign. What I need is a sign. Leave the rhetoric behind.
You won't be wasting my time.
Sometime it's cruel to be kind,
But that won't be out of line with me.

So tell me what I should know.
What will help me put my life back on track?
Is my ego in check?
Do I need to bolt my chair to the deck?
Help me find who I should be, help me find spirituality,
Not some mishmash ideology.
Please just help me find me.

1986

Chapter III

A Psychic Session

When I first started doing my psychometry sessions, I couldn't understand why some of my sessions were on track and others wrong. Some people were so stunned at the accuracy of their sessions that they sent other family members to me hoping for the same results, but I either couldn't get anything, or the information didn't make any sense to them at all. After I had followed the advice spirit had give me through John Appletree, to close off after each session, I still found this anomaly with some sessions.

It wasn't long before I found a common link with those I couldn't get the correct information. It was the person's state of mind and their attitude to life. Many times it seemed to be the way they were allowing problems to overtake their lives. That was when I twigged on the feeling that maybe the source of the information was not coming from me or from my guides, but from the person's own personal guides. And that the person's quality of guides wasn't necessarily serving in the best interest of that person.

I discovered that if the person had a worrying way of dealing with daily matters, then there was a good chance they were channelling that kind of attitude in their thinking. They would be the kind of person who were rarely happy and had a sad attitude toward life, no matter what the day may bring. They would pepper their conversations with complaints or sad stories concerning their partner or past partners, their children or neighbours. It wasn't a big step to assume that if they had lower level or mischievous guides around them, then their life would always be a misery. Any psychic reading, therefore, was going to be wrong, either partially or fully.

I had found meditation, and particularly a deliberate intention to want peace at a time when a negative energy would upset me. This seemed to be the best solution I could offer to such a person. When a person came to me for a session with that sort of energy around them, then they would be asked to do a very simple attuning meditation exercise with me. They were to ask their highest guides to pass on to my guides, and therefore me, whatever information their guides had for them. Following the exercise the quality of the information was usually totally different and far more accurate. The exercise made it clear that they determined the quality of their guides. It was important because their attitude not their guides or mine decided on the quality of their guides and information they received.

After I had started trance sessions it became the standard process my guides would use for anyone that had noticeable interference around them. I now realise this whole scenario came from my highest guides dropping seeds in my very fertile mind. It was further proof that they were indeed there helping me long before I recognised them and their help.

Usually I have a pretty clear session with most people after they have done the attuning exercise. There are still cases where the information is wrong or very hard to receive. This can be for a number of reasons. The first is the person may not be ready for the information they seek. There may be a time factor where the person has to wait for some period of time before they will get anything from their guides. Usually in

Chapter III

this case, my guides will say there is some kind of blockage, but not necessarily interference, and it is suggested that person comes back for a reading at another time. A second reason can be that their guides may not know. Now you might be surprised at this, and assume guides know everything. Because we have choice, what we may set in motion concerning certain matters, may not be clear to our guides. Though they can see the generic outcomes, they can't see the specifics. They will wait till the outcome is clearer and more in keeping with the long-term advantage, or disadvantage, in relation to our soul's journey.

Considering our guides can't lie to us, they may not be given the answers to our particular questions from their guides, and yes they too have high guides.

Another situation can be where a person has had so much interference around them, that even after the release, they could need up to two months before they are fully free from this interference. This was assuming they are willing to do the attuning meditation regularly and accept this highest guidance. This usually involves doing a complete review of their moral and conscience values as it relates to their spiritual beliefs.

Then there are the "prove you're a mind reader" types of clients who may well have given lip service to the attuning exercise, but still expect the psychic to get information without the aid of their guides. This is particularly those people that don't understand or believe in personal guides.

I can recall a particular case of this happening in Hervey Bay, when a woman kept telling me that the information I was giving her was totally wrong. In keeping with my policy that if in the session I can't get information that relates to the person in the first instance, they get their money back. I offered to return the woman's money. In a very insulting manner, she said she had never believe in psychics and believed we were all con artists.

I asked her if I was a con artist how could so many people have gained from their session and showed her the visitor's book. It contained the positive comments from the many hundreds who had visited me up to that time. She obviously didn't want explanations and brushed me off without reply.

Then my guides through me asked the woman;
"Did you do as Peter asked? Did you ask your guides to pass on the information to us?"

The woman replied no, saying that she thought it was a whole lot of rot, that there were no guides and that I was trying to justify my inadequacies. To which they replied: "Why not pacify us and do the exercise? In your mind just say, "If I have any guides, I give them permission to pass on information to Pete and his guides, so the information may be passed on to me."

She gave a huff, but seemed to do what she was asked. I immediately felt the difference. A huge flow of information came rushing out of my mouth on matters I couldn't possibly have known. Details concerning her parents back in Germany, her sister she hadn't seen for 30 years, her many relationships that had gone belly up. Finally a statement from her guides that if she would like her life to improve, which her guides lovingly said they had wanted for her for a long time all she had to do was to start believing that she was truly worthy. They added that the reason they had her to come for the session was to show her they were always with her. They further thanked her for allowing them to show her this was not a conjurer's trick.

Chapter III

I came out of the trance and slowly opened my eyes to find her sitting in a state of total shock. It was obvious she was trying to say something, but hadn't a clue what to say.

As my guides said to her as she left in a total daze, "Your guides have shown you they exist. Now we must start all over again and convince the next person they too have guides just waiting to be understood and recognised."

A most frustrating aspect of my work relates to those people that fence sit. They are the people who claim to support one ideology, while keeping very much in practice with another less rewarding one. They will agree fully with what I am saying and even have had major satisfaction from meditations or releases. But they still refuse or forget to do a regular attuning meditation or call on their guides. They will decline to call on their guides even during tough times. Because they have choice, for me to insist or even query if they have been following my suggestions, infers that I consider my process or beliefs superior to theirs. It takes a lot of patience to have to watch when such a person gets to the point where they are so desperate that they have to ask for help. It's even more heartbreaking when they don't ask.

Now that I am travelling up and down the coast of Queensland, south in the summer and north in the winter, the support needed from me by some is not available, because I am no longer available when they need me. I assume this is spirit, lovingly but purposefully, to mix metaphors, weaning them of the milk supply and at the same time gently move them away from their fence sitting.

Psychics will get it wrong, especially if they don't have an awareness of the complexities involved in the information transfer. This applies particularly to those who assume the tarot cards, the crystal ball, the crystals, or whatever tools they are using, are the source of their information, or are some kind of converter that transfers information from an unknown source. Clients will get a poor reading for the same reason. It is when the reader and the client both understand the importance of the process and deeper purpose and it's very special source that the psychic will give a good session and the person will be contented with the results.

A common complaint psychics get is when the information given is basically all is well, no changes coming and have a nice day. Psychics can't change a person's life, nor can they predict a person's future directions if there are no changes coming into that person's life. We psychics are not magicians with a magic wand. If in a psychic reading or session, we are told there are few if any changes coming in our life, then the psychic has still given us information and deserves payment. One can understand why some psychics find it easier if they make up little bits of information. This often done so the person asking for the reading or session feels that at least they got something for their money.

The problems with this of course is when the person doesn't receive their expectations such as winning the lotto, meeting someone special or life just continues as before it gives all psychics a bad name. This seems to happen regardless of psychic's best intentions.

If this person is therefore not receiving highest guidance, they will also start loosing clients, or find an increase in the more mischievous type of clients, or clients who could well take legal action against them. Their readings will often receive interference from low level guides. Higher guides always take care of their own.

A psychic who tells the truth and doesn't embellish the information may get abused from the dissatisfied person and end up giving them their money back. At least they know they

Chapter III

have been honourable to their client, themselves and their highest guides.

I remember being very concerned when, in the early days at Hervey Bay, I seemed to be giving more money back than I was keeping. I had just started writing a regular column in the local newspaper and the publicity generated a lot of clients. Many clients assumed I was like the other psychics giving pleasant, but not necessarily true messages to their clients. My guides quietly informed me that I would never be left without basic needs. All the time I have been doing sessions that has been a fact.

It only feeds myth when a client refers to a particular psychic as being good, because they happened to give pleasing information. If a person is appreciative of a psychic's excellent information then the client should thank his or her own personal guides. After all they are the source of the information and not the psychic. Of course the best thanks should go to the psychic, their guides, your guides and yourself. You must be doing something right if you are getting helpful information from them.

Here are some pointers that should help you get the best information in a psychic reading.
- Before going to a psychic, think over your reason for going.
- Take time to think what information of importance you would like answered.
- If you visit a psychic, knowing your life is pretty mundane, with no particular dramas happening and the psychic gets exactly that, remember the psychic it telling you the truth and not embellishing the facts.
- Put up to your guides the areas of your life that constantly bugging you, especially where solutions seem illusive.

- Reviewed all your concerns with your guides especially areas where you may have deliberately allowed some solutions to be overlooked because you don't like them.

When chatting with your guides, either before visiting a psychic or at any time, don't feel you have to use old English phrases, like thou, or thy, or similar. Simply talk to them as you would your best friends, for that is exactly who they are. Here is an example:

Hello to you my guides wherever you are. I don't really know, see or hear you, but I trust you can see, hear and know me. These matters I'm churning over, I leave with you, and if you think a psychic will assist me with these matters, I'll assume you are going to lead me to the right one. I'll leave it with you. Thanks

When you have chosen the psychic you wish to see, and organised a day and time to see them, it may seem like your decision, but it's more likely your guides who have set up this session for you. On the other hand you may have completely forgotten having put this thought up to them, and just happened to pass a shop with a psychic's sign out the front, and before you know it, are at the counter making a booking. Alternatively, you may find obstacles to the session seem to pop up everywhere. You may hear from the psychic that they are overbooked, or some unforseen situation may arise with your family that makes it impossible for you to get to the session. Either way there's a good chance it is your guides that have set up this blockage. If the psychic, timing, and circumstance are right, they will get you there. If however it isn't, they will set up obstacles until the timing is right and therefore the information that you seek is the best available for you.

Before going into the psychic's room, again within your mind, quickly think of the little chat you had with them, or say your own interpretation of it as you recall it, and then go into the room knowing you are not alone. Don't be concerned that

Chapter III

you may say the wrong word, or that you can't concentrate on what exactly to say. Remember your guides know you better than you know yourself. The moment you turn in your mind to the general thought of what you want to say, they will know exactly what that is. Remember you have the best team you could possibly have. Let them discern for you the information you are about to receive from the psychic. After all it is coming from them and not the psychic's opinion or interpretation. Believe that your guides are there with you, and they will be.

If you are disappointed when the session is finished, spend a quite moment with your guides and mull over what the psychic told you. If you strongly feel the psychic was off track, don't take immediate action, but wait a few months to see if what you were told happens. Again it must be stressed that neither the psychic nor your guide can make your life happen for you. You are the one who must instigate changes if change is going to happen. There are many who live lonely and sad lives who hope others will change it for them. Often these people come to psychics wishing to have someone come into their lives to make their lives more active and they usually leave disappointed.

One of the most common comments I have heard from people and particularly as a criticism from men, is why do we need to see a psychic? Their comments and arguments are based on the premise that there is very little point in knowing the future. Knowing what is to come won't change that future and rarely do psychics get accurate information on sports results, lotto or future fortunes. Knowing the future only causes distraction from what is at hand. What is the sense of having further disturbing information relating to the future, when we're having enough trouble dealing with the present?

There are those who claim it is against Christian belief and God's law to consult a psychic. They sight copious quotes from scripture usually out of context. The main reason a person comes to me is not to find out if they will win lotto or similar simple questions. Most of the questions are about relationships and usually are genuine and responsible ones. Others ask about spiritual, emotional, or soul based matters. They ask how to develop their spirituality, how to remove the worries and confusions in their mind, and why are they constantly being drawn into similar patterns in their lives.

Not all men are critical of psychics. The type of male who came to me for a psychic session, especially around the Mackay, Moranbah, Proserpine and Airlie Beach areas, was anything but the kind one would assume was interested in matters psychic. They consisted of miners, farmers, fishermen, business owners, entertainers, club performers, and even religious ministers. Most of my readings are to reassure a person of decisions they have taken, or plans to take, or that others may have taken that could impose or impact on them.

I am a "spiritually guided counsellor" and that is the title I'd prefer to use. I have been informed that in most States in Australia it is illegal to use the term Counsellor, unless you have the necessary degree in psychology. As to the usual comments from fundamental Christians claiming my work is against God's law, I answer in the following way:

The earliest part of the Old Testament, Genesis, has a story of Joseph being sold into bondage by his brothers, to the King of Egypt. While stuck in prison Joseph, who could interpret dreams, was summoned by the King to interpret his dream for him. Joseph told the King that there will be so many years of feast and so many of famine. He advises the King to store food to last through the famine. The King does, and when the prediction comes true, Joseph is rewarded. Joseph's process of interpreting the dream of the King is what we would call a psychic dream interpretation today. He told the fortune of the King, no different to what any psychic would tell anyone

Chapter III

about material wins or gains, or hard or bad times ahead in today's society. For this he was paid handsomely, no different to a psychic receiving payment for a reading or session.

The main difference to other mystics of that time was that Joseph claimed the information was not from his knowing, or the dreams themselves, but from his God, who he believed was the source of his knowledge.

Today we don't have dominance of one race and their beliefs over another. There is not the need for a race and its belief to fight for its' existence as was the case back when to simply exist the Jewish people had to fight against the many tribes and nations, including the Egyptians, and later the Romans. Whether it is Joseph interpreting a dream, Moses talking to a burning bush, a voice in the sky telling Abraham to kill his first born, there is one thing in common for all these psychic events; there must be a source. And it is the recognition of the source that determines the quality of the information received.

Some psychics believe that their tool is the source of information: Things such as tarot, crystal ball, or article that they may hold to concentrate on in psychometry. A second belief is that the psychics themselves are the source and that some of us are born psychic, just like some have natural talents as cooks, plumbers and artists. A third opinion believes all articles hold a psychic connection to previous owners or to those that have had the article in their possession. This can be anything from a ring, watch or similar article, to a tree, building or area of land.

I don't believe it matters what tools psychics use, be it rune stones, ouija boards or even an ordinary pack of playing cards. Nor do I believe certain tools are good and others are bad. These are simply tools for focusing the psychic's concentration. Psychics who believe their gift is of their own power, run the very serious risk of being blamed if their reading or interpretation of the information is incorrect, as is often the case with people of such conviction.

It is the guides of the person who are the source of information, whether they are visiting a psychic for a session, receiving messages for others, or sensing a one-of psychic occurrence. It is, of course they who determine which psychic tool best to use as a focal point for the channeler when passing on psychic information to or for that person.

If you want to train yourself in your psychic skills, so you may become a publicly accessible psychic, all you need to know to start is that your guides are your teachers. This source is all you really need to concentrate on. The source and the psychic must be in tune and alignment with each other for this combination or team to give the best quality information to the inquirer. This important foundation should be established first in order that a psychic practice their gift free of guilt, fear or apprehensions of any kind. The tarot, crystal ball, psychometric, medium, and playing card reader may seem to be the source of a psychic session, they are not. They are the conduits through which the information flows. A psychic is a finely attuned sensor of emotions and feelings.

A psychic must know their own feelings in as many different situations and circumstances as is possible. This will allow them to discriminate between their personal feelings and the peaceful energy of their guides. An accurate (good) psychic is aware of the differences between personal feelings, the inquirer's feelings, their guides and those of the inquirer. Now this may sound impossible to achieve, but just remember, your job is to trust your guides and let them work with you to expand this gift. To trust your guides you need to get to know them. This leads us back to daily meditations, and constant consultation with them.

Chapter III

No matter how seemingly simple the matter, with all things you do, there must be that willingness to have your guides override your thoughts, opinions and feelings. Trust they will only give you the best. Although everyone has the ability to feel, sense, or relate to that which we call psychic, not everyone necessarily develops or wants to develop their gift in a particular lifetime. A good rule of thumb is if you feel comfortable developing your psychic skill, in line with what I have said to this point, then there is no reason why you shouldn't give it a try.

Not all people sensing connections to past events, happenings or places are necessarily practicing psychics, or even conscious they have a psychic ability. They may only have had one or two memorable events occur in their life, and don't wish to push it further.

I have had many requests from people to cleanse or release energy and lost souls from their house or property that they feel have been stuck there. This usually happens with old homes, buildings, newly built homes, or vacant blocks of land where there may have been killings, such as the slaughtering of aboriginal people in the past. The assumption is that the energy is a part of the structure, property or artefacts at that location, and for reasons unknown, the energy only seems to present itself to certain people, usually to particular family members who seem more sensitive than others. Fearful that the energy may somehow transfer to these particularly sensitive members of the family I, a psychic, get asked to remove this energy.

In most instances I show the person how to connect to their guides. The guides in turn show them how to release any lost souls or negative energy links that may be connected to that particular place. I then leave it up to them and their guides as to what happens next. My guides and I simply act as witnesses. This is especially important when the persons asking

On the Light Path — Peter Lyons

for the release are very psychically gifted. By showing them how to connect to their guides, and then have them do the release, with my guides and me observing, We hoped this will encourage them to continue to improve their psychic skills and to interact more with their guides. I usually don't get into arguments, or discuss philosophy with those who may want lost souls to stay with them. I suggest they ask their guides for what is best, and leave the matter alone.

In a case in Hervey Bay, a young couple were woken from their sleep on more than one occasion, to the sound of something being dragged along the floor. Initially it was the woman who first heard the sound, but later on, both the husband and baby daughter also reacted to it. In separate incidents, the husband never felt comfortable sitting in a particular corner of the lounge room, and the wife rarely went out the front door. Their 2 year old was constantly chattering to an imaginary someone in her small room and they could not understand what was attracting the local parrots to sit on the front porch, when there was no food there to attract them.

During the house cleansing, both the wife and husband experienced a flash back to a time long ago that had no relationship to either of them. Neither had considered themselves psychic to that point. They could sense a severely crippled old man, who got great pleasure feeding the wild birds, living on the veranda. Sitting in the corner of the lounge room where the current male owner of the house felt uncomfortable when he passed there, was the presence of an old woman, most probably the wife of the old man. From the information we gathered, the old man took a turn for the worse one night and the wife, who we felt had been pretty seriously ill, must have tried to drag herself out to aid her husband, but died before she got there.

The interesting part of this story is that the house was not old. The young couple had built it from second hand materi-

Chapter III

als gathered from around the district. From the research that the young couple and I did at the time we were unable to find any connection to this house, and an actual couple who may have lived in the area. A month or so later I called back to see how the young couple were getting on, and couldn't believe how improved the feeling was in their home. The young couple had started doing regular attuning meditation, and were starting to get simple messages for family members, something they wouldn't have dared try previously. The little daughter started to become more relaxed in the evening, and there seemed to be a real sparkle in her beautiful blue eyes.

Now I can hear someone saying, he's contradicting himself. In one breath he says articles and places don't have feelings, but then he says people can get feeling when they touch thing or visit places of psychic significance. Well to be totally honest with you, this following information is hot off the Cuckoo's nest press release: Spirit is giving me an answer right now as I type. Articles, places or structures don't have feelings, we people do. They are nothing but tools of focus, just like tarot, crystal balls and tools used by psychometrists. Our guides use such articles, places or structures to trigger some situation or circumstance relating to a particular learning, experience or awareness we may be going through at that particular time.

For example, this old couple could easily have lived in Europe, with absolutely no connection whatsoever to this young couple or their newly built house. Then again there may have been a physical link to one or other of them and someone in spirit. Which ever was the case, spirit used the situation as a means of getting them to tune into their unknown gifts by imposing the old couple's history onto them, and using the house as the trigger.

Think back to times when you passed a building, were in a particular dwelling, saw someone in the street, heard a sound or smelt a perfume or scent, and this occurrence triggered a memory, which for the life of you, you couldn't recall actually happening. To some people this could be deja vous, but then again it may be that your guides are linking you to some past event for a specific purpose. Next time this happens to you, tune into your guides and see what happens. I am not saying anything necessarily will, but at least you are attuning to them, and are protected from any unwanted negative intrusions, should such a connection occur.

I must stress at this point that I don't consider psychic work, whether it is tarot card readings, rune stones, psychometry or even just playing around on an ouija board with friends, should be done lightly or carelessly, it is not a game. The tools are just tools, and like any tool in the hands of those that don't fully understand them they can do the unwary user harm. Always aim for the highest purest Truth and you will get only the best. For those of you keen to get started testing out your psychic skills, remember this is a God given gift. If you treat it with respect, especially the source, then you won't be working against the grain. Instead you will be working with that highest, purest power we call God. This applies not only to those wishing to become professional psychics, but also to anyone using any tools to interact with their understanding of God, spirits, souls, ghosts or similar. Remember it is not enough to call on God and assume we are on track, any more than the calling on white light is a perfect means of protection.

The religious ministers that parrot pious platitudes worthy of a saint, but whose moral conscience, lifestyle and example reflect the opposite can also draw to themselves the opposites in guides. We can't serve two masters. We must honour Truth, for to do otherwise can bring about major personal crises, including mental illness.

After establishing a link with our guides we can set about experimenting with our gift. To get started we will need an appropriate tool. Tarot cards for the clairvoyant, an article

Chapter III

such as a ring or watch for the psychometrist, or pendulum for dousing are ideal starting tools. The particular ability of the beginner coupled with their level of oneness with their guides, will determine the quality of the information they first receive. Most people start by writing down thoughts or feelings that come to mind without prompting. This may happen in the form of imagery, temperature sensation, feeling, emotions or moods the beginner may initially feel when concentrating on the subject.

It may be the beginner is holding the article and on concentrating on it, begins to see a particular image in their mind, or the article may seem to be particularly hot or cold, or the beginner may get some feelings or emotions that only seemed to come to them once they touched the article. This is similar with the beginner and clairvoyance when they first start interacting with the tarot cards. In the case of trance work, the beginner needs to totally still their own mind while allowing words to be spoken, words that at first may make no sense to them.

After this kind of experimenting certain tools will become more attractive and comfortable to the user than others. Some may start with Angel cards and then progress to expressing feelings and end up a trance medium. Others may find tarot cards are comfortable and move on to aura readings. Whatever tools you initially use, your guides will lead you onto what suits you best. Usually most good psychics eventually grow out of the need for tools as their interaction with the source grows stronger and their understanding of their individual spiritual gift increases.

Remember this exercise is a two way street. In the first instance you are practicing to open your psychic channel, which is actually your guide showing you the difference between your own feelings and fears, and the peace that only your guides can give you. However in the second, you are helping your guides to determine how best they can serve God in the way they guide you. There is no plateau of permanence, no sitting in one place, assuming that you have a gift and that is it. You will be in a constant process of discerning, upgrading, reviewing and adjusting as you grow to your limit this life, and on into the next.

Too often I have heard psychics claim they never question their gift, never try looking too deeply as to how it works, never consider that maybe they are just at the doorway of something far bigger, which needs to be expressed further. Sadly it is often these psychics who just give what they get without thought to the source, or the consequences of their actions, and eventually loose their accuracy and their ability. And even sadder, in the process of their demise which leaves them wide open to interference, their readings take on a reflection of this ever-increasing negativity. These fear-based messages eventually manifest in their life, but also into the lives of those seeking their council. In some cases the psychic, psychological and physical damage caused by these psychics can never be fully repaired in that particular life.

If a person takes up psychic work simply as a means of make a living, they are doing it for the wrong reason. We have to live, and there is nothing wrong with charging for our services, but it is not the reason we should be doing psychic work. The money is there to allow us to live, pay taxes, pay debts and survive, so that we can concentrate on the purpose at hand, namely serving the greater good who through our guides has us doing this particular work. If there were some way that I could give sessions without having to charge a person, and knowing that the person concerned was a genuine seeker of the highest Truth, I would. If some benevolent someone were willing to pay my debts and expenses in this physical world, I would be more than happy to do this work for free. Of course, other than winning lotto or the lottery, or selling millions of copies of this book, the chances are most unlikely.

Chapter III

For those seriously interested in becoming a psychic reader, or wishing to do psychic sessions, or for those wanting an understanding of what a psychic does in a particular session, I will now go through my process, as shown me by my guides. Feel free to adapt it to your own circumstances and needs, but remember; it is your guides that have the information, not you. So let them lead you in what they do best, and only use this process I am now giving you as a starting point.

It is now understood by those that come to me for a session that through me my guides give only the best to those truly seeking Truth, for which they pay a set and fair fee. As part of the process the seeker gets the chance to determine if I am speaking relevant to their circumstance and if not, they get their money back. It is spirit that sets the amount of money I charge a person. I have determined this by firstly checking the figure I got from them with my psychic friends using the 'yes-no' method I explain further on. There have been a number of cases where I have not charged a person. In these instances the information guides wanted to pass on to this person was far more important that the money I might have been entitled to.

I have never considered a person's payment was for a certain amount of information within a certain time frame, and then that's it. The money is simply a means of showing the person that what I give has a monetary value as well as a spiritual one. For example, when I worked for donations, in the early days of my doing psychometry readings, there was very little respect shown for the information I was giving. It was usual for people to get a reading done to kill time while they were waiting for a healing, or a "lets see if he's better than Madam Blavadsky's student." Then there were those that would ask the same questions every time I visited that particular place, and pounce on me if the answers were the slightest bit different. It was a game they played, which was blinding them from what they should have been gaining from such a session. As soon as I started to charge for the sessions, this kind of person rapidly disappeared. Thankfully, genuinely interested people wanting to improve their lot in life began replacing them.

OK to get started doing a public psychic reading or session, you need to dedicate the room you plan to use and all its contents. This applies to anyone doing tarot, psychometry, trance, spiritual healing, Reiki, crystal work, meditation circles, beginner's psychic circles, or any form of psychic session, where contacting spirit is part of the procedure. Remember intuition, gut feelings, "I just know things" or "I just feel things" are all part of this psychic process. Remember you are not the source; you are the receiver.

Not everyone who comes for a reading is necessarily a decent, spiritually attuned or trustworthy person, even if they are your best friends. Nor is everyone necessarily without interference, mischievous energy or lost souls. I have been quite shocked at some of my clients I thought to be quite decent who have turned out to be anything but. That is not to say you need to be fearful of them, or that you refuse anyone coming to you for a session, just that you need to be ever vigilant, and therefore always protected, and that means you must let your guides lead.

For those who feel they have adequately protected themselves by burning sage, chanting some ancient mantra, placement of crystals, drawing in the white light, calling on the universe or similar, with the greatest respect to you, you would probably get better protection by wrapping yourself in toilet paper.

The protection against psychic interference comes from within your core centre, called you psychos. This is a Greek word, pronounced sick-os, which means of the breath, soul or spirit, and from which we get the terms psychosis, psychiatry, psychic, psychoanalyse etc. This inner centre has to be made safe

Chapter III

and strong, and this is done when we becoming at one with our guides. This is where the true White Light lives.

Before moving on to actually doing a psychic session, I would suggest you keep in mind the process I have set myself, as a part of my discipline, to refine my alertness. I constantly check and recheck the clarity of the information I receive, to ensure it is from my guides and not from my own hopes and wishes. The basis of this alertness is Truth at all cost. No matter how it may affect the client or my self. Truth must not be compromised. This discipline is particularly necessary for any psychic, but particularly for trance mediums. When in trance, the medium must be constantly aware of all feeling, not unlike that of someone flying a plane in foggy conditions. In my case I am always on the edge, aware that the slightest small thing could be a sign of something bigger; the possible tip of a mountain. Something not being obvious could easily lead to a very wrong statement or incorrect interpretation of the information being given through me. A similar analogy is of someone working on an assembly line at a fruit factory; constantly watching the belt, ensuring the fruit isn't inferior or second rate.

Yet almost as a contradiction to this statement, I am totally calm and at ease and at peace with my Guides, as if I don't have a care in the world. It is like the two opposites are operating in harmony at the same time. On the one hand I have total trust in my Guides' Truth, while at the same time, being ever conscious of my humanness and how I can unintentionally interfere in the delicate process of channelling. It is the dedication, hard work and commitment both my Guides and I put in before a session that keeps this balance perfectly pivoted.

I strongly suggest that all psychics start every day by setting aside a time for meditation. I prefer the mornings, as a replacement of my very Catholic Morning Offerings, and at night my Evening Prayers. The difference with those kind of prayers compared with what I have replaced them with, is I don't plead, ask or request in a manner that separates my guides from me. Instead I address them as friends, so that it is simply a matter of:

"Hi guys (later replace by "Hi guides" which means the same thing to me now) how are you? Any information you need, or want me to know to improve my link with you, including anything I may be doing contrary to your way, please show me now, or correct me through circumstances in my daily life. Thanks as always."

And then I simply go about my normal daily chores, ever mindful that if I were to get thoughts that had me feeling agitated about some matter, particularly for something I hadn't done, or had done that I felt uncomfortable about, I immediately sit quietly and mull over the pros and cons of that matter with them. I am aware that Truth is the Chairperson. Usually at a later time I will get a peaceful thought or feeling telling me one way or the other what the right course concerning this matter might be.

I will then say in my mind "I assume this information is from you, my guides, and if not, please show me otherwise." To this I usually get a reply in the form of a smile, deep within, or through some pleasant action in my life's circumstances, and I accept it is from them. It takes practice and there have been many a time I wonder if they had taken a ten-year vacation. That is when I know I have to trust them more and build further on my faith in them. I continually commune with my guides, whether at home, in the garden, driving to the various centres where I do sessions, even writing this book, as if I am talking to my best friends. After all, that is exactly what they are to me, as they are to anyone that wants them. It is with this understanding of Truth and trust in my guides that I offer my services with confidence to those interested in a session.

Chapter III

When it comes to the sessions, I never know who is coming to see me until the actual morning. Even then, I only know them by first names on a list. . It is at this time I may get an idea of how many people I will have in that particular session and generally the kind of day that lays ahead for me. I must stress that I don't ask for information, for to do so could draw interference. Often, my guides bring information to me when I least expect it.

There have been times when I have been feeling quite restless and uncertain prior to the next day's session, only to find one of the clients coming to see me was not who they claim to be, or that there was an irate interrogator waiting for me when I arrive. Such was the case when a fundamentalist Christian chose to challenge me "in God's name" at a health food store in Maryborough back in early 2000. I arrived as per usual, greeted the owners, and made my way to the small room at the back of the shop to prepare myself for the day's sessions.

One of the owners tucked her head around the corner to say I had someone wanting to have a quick word with me before I started my first session. I returned to the shop to find a rather tall, elderly, bespectacled man sitting at one of the tables provided for customers. He had an opened soft brief case, exposing a large quantity of literature. As I got close enough to read I realised it was Christian literature. I introduced myself and offered my hand. He didn't respond. Instead he asked, "With whose authority do you do your psychic work?" To which I replied God's. This shook him a little. I assume he was expecting me to say Satan. "Aren't you a psychic?" He then asked, to which I replied, 'Yes, that is the modern word for it." "Then how can you work for God when you are doing the work of Satan?" He retorted.

Now I must explain here that this kind of address to psychics by fundamental Christians is not exclusive to me and further that the premise on which they start their argument is usually based on assumptions they have rarely thought through fully. I asked him if it were possible, that is, if he had the ability to receive God's word, like the prophets in the Bible, what name would he use? My intention was to show him that by using the term prophet, I would be just as much under attack as I would by using the psychic term. Instead he replied that the coming of Jesus meant there was no longer need for prophets, as the Bible was now a living prophecy. That one stung me a little, as I wasn't expecting it. At first I felt if I didn't have answers for this man's questions, I would be letting down my guides, and therefore God. The fact that I baulked, and he expressed a smug smile, didn't help settle my feelings at all.

In a flash, I realised I hadn't had time to attune to my guides, and so was vulnerable to my own humanness, and personal feelings. I immediately thought of them; the best I could do in such a short time, and smiled inwardly my respect for them. It was then I heard my mouth saying, "I am not here to judge you or the work you do, and nor will I. You have your responsibilities for God's work, but I also have mine. We will never get this matter sorted out here in a few moments, when churches all over the world, right now, are arguing the differences of their belief."

I offered him my hand as I rose to leave, but he replied he was not finished with me yet. My mouth said that I was, and I started to walk off to the room. The owner caught my attention to say my first client had arrived, and I went to her to introduce myself, and then led her to the room. When the session had ended, I returned to the shop expecting to find the fundamentalist Christian waiting for me. The owner said with a chuckle that he had left the shop after recognising the woman who had just had the session with me was a local church minister's wife.

The feelings in advance are not only warnings, but also a reminder of who is doing the talking. In this case it was their

Chapter III

way of getting me in a mind set so that I automatically tune into them and not tried to protect their honour. They are big enough to look after themselves, and usually do a far better job than I could ever do. Hence why they are the puppeteers and I, and any good psychic, are their puppets.

On arriving at the place where I do my sessions and after setting up my tape recorder, brochures, making a list of the people that will be seeing me for the day and having my mandatory cup of tea or "cuppa," I sit alone in the room and dedicate it to my guides, in this manner:

Hi guides, and welcome. To any entities, energies, souls or spirits that are not my highest Truth, my guides and their quality of light, you won't be comfortable here, so best you find somewhere else to go. I wish you no harm or hurt, and in fact welcome you to stay so long as you understand that my guides determine how this session will be run. They are the overriding power this day, in accordance with God's will and therefore Spirit Law.

I then have the overwhelming feeling of peace expanding from deep within; the sign from them that we are ready to start. I always do a discernment check to make sure I am fully aware of anything that is not feeling perfect within. If there are any doubts, I will throw it over to them to thoroughly check out whatever that feeling or concern may be. This is a bit like doing a computer virus check a second time, just in case.

I can recall one time arriving to do my session at Hervey Bay, and not long after I had started to prepare myself for the day's clients and was feeling strange and almost sickly. I had no choice but to cancel the two-day's readings, which didn't help my very low bank account. Later I found there had been a robbery and an arson attempt in the small alleyway right next to the room where I did my sessions the night before. The police suspected both the shop owner and the next-door owner, though I never found out if charges were laid. I assume my guides, knowing in advance what kind of negative energy would have drawn this kind of person or persons to the shop in the first place, and how that energy could have caused interference with my sessions, closed me down for those days. In fact I never went to that place again.

Next step in the process is the actual psychic session. I usually greet my client at the shop counter and invite them into the room. I try as much as possible not to make eye contact or to interact with the person, as this can lead to a front end loading. This can happen when the psychic, intentionally or unintentionally, gleans sippets of information from the client, either from observations of body language or mood, which could influence the session. Instead I try to make the person feel at ease by making some humorous comment, such as; "Well here's hoping I get something decent for you, otherwise I won't get paid and you won't get the message."

It is from the person's reaction to this comment that my guides will confirm the person's emotional status with me, particularly if they have any interference around them. I don't mean by this that everyone that laughs is necessarily without interference, nor that anyone that doesn't respond necessarily has interference around him or her. I mean that spirit picks up on the person's internal or intuitive reaction to my comment.

I then go through an explanation of how I work. I basically explain that I am a trance medium and that the source of the information they are about to receive is from their own guides, who pass on the information to my guides, who in turn speak through me.

I explain that though some people think to the contrary, psychics are not mind readers, and humorously add that if I were an unscrupulous mind reader with such ability, I would head down to their bank immediately after the session, to steal

Chapter III

whatever money they may have in their account, as I would surely know the access code. In some instances I get the reply, "The small amount I have there you can keep," with a chuckle.

This helps the client to understand there is no hidden skulduggery going on, and also to assure them that the session, which may seem to them quite an amazing process, is proof of the existence of the client's own guides. It helps them see that there is no way I or my guides could know anything about them without their guides passing this information on. In other words, it is their guides running the session, not my guides or I. If the client is a serious worrier; if they have a tendency to let others undermine their self esteem; if currently they are having something or someone overriding or interfering in their life; if they don't have a good understanding of their moral conscience value (that is they rarely check to determine their true belief in relation to what they know to be right, pure, true and good), and may well have interference guiding them, it usually shows up at this time. It will show in the form of a lack of humour or understanding of what I have said.

I then put them at ease by explaining that my guides will check to ensure that the guidance around them is coming from their guides. If my guides feel there is interference, they will show the person how to draw their guides, which in turn aligns their chakras, balances their overall vibrations and cleanses their aura of any negative or low level entities.

This process usually involves a very short but effective attuning meditation that they are encouraged to continue saying daily after they have left the session. I have included a version of this meditation further on in the book. I always tape record my sessions for the person and insist that if there should be a reason for why they would want their money back, I will return the money after they have returned the tape. I then continue on with the session for both the person that needed the attuning, and those that don't.

Using three chakras or energy centres as focal points, my guides then gives that person information that should related personally to them on matters to do with the psychic-spiritual, communication and self esteem, and personal relationship area of their life. If the information my guides through me give the person makes sense and they feel it is appropriate, then the session proceeds. If however the person feels the information is too vague, inappropriate to why they have come, don't like my looks, or thought I was a fundamentalist Christian (yes again another fun aspect to make the client feel comfortable) they get their money back. Assuming they are happy with what I have said as being relevant to them, my guides then give whatever other information They may have for the person, which they will have got from that person's guides. This is the bulk time of the session.

Then comes question time, where the person gets to ask any question, firstly on what has been said, and then on any matter that is of importance to them. Usually by the time we get to question time, the person will indicate that the questions they had planned to ask were answered in the first section during the chakra check. After all, if their guides were responsible for them coming for a session, the most important matters on the client's mind would have to be the first things their guides would pass on to my guides and therefore to me.

Most people will say they have run out of questions at about the three quarter hour mark, or they may ask questions that are simply an attempt to make sure they get all the information they came for. I allow people to email or post further questions to me after they have left the session, because invariably they will remember important questions, some coming out of the reading, after they have replayed the tape at home. I recommend this process to any psychic, as it allows feedback from any clients that choose to do so.

The information I have given here obviously applies to my trance psychic sessions, but anyone doing any form of psychic sessions can use this same basic format. Your guides will select the particular tool to use to pass on the relevant information and they will also give you the thoughts, words and feelings you need to properly interpret this information.

By practicing the daily attuning meditations, reviewing your moral conscience value in accordance with what you know to be right, pure, true and good, and treating the whole matter with the respect you know it deserves, you will soon have the relevant information flowing freely through you. It is your guides that are happily doing all the hard work, while you rake in the money, although I wouldn't be suggesting you open a Swiss bank account.

Of course not everyone wants to be a psychic. Most people are happy visiting a decent local psychic who makes sense and gives clear and honest messages. Sadly these truly gifted psychics are getting harder to find. I repeatedly hear complaints from people who say some psychics say what they think the person would like them to say, and sadly I know this to be so with a number of psychics I have known. Take the example of the psychic that told me she will never tell anyone they are going to have a marriage or relationship break-up, even if the psychic strongly felt that will happen.

On the other hand there are those psychics that think it quite acceptable to tell someone that a relative, friend or someone they know, is going to die or take ill soon. It's no wonder people feel psychics and the work they do is dangerous, worrying, upsetting or totally unnecessary.

The whole idea of a psychic session is to help people through difficult circumstances, with information that should either reassure the person concerned as to whether they have made the right decision in a particular matter, or to show an alternative way for those that are lost and needing assistance. Primarily it should show the person that they are not alone and that they have very highly evolved friends in spirit working as God's messengers, just waiting to guide them through the rough roads of life.

Giving people information, without understanding or caring about the consequences, is the primary reason many people, who have confirmed their satisfaction with me and my work, say they were originally reluctant to visit a psychic. Sadly the most common complaint I hear is against tarot readers. Here is an example of someone who went to a psychic at a travelling expo, wanting reassurance concerning an important coming event in her life.

Psychic: OK now this card indicates your personal relationship. I feel there is a person in your life at the moment, possibly a boyfriend, partner or husband?

Client: Yes I have a husband.

Psychic: I feel there is something he is having trouble trying to tell you. I think it has something to do with a previous relationship.

Client: Oh! (Very surprised)

Psychic: Have you known him very long?

Client: Yes, four years.

Chapter III

Psychic: Then again it could indicate that there may be some difficulties coming up between you both. Are you having difficulties in this relationship at the moment?

Client: No, we just got married and we are planning to go on our honeymoon.

Psychic: (Turns over another card.) This card says it is not of a serious nature and I can see you both working through this with very little consequence. Maybe he has something to tell you later about an old love. Has he said anything to you, or hinted at anything before you got married?

Client: No absolutely not. I have known him since my school days and none of this makes sense.

Psychic: (Pause) Oh OK. Have there been any problems with the plans for the honeymoon?

Client: No the honeymoon was planned long ago. We had a few minor problems before the wedding, to do with the cake decorations, but nothing serious. In fact everything just flowed along wonderfully.

Psychic: Well it's possible something may happen later, but I'm sure it will be solved very quickly. (A pat on the hand and a reassuring smile as if that would solve any misunderstandings she may have caused.)

Let's look at what happened or at least what didn't happen. The tarot reader has let the cards dictate the information to her based on their face value, and her own feelings and opinions, instead of using the cards as a focal tool for the source coming from the young client's guides. Then when she realized she was starting to dig a hole for herself, instead of admitting she may have got it wrong and restarting the proceedings, she just dug deeper.

Using the cards as a focal tool, the tarot reader should be able to discern between what the cards indicate, based on their face value and the feelings that the tarot reader gets as she is reading them. When this woman came to see another tarot card reader she was quite reticent, even though her friend had told her of how good she believed this psychic to be, she was still reluctant. This is roughly how the second session went, recalled by her sometime later:

Second psychic: OK now this card indicates difficulties in a personal relationship. (Pause as the tarot reader checks or focuses on the source, before continuing.) This is confusing me here, because even though this particular card indicates difficulties with a personal relationship, I get the very opposite with you. I feel you are very happy and contented, and something special has recently happened to you, either you've met someone new, or made a commitment to someone. Am I correct?

Client: Yes I have just got married

Psychic: That makes sense with what I feel. And the whole thing went without a hitch, correct?

Client: Yes it was wonderful

Psychic: How wonderful for you. Congratulations. (Pause as the psychic allowed her guides to pass on further relevant information) Have either of you had cause for concern about future plans? I think it may be concerning money, an investment, home or property? I think it is you, and I feel you are unsure about your partner's plan to buy something, a house or land I think. Is this making any sense to you?

Now this didn't shown up in a particular cards, but the guides of this tarot reader were feeding her the relevant information in relation to this young woman's particular circumstances.

Chapter III

Client: Absolutely. I want us to buy a particular place now in another town, but my husband wants to buy two cheaper places, fix them up, sell them and make a profit, then buy what we both want later.

Psychic: OK I feel you will end up with your dream home in a few years time, and I feel your husband's ideal of doing up two houses and selling them, is how you will get the money to achieve this. So you are both right and it is going to bond you even closer as you each develop this trust you have for each other. You both need to swallow your pride, trust your instinct, which is really your guides, and discuss matters from a dual perspective, not as two singles people. Don't forget you are married now *Smile*

I feel you are going to have a very enjoyable and long term relationship with this man.

The first psychic was fishing for information from the client to make the circumstances fit the card. The second psychic made the circumstances dictate the cards. She let the guides speak what they wanted to say, not what she thought appropriate. It takes a very special discipline on the part of the psychic, not to let personal feelings; thoughts, hopes or wishes interfere in a psychic session. Those that do let their feelings overrule the session, tend to assume they are the source and forget, or don't even recognise, the information didn't come from their own knowing, but from the client's own guides.

Another aspect of this kind of reading is the first psychic unintentionally front end loaded, which happens to too many psychics. Front end loading is when the client is either asked to give more information that is necessary for a good session, or the client, unintentionally, gives over too much information. Here is an example of a client unintentionally front-end loading the psychic:

Client: Can you tell me if this man I have just met is my soul mate? Oh I just know he loves me and he is so kind and loving. In the three weeks I've known him he's already better than the last awful man I was with. Bobby, that's his name, has told me I am exactly what he is looking for, and I know his past relationship is over and that he plans to tell his old girlfriend about us soon. He is the right one for me isn't he? The client has told the psychic,

- She has recently met someone and his name is Bobby.
- She didn't like her last boyfriend.
- She has set her heart on this new relationship with Bobby.
- She has only known Bobby a short time.
- She intends a long-term relationship with him.
- She has probably already given this impression to him.
- She is aware he still has contact or a relationship with another person, possibly a current lover.
- She may feel very strongly about this particular new person, but it is obvious from what she has said, most of it is more her hopes and wishes, rather than how he truly feels about her.

She has given more information and trust to the psychic than the psychic should know in such a situation, which can easily affect what the psychic's reply will be. It takes a very strong and well-disciplined psychic in such a situation to not be influenced. I know of a psychic, who simply said, as a standard answer in such cases, "Oh I see your love life being much better than it has been, and there will be a special reward coming your way in 12 months time." When the client asks, as invariably they do, "Yes but can you see us together?" she replies, "Oh now you know what men are like. He'll come around, just be patient."

Even thought the psychic knows the relationship is doomed before it has even started. The psychic doesn't want to disappoint or upset the client, but in giving such an answer has compromised Truth, and the source of that Truth.

There isn't a session I do that doesn't have some front-end loading, it can't be helped.

I try to prevent this as much as possible, by asking the person not to say anything until I have given the information spirit has asked me to pass on first. In question time, it is mostly front end loading, but by that time the session has got to the point where the person is asking their questions, matters of importance have already been dealt with. There is already established a very strong knowing by the client that what is coming through me in trance, is come from their guides, or they would have already left.

It is a natural human process to have an opinion. However, a psychic's opinion isn't necessarily coming from the client's guides. The less the psychic knows, the less the chances of them having an opinion, and the more accurate the information from the client's guides. So as a general rule in the early stages of a reading, a psychic should not be asking questions as a means of getting the session started because that could cause front end loading. If you are the client going to a psychic, the less the psychic knows about you or your questions, the better and more accurate the information should be.

Now you might say that in the example I gave of the psychic who did the second reading for the newly wed, she asked questions which were front end loaded. The difference is the second psychic was making more of a statement in the questions, rather than a genuine question that didn't, to that point, have an answer. In other words the psychic showed the woman, in the form of questions, what she already knew, and was asking for confirmation. As an example at variance with the second psychic's reading, let's see what should have happened when she got it wrong:

Psychic: OK now this card indicates difficulties in a personal relationship. (Pause as the tarot reader checks or focuses on the source, before continuing.) This is confusing me here, because even though this particular card indicates difficulties with a personal relationship, I get the very opposite with you.

I feel you are very happy and contented, and something special has recently happened to you, either you've met someone new, or made a commitment to someone. Am I correct?

Client: Well no not really. You see I have just recently separated from my fiancé.

Psychic: Oh dear, I'm not even close. Oh I'm sorry. I'll have to give you your money back, because for some reason, the information is totally off track.

Or another possible scenario,

Psychic: Oh dear I am off track aren't I. (Pause) is this something that has just happened in the past week or so? Like you and he have had some kind of disagreement or you have a strong reason to doubt him and his sincerity? Does that make sense?

Client: Yes, my best friend told me she had an affair with him.

Psychic: And what did he say to this?

Client: Oh he denied it of course, they all do.

Psychic: Well I feel your friend wasn't telling you the truth, your fiancé didn't have an affair and he is heart-broken, because he truly loves you. I feel you will find out the truth by the end of next week, and you and this so called friend will

Chapter III

part company. I see you and your man getting married as planned but you will need a new bride's maid.

OK now in this scenario, even though the psychic asked questions and seemingly front end loaded, those questions were in relation to something the psychic already knew or felt before the client had answered. In other words, the client, indicating the information the psychic had received was correct, answered the psychic's questions in the affirmative. This included telling the client that the friend, who had lied to her, was to have been the bride's maid. Something the client hadn't told the psychic, and which the psychic couldn't possibly have known.

A number of years ago, in fact in the early 90's, because front end loading is so hard to prevent, and as a means of finding a purer way of receiving simple answers to questions for people, I asked my guides if They could come up with a simple system to help in such circumstances. I had already known of the pendulum system of Yes and No, which I had used very early in my learning. This is where the pendulum turning one way was Yes and the opposite way was No. However, what I was looking for was a totally independent system, one that used no tools at all. Based on the pendulum system they introduced me to the Yes-Nos and ABCs method. As far as I know, there is no one else using such a system, other than those that spirit has taught through me. This process is where the person thinks of a question, the contents of which they keep to themselves, and once the person has the question constructed in their mind, the psychic tunes into their guides who receives the answer from that person's guides, which the psychic then passes on to that person.

Lets look at an example of a Yes-No, and lets say the person in their mind asks, "Will my husband and I ever fully love each other, yes or no?" Now remember this person has said nothing out loud, the question is in their mind, so the psychic has no idea of the question.

The psychic's reply could be similar to this: "I'm seeing a yes and a no. I can see a tennis court and there are two people on the court, but they gave up playing a long time ago. I see lots of tennis balls around both these people's feet, but neither seems too keen to pass them on. It is like each expects the other to take some kind of action, and I feel your guides are saying it will continue this way until one or other person plays ball."

The advantage of this process is it allows no room for front end loading. This is the best system to be used, for example, when the police or authorities wish to use the services of a psychic. The authority concerned can put questions, or even just call to mind a person of interest, and the psychic should be able to give the relevant information without the police or the authority having to divulge confidential information to the psychic.

The ABCs are used for multiple questions or questions with multiple answers and are a little more complicated to explain. Lets say a young woman has a question concerning choosing her future partner from a number of candidates, "Will I end up with Robert, Julian, James or someone else? " This person then puts up the three names, plus "someone else" separately, as ABC and in this case D, so that person's question, in their mind, is: "Will I end up with A = Julian, B = someone else, C = Robert, D = James? "

You'll notice I have shuffled the letters and names around, so as to prevent the psychic being accused of guessing, an accusation that can be made against the Yes-No system. The psychic then allows their guides to give them a single letter or the strongest one first and the less strong following, especially in the case where there may be more than one letter, eg: "I am

Chapter III

getting B very strong, but I am also getting D. The D seems to be short term but the B is longer term."

This means the young lady will spend a special time with James, but not necessarily long term, and there will not be much if any contact with Julian or Robert. In other words this person will still be looking for Mr. Right, after she has finished her fling with James. Of course this person would then ask further questions, either ABCs or Yes – Nos to clarify this matter. I have often had a person putting up exactly the same question a second or a third time, just to ensure that I am on track, only with different letters corresponding to the same matters, such as the question above, only this time it would have been: "Will I end up with A = James, B = Robert, C = someone else, D = Julian?" Usually the answer is the same every time.

In the instance where the answers are different, it can indicate that the question has been put in a confusing way, or that there is more to the matter than the question indicated. An example of this, a few years ago a person asked me this ABCD: "Will we A = Take up my parent's offer of accommodation, B = Move to Mackay, C = Move to Sarina, D = Move to Koumala." In reply I got B, but I also felt C, though not as strong. So she asked again, but this time she changed the letters around: "Will we A = Move to Mackay, B = Move to Koumala, C = Stay with my parents, D = Move to Sarina." To which I got B then a vague D and then confusion. Can you see the mistake she made? She had not given spirit an option in the answer to say something else, so they answered confusion with confusion. When she added an E to the question: "Will we A = Take up my parent's offer, B = something different or not yet know, C = Mackay, D = Koumala, E = Sarina." I got, "Ah now it's making sense to them. They are saying B again, but it feels much clearer this time."

After many other ABCs it turned out that she had assumed rentals in all places. However spirit could see an option for them renting in one town and buying in another, but we weren't getting which town was the rental and which was the buying. She couldn't see them buying as they had no money and his job was insecure. A week or so later, they heard that a loan he had applied for, had been accepted, but that they had to wait a given period of a month or two, before they could get the loan. So, they had the option of renting first and then buying later, but just where had not been decided by them, so their guides couldn't answer.

Some weeks later they contacted me to say they had decided, almost irrationally, to move to a totally different town, where he had the chance of getting his old job back, where the cost of living was far cheaper and the lifestyle for the kids was far better. It is important to stress that the psychic should not ask what the question was, as this can be very personal for the person asking. If the person chooses to tell the psychic then there is no problem. The psychic can certainly ask if the answer he or she has given is making sense, without needing to know the actual contents. These methods are particularly good when there may be a conflict of interest between the psychic and the questions being asked.

Let's take the first instance, where the girl asked: "Will I end up with A = James, B = Robert, C = someone else, D = Julian?" Can you see the advantage to this method had the psychic answering the above questions been the sister of one of these young men?

A third and more advanced method to the Yes-No, ABC is when the person puts a question up in their mind, and the psychic has to give whatever information they may receive without the added Yes-No or ABC. The groups I associate with use this method the most, not only because it is quicker, but

Chapter III

also because it keeps the psychic closely tuned to their guides, and usually in conjunction with the full circle energy.

Here is an example of how this method works and is different to Yes - No or ABC. For quite some time a few years ago, I lent my friends my Kia as their car had broken down and they were without transport. On one of my visits to their place, they put up to their guides:

What information can spirit give us on future transport needs, a new car, and the possibility of buying Pete's Kia.
The reply I got for them was something like,

"I see you both merrily running down the highway, like you are in a cartoon-like car, and very happy. I can see light colours around you, possibly light yellow, cream or white, and it seems to be quite roomy".

Remember I had no idea the question related to a car or transport in general. There was no way they could afford a car, even a decent second hand one. They simply didn't have the money as they were paying off a house. I kept saying, I can see this all happening very soon. Four months later, just prior to Christmas 2004, they bought a decent second hand, white station wagon, which was just perfect for their needs. This had come about when their bank had notified them they could organise a loan extension, considering they were good customers, and the interest would be locked in over the time of the loan. Of course on dusty country roads, most cars soon take on a dirty yellow appearance, the colour I had described. As to the carton-like car, they laughingly refer to themselves as the strange but harmless neighbours, which is why I got the humorous aspect. I had no idea the question related to them.

So how does this process work? How can the psychic know this kind of information without having any obvious knowledge of the question the person is asking? Is it still the same system as other psychic sessions, where the information coming from the person's own guides? Yes, assuming the persons concerned interact with their guides as I have previously outlined. When the person asks a question of a psychic, whether the question is out front at a psychic session, or in the form of Yes-Nos or ABC's, as is the case with all psychic sessions, the person's own personal guides are the source of the information. When the person asks the psychic a question, they are actually asking their own guides, and that person's own guides then pass the answer on to the psychic's guides, who then pass it on to the person.

If the person asking the question doesn't have full knowing of this process, if they don't give permission to their guides, or if they have an attitude that they will do everything in their power to stop the psychic getting the answer to their question, then the psychic will not get a correct answer.

It is very important therefore, that the person asking the question of the psychic, especially using the Yes-No or ABC system, gives a respectful authorisation to his or her own personal guides to pass on whatever information will be in that person's best interest, in relation to this matter. This then allows the psychic to pass onto the person the best information available for them at this time.

There can still be difficulties for the psychic getting the correct information if the person asking the question has psychic interference or they are blocked psychically. The answers will invariably be wrong, or so vague as to be of no worth to the person asking.

Yes-Nos and ABC's tend to be asked of me when I am not prepared, as opposed to when I am in a reading room or doing regular sessions. In this situation I usually ask my guides to do a quick check of both the person asking the question and of

Chapter III

myself, before I commence. If there is any interference around me, (and I am as vulnerable as anyone else) I excuse myself from the person and quietly attune myself to my guides before returning to answer his or her questions. If there is any serious interference around the person asking the question, I will try and encourage them to join me in a quiet room or quiet corner somewhere, often with a cup of coffee or tea if practicable. Not that the coffee or tea affects the status of the reading, it simply creates a relaxed and friendly atmosphere. I then get them to join me in the simple attuning meditation.

I don't recommend a person ask a psychic a question, whether an open question or the Yes-No, ABC method, without firstly getting to know your own personal guides. Meditating regularly over at least a five to six month period and following my suggestions concerning improving your moral conscious values, will almost guarantee you will get good responses from any psychic. This of course is assuming your guides have something worth while to pass on to you. In many cases, after doing meditations regularly, the person will find they have answers to their question without having to ask a psychic.

Now there are going to be those, no matter what I say to the contrary, who will still believe the psychic system is basically the ability for some gifted people to read the minds of other, less gifted, people. I will add to what I have already said in reply to this belief: If these gifted people were mind readers, wouldn't they be able to answer almost any question asked of them? What would restrict their knowing? Wouldn't they have queues at their door of people wanting to know answers to the most puzzling of questions?

The information a psychic receives is usually limited to specific areas of a person's life, and so it stands to reason that whatever information the psychic receives must come from a specific source. The person's own guides give out the relevant information when requested. They also protect the person by only allowing the psychic to know the appropriate information to the person's specific question and area of inquiry. It is logically to assume that the quality of the information a person receives is also an indication of the level of guidance that person has.

This also brings us to the question of ethics and invasion of privacy. If a psychic were to give information of a psychic nature without being asked to do so, it would be the same as if a professional person were to talk to a person openly about privileged information. Confidential information is just that, confidential. Even if the psychic doesn't realise it, the information they receive, or think they receive for another person, could well be of an extremely personal nature. As a general rule, psychics should only give information to those that ask for it.

It could be said as a counter point that if a psychic felt the information was coming from that person's guides, or that as a psychic they feel duty bound to pass on this particular information, that it would be wrong for the psychic not to do so. I would answer this by saying it is highly unusual for spiritual guides of that calibre to pass on information in this manner. If the psychic were to just blab out whatever they have received, it could cause serious worry, concern and possibly plant a negative thought in a person mind, or worse, reinforce an existing negativity within that person.

Take as an example the mother of a friend of mine, who recently visited a naturopath for a consultation. As part of the initial discussion, my friend's mother mentioned she hadn't sleeping well since her father died some twelve months before. Both my friend and my self had said it was more diet than anything psychic to which she agreed to later. However, on visiting the naturopath and repeating what she told us, the naturopath immediately told her she could see her father standing beside her. She didn't ask what that meant, and the naturopath didn't reiterate further, with the result the woman's worrying and lack of sleep increased.

The message this naturopath gave in itself wasn't all that troubling, it was the fact that this naturopath said something of a psychic nature, without telling the mother she was, or wasn't, a psychic, which caused the concern. The mother kept churning over in her mind that there must have been a reason for why this qualified naturopath could see her father there around her. Regardless of points to the contrary being put by her daughter, the mother still felt that it had to be for some important reason, otherwise why would this naturopath have received this information. The mother assumed the information had come from a spiritual source, possibly her father, when it was more likely the naturopath's own best intended, but indiscreet, personal thoughts.

Another point in this saga was when the mother had mentioned to the naturopath her concerns about her husband's health. Her husband was waiting out the front of the shop so the naturopath, without any request or authority from the husband, approached him insisting that he visit her at his earliest convenience. As it turned out the husband did need naturopathic assistance, which he wouldn't have got had it been left to him. The point is where does the choice boundary lay? When should someone approach another, no matter how serious it may seem to the one approaching?

The information given by a psychic should be helpful, non-worrying and ease a person's concerns relating to such matters, not as the psychic perceives it, but as the person perceives it. It is one thing to be given permission to give information as a psychic, and another to have someone else ask for someone else.

A case that comes to mind was when I was waiting at one of my outlets for a client to arrive for a session. A woman, who was talking to one of the shop assistants, started to become agitated. I didn't know what the subject was about, but just from her body language, I knew there was something happening to and around her, that was anything but good. My normal action in such circumstances is to move away, or even to walk out of the shop, as it has nothing to do with me unless I'm asked. As I made my way slowly towards the door, the assistant subtly caught my eye, and before I knew it, I was talking pleasantly to them both. The woman had had a dreadful repetitive dream over the past few months in which a loved one had been murdered and she was convinced something was going to happen to someone in her family. The assistant introduced me to her as the resident psychic, and the customer retreated slightly. I made it clear from the outset that if whatever I said made her uncomfortable, or if she didn't want to continue the discussion, she just had to say so and I would stop.

With her reserved consent I took her to a discreet corner of the shop. I started to ask her a series of helpful and caring based questions, all offered by my guides, to which she volunteered answers. From this I was able to build a picture that she could easily understand. I was able to determine that she had been on medication for a mental illness and had stopped taking it a few weeks prior to the dreams starting. This has been when the dreams seemed to become more prophetic to her. She agreed that she had been under a psychiatrist for bi polar disorder. And further she felt uncomfortable with the medication. I asked her if she would like to try the release meditation. Reluctant at first she followed me into my session room. The meditation was only about fifteen minutes in all, but the person who left was nothing like the person who had sat down. I told her the importance of revisiting her psychiatrist and to stick to whatever medication she was prescribed. She said that she felt she was a slave to the medication and I asked did she tell the doctor this, to which she replied no. I said that she had a right to refuse medication, but that she

Chapter III

had to tell the doctor, as some mental illness medications need special care in how they were used. She called back a few months later to tell the shop assistant she had visited the psychiatrist and he had adjusted the dosage, resulting in her feeling much more balanced, and less groggy.

It is not that unusual for a psychic to have a situation where they get called to pass on information outside of a designated session, as happened in this case. If such a situation was to happen to a psychic and they felt their guides had matters to be passed on, it could possibly happen the following way:
Psychic: Please excuse me, I am a psychic and I usually would never do this without being asked, but I feel very strongly I have to say this to you. Do you mind? This then gives the person a right to say yes or no to the information.

Assuming authority has been given to the psychic, the way they pass on this information is very important also. As a general rule the information should never be given in public, that is, in front of others. It is important to call the person to one side, so as not to embarrass that person, or others that may be present. Even if the person says something like, "Oh it's alright, this person is my friend. We don't have any secrets from each other." The psychic should explain to the person that the information might be for his or her ears only, and that it best for this person to make the decision to share with their friend after they have heard the information. The psychic would then give a gentle run-in of the basics of the message they have received. As an example they could say something like: "I am getting you are currently making or are about to make a decision concerning (whatever the matter may be), does this make any sense to you?"

In all instances the psychic should not lead the person or try to interpret this information for the person, unless asked. Even though the person has given the psychic permission to pass on the information, it could be limited permission based on politeness, mingled with good faith and possibly embarrassment on the part of the participant. They may be petrified to think someone knows such matters about them, not knowing that the information source is their own personal guides. Under no circumstance should a psychic ask for payment or even suggest a full reading at that time, as the person could be very confused and vulnerable. It would be best, even if the person were to ask for a reading or session, that the psychic defer such for another time, so as to allow the person to reappraise their circumstances and therefore to determine how the psychic may be of some assistance to them. There is no harm in the psychic giving the person their card or brochure to allow the person to contact them at a later date.

As was the case with the naturopath, it can be a psychic person's well meaning and good intent that can instigate a message. This message may not necessarily have come from either the person's guides or the guidance of the psychic. Hence why I repeat that there is need for the psychic to identify between their own emotions and feelings and that of their guides and the differences to be clearly defined in their mind. Discernment is the psychics imperative.

Another case concerning this particular naturopath was when she told her client she urgently needed to visit her mother, as the client's mother was very ill and wouldn't last the month. When this woman challenged the naturopath as to her credentials, the naturopath replied "Oh no I am not a psychic. I don't use tarot cards or things like that, I am empathic. All my information comes from angels, and I confirm this information with kinesiology."

A few months later this woman revisited this naturopath to say she had visited the relative and there was nothing wrong with her. She further suggested this naturopath trade in her angels, as they were totally wrong in this instance. If this had been said to a lesser person, that person could have sued the naturopath. Had this naturopath known anything about empathy, kinesiology, or angels, she would have known they are all part of the one system, and the source she was tapping into was not pure Truth.

Learning To Work With Your Guides

Before we move on from the Yes-No, ABC system, for those that may want to experiment with it, here is a simple process you can follow. The preparation with your guides is extremely important, as they are the source of this information, so it is necessary to do the attuning meditation regularly before you even attempt to try this. Remember that the question you are asking your guides may not be answerable, or they may have reasons why they can't answer you, so don't have expectations. Look on the experiment as an exercise. If you don't have someone to assist you, try this Yes-No method.

Write down four, five or six questions onto separate pieces of paper. Make sure they are separate questions and not related to the same matter, and pose the questions so that they can be answered yes, no or something else. Once you have written your questions, fold each piece separately, and then shuffle them so you have no idea which question is on which piece of paper. Taking each folded piece of paper and write on the outside the words: Yes-No-Something Else separately. Shuffle the pieces of paper in your hands so that you don't know which questions are on which sheet of paper. Now spread the still folded separate sheets of paper over a flat area. Ask your guides in your mind if they could please help you with this experiment. Don't be concerned if you don't know whether your guides can hear you, they will show you they are present if they can, either by their answer, or by the way you feel.

With the thought in mind that you are purely a channel for them, not only on these questions, but for future ones as well, pick up one of the folded pieces of paper with the questions inside and hold it in your hands. With your eyes closed, and no expectations, let your mind go completely still. Remember you are not the source and therefore you don't have to do anything, other than to be completely at peace with the knowledge that if there is an answer forthcoming from your guide, you will feel it.

If you get a very quiet, hard to discern feeling that goes one way or the other, that is, you get a Yes or a No, but it feels very weak, tick or circle that particular word on the outside of that particular folded question. Don't look at the question till you have finished the exercise with all the questions.

Do this with each question till you have completed all questions, then thank your guides within your mind, and then unfold the questions and check your answers against them.

It is important not to act on these answers, or to assume them to be right till you have practiced often and got the hang of the exercise, gaining confidence so that you are truly interacting with your guides.

If you are used to using a pendulum of course you can do the same thing by holding the pendulum over each question, after determining which directional turn of the pendulum is Yes or No. Once you have got quite used to this system and you feel pretty confident that you and your guides are communing, reasonably well, you might like to try the ABC process.

To do this you need to write one question and fold it the same way you did in the Yes-No exercise. On the outside of this question however, you write the letters A = Yes, B = No and C = X (something else). You don't have to have A for Yes or B for No, you could swap the letters around, and it's not a bad idea to do this, just so you know you aren't pre-empting the answers, not that you possibly could.

Again you write up a number of questions in this way and scatter them so that you don't know which question you are

Chapter III

holding. It is important not to know which questions you are asking your guides. Making sure you don't try to influence the answer, or try to hard to get an answer, circle whichever letter seems strongest to you on each question, and when you have finished all the questions, you can read the answers.
If you wanted to double check, with either Yes-No's or ABC's, you could turn your question over and after you have written down your answer, re shuffle them when you have done them all the first time, and then re-do the exercise again, writing down on the blank side whatever feeling is the strongest.

Remember experimenting is a wonderful way of finding out more about your wonderful guides. So long as you have respect for them as being the representatives of God, Goodness, the Creator etc. you can't do any wrong. Often, after you have been doing this for some time, when you read the answers, you'll find they are the same as you already knew, which is a true sign that your guides have been helping you all along. It is important not to cheat in any way. By that I mean when you ask the questions, do it so that you don't have a clue what the answers are going to be.

If you have a friend to help you, ask your friend to think of a question using the same rules and conditions I suggested for the questions above. While he or she is preparing their question, go still and quiet and ask your guides to assist you. Once your friend has organised his or her question ask them to give permission to their guides to allow this information to be passed on to your guides. Remember it is their guides who will be passing on the information.

There are different ways you may assist the process of receiving information from your guides. One is to imagine you are flying through a sky filled with the words Yes and No, or the letters corresponding to your friend's options. The particular word or letter that seems strongest to you is the one you can choose as the answer to the particular question your friend asked.

Again remember, you are only a beginner and you are not expected to get it right the first time, any more than your guides will get it right that first time either. It is simply allowing the psychic channel between you and your guides to be attuned, so that after enough practice, you will start receiving correct answers about 40% or 50% of the time.

For those that find no answers seem forthcoming, no matter how hard they try, here is a suggestion. To a specific question you have written down, and after asking for a Yes or No and not getting anything, ask yourself: What would my guides say to this question, Yes or No?' And then write down either Yes or No and wait to see if that answer feels comfortable. Remember our guides work through our feelings and we then interpret those feelings. For a raw beginner, the process needs to be built, just like a computer getting used to interpreting new software.

On the Light Path   Peter Lyons

Yours In Embryo

Oh! Lord here I am, a thousand light years
from where I was yesterday.
Thinking good times were a stone's throw away.
What a fool I've been.
And where I am now, can be best measured
by the things taken away.
Man made images that led my mind astray,
I now have peaceful dreams.

And yes I try hard, there's no sitting back
and letting good works slide.
I work hard each day, till I know that
we're both satisfied - inside.
So Lord, watch me grow, please
don't neglect this special seed that you've sown.
Help me hang in there when growing seems so slow.
I'm yours in embryo.

And Lord, hold me firm, when there are hurtful
kinds of lessons to be learned.
Oh please hold me tight. I'm so frightened
I might somehow get burned. I'm scared.
My Friends here I am, a thousand light years from where
I was yesterday.
Knowing you're less than a stone's throw away.
I now have peaceful dreams.

1983

Chapter IV

Revisiting The Past

There is no doubt that we are living in very hard and difficult times; unlike any time we have known since recorded history. We certainly have had harder times in a physical sense in the past, where loss of life was common and life expectancy was short. However, this new hardship comes from the saturation we have created as a result of the new choices we now have to make, and the little to no guidance on how we should make them. Choices that may have seemed benign and pleasurable have made us totally unsure and vulnerable as to the consequences. Noise, movement, action and distractions go on around us; some we create and others we have to tolerate. The mobile phone has almost become a natural appendage to most of us.

We have learned to survive through this bedlam, and often we do this by creating an opposite energy to that imposed on us. Take sounds for example. Not everyone uses iPods because they like the music. Some are blowing their eardrums away so that they don't have to listen to the perpetual cacophony of our industrious cities. If we were to try and individually identify or recognise even half of these distractions we face each day, we'd surely get bowled over by the enormity of the intensity and complexity. Is it any wonder we use distractive tools to help us block most of it from our tired and overworked conscious minds. We have desensitised ourselves.

On the Light Path — Peter Lyons

This frenzy of activity still has a greater bearing on our stability and mind status than we may realize, even when we use this anaesthetic-like tool, so that at the end of a very busy working day, we continue to whirl around somewhere back where we were an hour or so earlier. Then we have the family commitments, pressures and expectations. We finish one occupation and jump straight into another more personal one, our family commitments. We need to wind down, chill out, cut off and relax. We often partake of a glass or two of wine, beer or stronger drink. In the case of many now, some happy pills or self-diagnosed medication that our doctor wouldn't recommend, and which the police might not tolerate. And then we repeat the process the next day. Most of today's stress comes from the expectations we and others put on us.

It all tends to start when we made those original choices, usually as teenagers, when we buy our first car, join a sport club or sporting organization, all of which usually costs more that we'll ever earn, so we get ourselves a loan. The purchases continue and the debt grows. It's not long after this that we make a commitment to that significant other, and often unplanned. The already stretched loan now has to include the cost of a house purchase or rental, new car, electrical items for that house, and of course the expenses of the inevitable bi product of your relationship, children. So it's off to the banks and other lending institutions where we further sign our life away. In order that we pay back these loans and borrowings, we tie ourselves to work commitments, often extending ourselves beyond our abilities. We dare not admit to our failings or over committed status because to do so has us believe we would be looked upon in the larger community as being less capable than anyone else.

Employment becomes less to do with particular skills, and more about how much money we can make in the shortest amount of time. So there we are, as younger workers, debt ridden from over spending, trying desperately to pay it all

Chapter IV

off. With any employment we are expected to be the company's man or woman, the business representative, the face of those who employs us. Because of our debt, the company virtually owns us and therefore dictates diversions to our soul's journey.

This means we compromise our values in order that we serve that business or we don't get paid. So skilled are we at this compromising, that we loose sight of the fact we are no longer respecting, or fully conscious of, our own personal values. We quickly loose sight of our true soul's journey, as we become nothing more than a cog in a very complicated human-made machine.

We may think this doesn't apply to us, that we are actually our own person, and that we are fully in control of our physical, as well as spiritual, journey. As a means of determining exactly whose road we are following, try this questionnaire.

- How much of what you do, on a day-to-day basis, is for the material world and how much is towards your spiritual journey?
- How much influence does sensational radio, TV, glossy gossip magazines, or similar Internet sources have on your life?
- How many of the products that you have in your home didn't come from advertising?
- What are your long-term goals, and if you don't have any, is it because you can't afford them?
- Are you achieving your highest potential in your occupation, or are you primarily working to pay bills?
- Can you recall having a high occupational goal and if you didn't achieve it, what prevented it?
- Do you still live with a mind filled with unfulfilled dreams, hopes and wishes that you rarely address practically?

- Do you still ignore those old festering, smelly aspects of your past still deeply affecting your personal ego?
- Are you still letting other people and collective organizations, past or present, negatively affecting your life path, both spiritually and materially?
- Are you your own man woman or are you a mishmash of other people's desires?

After taking this exercise if you feel anywhere from a little touchy to down right despair don't. Remember all things are changeable and most of what we do in our life comes from the influence of the material world-supporting gurus. These popular conservative radio and TV jocks' whole purpose in life is to create income by causing us to feel inferior and second rate if we don't buy their products, follow their line of politics, or strive to live outside of our means. Though many claim to follow Christian values, rarely do they tell us we need to regularly review our goals, both spiritually and materially, from a moral perspective.

In order that we fight back against this very insidious and powerful force, we must first take control of ourselves, and we do this by reviewing the basics of our belief system.
Who is God to us? Do we believe in a God? If not, what do we use as an absolute on which to base our moral and spiritual values? On what do we base our rights and wrongs or moral ideas, conceptions and beliefs?

How much of our life is based on our physical needs and wants, as opposed to what we know is right? Is our knowing in accordance with our highest reasoning, or spiritual beliefs? How many times do we compromise our highest virtues and values in order that we attain certain material gains? How many times do we tell a lie, which we may call a white one, in order that we protect our self-esteem, our material goods or possessions? Technically a white lie is when we tell an untruth to protect another from something that may harm them.

Chapter IV

When we tell an untruth to protect our self it is a straight out lie. There is no excusing this if we are to be truly honest with ourselves. How many times have we borrowed something from another person and never returned it? Aren't we potentially thieves when we borrow goods, money or emotions from another, till we have repaid or returned what we have borrowed? When was the last time we looked at our personal values in this way?

It is so easy for someone to justify whatever they are doing, based on their unchecked values, or the values of others, which they accept and blindly follow without question.
From the very beginning of our life here on earth, from the moment we first understand what others are saying to us, we begin to learn the complexities of being human. When someone in authority asks us a question and we know we will be in trouble if we admit to the accusation, how do we answer?

I'll bet most of us will begrudgingly admit we would deny the charges, or at least find justification for our actions, if we could get away with it. We are inducted into the school of multiple manipulations where what is right in one circumstance can be totally wrong in another, or to another person, circumstance or situation. It is from this basis that we learn a very complex understanding of what is right and what is wrong. It is also how we, often unknowingly, use our choice mechanism to put self-survival above all else.
"Who spilt this milk?" Asks a very angry parent. Silence.
"I won't ask again, who spilt this milk?"
Now what child is going to say 'me mummy, it was me'
"Johnny, did you spill this milk?"
"No, no it was...well you know that cat from next door, well, it got in through the window and...and..."

As the little mind works feverishly to defend itself from a fate perceived to be far worse than spilt milk, it is also trying to juggle between being honest and truthful, and not getting into trouble for something as trivial as spilt milk. And to children, many matters adults see as definite no-nos, children see as trivial. As we grow into adults, we bring these learned behaviours of dismissing authority in certain instances, with us. When we drive on the highway, do we really drive at or below the speed limits, or do we see this as an adult version of one of those learned behaviours? That is, we see the law and therefore the police, in the same way as we saw our parents' corrections?

Deep within our psyche we develop a basic understanding of what we see as unchangeable values and what we see as trivia, as they relate to us personally. Take for instance this mother that insists on treating the spilt milk as an unchangeable. How did she get to this point where spilling milk became so important? Was it the cost of the milk and its effect on the budget? Though this may be the case, it is more likely the original event was so strongly instilled in her mind, either by herself or by others, that she felt obligated to continue instilling this value in her child. It is as if a permanent post had been concreted into her psyche; 'you just don't spill milk, because my subconscious can remember when...

From the moment we start to walk and talk, we start exerting our choices, although not necessarily all that informed, for the things we want or need. Invariably once a child has developed reasonable motor skills, that child will tend to put whatever new attractive object they find into their mouth. This also coincides with a need caused when they first start cutting their teeth, and so they associate the choice of these objects with the need to overcome pain. When the child is tired, hungry, dirty nappies or diapers, or gets a fright, they immediately cry out and in return receive affection, love and nurturing. In this process of building block formation, the child learns to determine what is right and what is wrong, based on what works for them.

Chapter IV

The child that cries out constantly, but doesn't get the desired response, soon learns to add a secondary attention protocol. Holding onto or running after the fast disappearing parent, and pleading, is one example. In other ways the child also learns controlling skills based on what they consider a priority at a particular time. What may be a very important choice at one moment can soon get discarded for something else.

A good example of this is when the child has a particular toy taken from them. They become quite vocal and expressive till they get the article back, yet within twenty four hours or less, that same toy can become as interesting to the child as any other discarded article scattered around the floor. As we grow we also learn to use these very same building block skills to make our choices, and it depends on the input as to the quality of these choices, so that we build a unique self-choice based value system. How often have we prioritised something, just like the child's toy, only to discard it for something, more meaningful at another time? The difference with us as adults compared to the child is that our parents are no longer there to pay for our whims.

How informed our choices, determines how much learning we have to do in any particular life. In tribal times there was a basic understanding of this, and in some communities it was assumed the more experiences we had, particularly painful ones, the better the person performed for their community, and the better they served themselves. Thankfully we no longer encourage that kind of behaviour, or do we?

Let me explain my understanding of ego a little further. Ego is often a misused description. There is nothing wrong with having an ego; in fact, we would not be the individuals we are if it weren't for our ego. It is when we inflate the ego with pride, self-righteousness, vanity and even uses it as a defence against fear, that we can rightly be accused of being egocentric or having an overly inflated ego that blinds us to our own shortcomings and weaknesses. Now let's look at what happens when we as individuals become a part of a group or collective ego. This is when the individual denies, or even in the smallest of ways, gives power to a group, body or organization at the expense of self. This of course is what happens when we create our societies, communities, business organizations, Churches, sporting and social clubs, where we willingly give a part of our own ego for the benefit and advantage of that collective.

In the same way, when an individual wrongly centres their ego, so it can apply to the collective ego. Companies, businesses, Churches, clubs and the like that are willing to sacrifice the individual members or employees for the good of that organization or group are an egocentric collective that are wrongly using their power. In many countries these actions are going against that nation's laws. As we all know laws can easily be overlooked or overruled and the activities of many egocentric collectives can remain hidden for long periods of time. This happens especially when the larger or more influential members of that particular collective are behind the power trip.

Our Life Path is a hard enough journey without all the complicated pressures others put on us and we can so easily get caught up in the injustices of it all. We must sail away from the troubled waters, especially if our personal history shows we tend to get caught up in the backwash of such matters. If we don't deny these frustrations, injustices and the negative feelings they create, we become a part of that problem and eventually start suffering mentally. We can end up very confused and unable to carry out our proper function in our job, relationship or community. We can easily get left along the side of the road, feeling the guilt and scorn poured upon us, either from what we feel others have said or done, or from what we ourselves have created. We must speak up for what we know is right by our conscience, even though we run the risk of loosing a good income, stand to be ridiculed by other

Chapter IV

employees and no doubt our partner, and possibly end up on a dole queue. Anyone who has had this kind of experience in their life knows full well that down the track, life somehow turns in their favour. When we honour our true values, our guides will protect us.

To some this whole concept of taking a stand on a moral issue brings fear to mind. The very thought that such an action could destroy their career, marriage, and standing in their community, is beyond their comprehension. Yet it is often this kind of person who claims to have a religious faith.

What beliefs are they really holding onto? Is their God a deaf mute who can't or won't listen to their daily prayers? Is their belief based on the Benjamin Franklin adage "God helps those that help themselves?" which many believe is a Bible quote but is actually the total opposite to Christian teaching? When does the self help end and the God help begin? Or has God become a figment of our New Age minds?

At certain times in our life, and when we least expect it, we enter a period of review, usually over which we have no control. This is when we get to reassess our values, goals and long-term plans. There is no set time frame or pattern to when these reviews occur they just happen. The life we assume was right for us when we were younger isn't necessarily how it will be for us for the rest of our life. Not everyone had a life path with slow gradual and gentle curves to take them through or away from traumatic and turbulent times. In fact there are very few people, if any, who can claim to have had such a life. We are here to experience and deal with all emotions, the good and painful ones that life throws at us.

Cycles

If you look back over your life, especially since puberty, you might notice you have experienced a cyclical pattern of similar occurrences, where what happened to you previously seems to be revisited in a particular pattern. In my case it is usually around 7 to 10 years. These similarities are usually not exact copies of that previous time, but more a return in the form of a spiral. Actually there can be numerous interacting cycles going on at the same time: Some five, some twenty and others thirty year cycles. It is when a number of cycles coincide, especially in areas we aren't properly dealing with, or possibly not aware need addressing, that painful situations can arise.

In my own case I certainly have had such a situation, which occurred at the end of one of my regular seven to ten year cycles when I was 47. It was a major ending cycle for me and three years later I began a brand new cycle, which lead me into my spiritual path and away from my then personal relationship. This was when my wife and I separated. Back then I used astrology as a means of understanding this as well as advice from the very good psychic who helped me make sense of it all. I suggest to anyone wishing to know more about particular patterns and cycles in their lives, that they also have an astrology reading. Not a sun sign reading that most people associate with astrology, but a proper astrology chart prepared by someone who knows what they are doing, and preferably someone who is also a decent psychic.

Not everyone's road to Damascus experience is as simple as being bucked off a horse as was the case with Paul the Evangelist in the New Testament. As a very dedicated follower of my Christian belief, I was led to think that to consult a psychic or an astrologer meant that I was deliberately going off the rails, or at least going away from the God that Paul embraced. I had diligently followed all of the Churches teachings, and had deliberately stayed a healthy distance from psychic matters, even in those early days at the Spiritualist Church; yet I still felt I'd lost out from the circumstantial changes I had experienced at that time. Why?

Chapter IV

Finding Your Path

I believe now that by assuming and following the journey other family members had found right for them, I had unintentionally strayed from the path I was to have taken this particular life, even though I had consulted God regularly by praying daily and regularly attending Mass. Not that what I had done was wrong, simply that I had followed in someone else's footsteps. It was after I started to look more seriously at where "Angels" and "God" fitted into my life, in a way that made sense to me, that I started to see the pieces of the puzzle fit more comfortably. Guides and guardian angels are God's personal representatives to us. We don't have to follow what our guides choose for us and nor will They override our decisions, They can't. We here in the physical world are the ones with free will.

Of course I didn't then know this or my guides, the way I do now. There was no way I could just have "tuned in" to them and "turned off" from my original journey. So my guides, unable to direct me or even to get through to me, had no choice but to pull back, leaving me wide open to all the matters that finally distracted me, till I found what was right and comfortable. Had it not been for my "intent" in the first place, my dedication to Truth, and my only wanting the highest, I probably would have ended up like so many others blaming an unfair God and his Church and Clergy for having discarded me. There is no right or wrong, correct or incorrect way: It's more that we have to learn to deal with the curve ball in the great game of life.

When a cycle or a review like this one suddenly appears in our life, all that we believe in is challenged, not unlike Job's story in the Old Testament. We cry out to that which we believe in, but because our prayers are not answered as we would like, we assume our belief structure has lets us down, and we are left feeling lonely and alone. In review of such a situation we would no doubt understand that the expectation we had of God, and God's ways, were incorrect. Had we had less expectation of God and God's ways, we would have be more aware of the longer term means God uses compared to our short term expectations.

It is at times like these that we can be wide open for well meaning, but not very adequate, spirits, souls or guides of a lower level. These guides are more than willing to assist in the best way they can, but are totally inadequate for the job. Because we are very vulnerable at such a time, and are willing to grab onto anything that holds similar feelings or answers to what we now feel is right, we take this guidance gladly. Eventually however, we either feel like we are being guided to hell in a hand basket when our plans, hopes and wishes start to disintegrate, or we will suddenly have our circumstance drag us to a halt.

The most important rule to follow at this time is to go after what you know to be right in your own moral conscience value and not to make impulsive or popular choices, because that will only prolong the inevitable.

The whole reason we are going through such testings is to see just how much of our faith, trust, and belief has really worked for us to this point in our lives. If our faith and trust have been based in the material and they are not serving us according to our particular spiritual life path. We will continue to face these particular challenges. After trying all the alternative ways open to us we will find what suits us best is the one we were meant to following in the first place. In so doing we are focusing in on the guides we were meant to have assisting us all along. Not that we are necessarily going to know that from day one. In fact, it's not till we have the floor drawn away from under us, that we feel our vulnerability and either grab onto the nearest secure structure only to get a hand full of splinters, or we fall. Often, after the event, we realise the fall is nowhere near as frightening as we envisaged, and our first major lesson in trust has been learned.

Starting With Your Guides

Imagine a person using an elevator for the first time, trying desperately to hold onto the sidewalls as it plummets towards their floor only to find that the entire fear was totally unnecessary. We trust man made machines that often fail. However, we rarely trust the very power that created us. Why?

Once you have reached this knowledge, or if you happen to have one of these cycles after you've made acquaintance with your guides, remember to take time and consult them. Choose only that which you know is right by your own values no matter how much it may hurt you or others.

Now some may say they thought they were already in alignment with their guides when a disaster befell them. There is a very good chance they may have been living a blend of what were their own values, in harmony with their true guide, mixed with the values of other, lower level spiritual entities.

Normally as we grow, our guides change automatically. If we hold onto old ideals and limit our thinking for sentimental reasons, fear of letting go, or simply because we have not reviewed our moral conscious values we then are preventing the natural change in our guides. Though we don't know it, by not growing and expanding into our future, in accordance with our original spiritual blueprint, we are not only holding our self back, but we are also delaying the upgrading of our guidance.

This leaves us in a situation where we are receiving confusing messages. On one side from our guides trying to move us, and on the other, from well-meaning entities trying to satisfy our need to stay where we are. Even though we are unintentionally rejecting our true guides, they will still try to assist us in our daily life. The combination is now totally overwhelming for us and eventually something has to give. The result can be a breakdown, a complete life change or the disaster that befell us. It is usual, after such a huge upheaval, for us to discard those thoughts, feelings, emotions etc we originally held onto. This in turn opens the door for our guides to continue us on our journey. It is natural after such an event to feel alone, empty, or that you're guides have gone missing. Don't be concerned; your mind is actually in a true state of peace, which is how it is meant to be. As you learn to accept this new mindset the more likely you are to receive high quality guidance.

We have addressed previously the possibility that in our younger days we made decisions without fully knowing our souls journey, or our real needs for this life. We may have merrily sailed along this particular path, totally oblivious to the fact we are off course. What if it is our partner we are talking about? We would have major difficulty understanding why suddenly after so many years he or she suddenly decides to try another life path that does not include us. We are not going to make any gains by rubbing salt into their wounds. We do have a right to state our case. It is how it is stated that may be the difference between the person we love taking time out and then returning to us better than before. Or they may leave us permanently, riddled with guilt feelings, or unanswered questions, never to return.

It depends on where we are as a soul, on the scale between the material and the spiritual world, as to the relevance of the particular life we live. If in this particular life we have strong desires towards all things material such as home, family, children, money and what it can buy, so that generally we live with the material being paramount for us, then we will be drawn to that kind of life and a relationship that best suites that need.

Chapter IV

If our partner or circumstance changes in such a way that we feel we are being drawn away from our particular road, for example if our partner suddenly finds religion or spirituality, or has an interest in a different kind of religion or spirituality from what we are used to, we or they may feel it is time also to make some important changes.

Of course there are different ways this could apply, as was the case with some of those in the Hippy movement of the seventies when they realized their living off the land in a glorified cardboard box with the barest of essentials wasn't what they really wanted after all. The theory may have been appealing but the reality was something else again. Many of them came to a point where they tired with the laboriousness of that form of living and soon became the wheelers and dealers of the eighties and nineties. Many left their alternative multi partnership lifestyle and became quite conservative. One family I knew went from dope smoking, partner swapping and feral living to moving into the nearest town and started up a branch of a Christian Fundamentalist Church. Lucky for them, they both had this life change happen simultaneously and as far as I know they remained together.

Where our soul's values are in relation to this particular incarnation determines the quality and expertise of our guides. The last thing we want from our guides is information that opposes our wishes, dreams and expectations. We all know what happens when people try to advise us against our wishes. We rebel, ignore, disregard or show disrespect in some way towards those trying to help us as we possibly did with our parents, friends, our school or university teachers, religious ministers, and law enforcers in our early days.

The same applies with our level of guides. There is no sense in having 'Jesus' guiding us when we want to amass a fortune. Better we have a Rockefeller or some other deceased billionaire.

Think of what you have been praying, putting out into the universe, wishing, plotting or planning for. How many brick walls have stopped you from finding this happiness you seek? Could it be you are praying for the wrong thing, or asking for that which goes against what this particular life path has to teach you? Interestingly enough, this is often the reason people give for no longer having a Christian belief system; "Oh! Don't talk to me about God. Where was God when my daughter was killed?" "Where was God when the bank came and re-possessed our farm?"

"Where was God when the marriage He was supposed to have blessed and protected fell apart?"

When adjustments come into our live they are usually major ones, which invariably sends shock waves through our entire life. Much like an earthquake shakes and destroys all that is not secured leaving a pile of misery, devastation and heartache amongst the rubble.

There are two ways we can deal with these. One is to be prepared, which hopefully you will be after reading this, so that you can take the necessary steps to ensure you are ready when and if such a situation happens. The other is to blindly ride the train of life with little or no thought to what may happen if there is a derailment, and then to accuse everyone from the owner of the railway down to the driver for whatever has gone wrong.

All I Have Belongs To God

An attitude I found that helped me after my particular tsunami was that we own nothing; the Creator owns everything. When Jesus said 'give unto Caesar that which is Caesar's and to God that which is Gods,' he knew that all things were God's. Nothing was Caesar's. There is also that overly used expression of Ben Franklin I mentioned earlier: God helps those that

Chapter IV

help themselves, to which a well-known Sydney radio personality wickedly added: And God help those caught helping themselves.

If we have lived to a point in our life where we have instigated, created or fought for a particular way or point of view, without asking for guidance, do we have the right to ask our guides to help us out of what we ourselves have created? Aren't we to reap that which we have sown as a part of our learning?

Did we create our children, or did the Creator? Are our children ours, or God's? What of our children's journey, intentions or purposes in this particular life? Do we have a right to override their intentions or purposes because they are our offspring? Think back to how you felt when your parents tried to override your decisions and how you still carry scars from that time.

I refer back to the statement "Oh! Don't talk to me about God. Where was God when my daughter was killed?" What if it was mutually agreed between her soul and the Creator, before the daughter came into this life, that she would burn off some short term Karmic energy to aid her or someone else's spiritual growing in this or another life? To do this meant either she died very young, was killed tragically as a young woman, or died in a way that caused others to question their own faith or belief. Such a decision is best left unknown to those who it can hurt the most. In fact, if while in spirit, I knew that was to be my journey's end and next reincarnation, I think I'd be telling the Creator not to let me know when the end is near, and to have the event made as painless a possible. All in all such a scenario is one I wouldn't like to have to partake in.

In the same way, for those angry with their guides because they lost their property, or because their marriage fell apart, would they have felt the same if they had know the full extent of their life path from past lives as well as this one? Knowing that by loosing property and a marriage they were quickening their soul's journey? One can only speculate as to their opinion with such advanced knowledge.

Considering our societal decline, we are more likely now than ever before to be possessed by negative energies and less so by positive ones. The more self-righteous our stance, the more likely we are to be displaying this possession. No doubt you have seen in others or had it occur to yourself, a mind matter so debilitating that nothing and no one can pull you out from this quagmire. In this state, we are most likely the last ones to see how totally off the spiritual track we really are. All the medication, the soothsayers, the doctors or religious ministers have to offer still doesn't clear up this bottomless pit we feel we are stuck in.

How and when did this process start? We usually move out of synchronisation when we put our opinion or point of view above others. It may be that we deny our own weaknesses and refuse to accept that others know better than us. We may hear criticisms from our friends for what they perceive we have said or done, but we dismiss the criticism. There may even be proof beyond doubt that what they have said is the truth, and still we deny it happening. Others may have to compromise their values or themselves to keep the peace, after something we have said or done.

Despair

There are different kinds of mind states that can unintentionally feed this righteousness and self based ego. A particular kind can appear to some when they face a specific tragedy such as the sudden death of a significant other, the death of a special pet, or being told they have a terminal illness. The sudden loss of a friend, including that of a pet, reminds us of

Chapter IV

how interwoven our life was with that friend. The shock of living alone, or in the case of terminal illness, having to face death ourselves, usually has us reviewing our own belief system, with little to no serious repercussions. Naturally there is going to be shock at the news of the termination of life. This is followed by the grieving process and then the learning to cope after the event.

It is those that are so shocked at the finality of life that suffers the most. It is as if they were so imbedded in their own life that finality didn't exist, till they were forced to face it, and then their life crumbled around them.

A similar situation can be when we discover our partner, whom we totally trusted, is or was having an affair, or worse, that they are leaving us for this other person. The discovery by some women, particularly a teenager, that they have fallen pregnant, can induce a suicidal despair.

Other lesser matters coupled together, can bring us to the brink. We can be brought to the brink by such things as the realization of the inappropriateness of our marriage or relationship, problems associated with our career choice, residential upheavals, or decisions or matters caused by our children's actions. On their own we may be able to cope with these upheavals but bundled together they can become almost insurmountable, especially if we know we need to make changes but have nowhere to go as an alternative that is appropriate and safe. Much as we try putting out to the universe or praying to our particular denomination's God, we still receive no satisfactory answers.

It is when we are at this lowest point that we are more inclined to examine our faith, if we have one, and what principles that faith is based on. If we are honest with ourselves, we may find our only commitment to that belief is lip service, or that we have only been accepting those parts that suit us. It's possible we have been holding onto an ideology more for sentimental reason than for its' true strength. If, at such a time in our life, we don't have a rock solid understanding of a God and where he, she or it stands in our life, then we are vulnerable to the devil Jesus said was the worst of sins, despair.

Despair is when we feel so totally alone, beyond just feeling isolated from other people. It is when we feel so utterly guilt ridden that we feel even the attempt to try and express our self is beyond our abilities. When we get this far down our one-way tunnel there are two main choices we have. One is to continue on despair's highway, which can lead to suicide and self-harm, or we force ourselves up the tight narrow and difficult path to safety. We have to admit, submit, and then commit.

We must first admit that we are out of control and unable to deal with the despair or depression. Then we must submit ourselves to others such as professional counsellors or our family doctor. Finally we must commit ourselves to taking the steps necessary to improve our self-esteem and self worth in order that we don't wind up back at this same sad and debilitating place.

Embracing Life

As we gain strength and are able to cope in a basic fashion, we then need to do the spiritual equivalent of the above. We must first admit we are not as attuned to our highest beliefs as we ought to be, and that whatever we believed in has been found to be inadequate. We have to search for something stronger, and more reliable. For some, this may be visiting different religious beliefs till one that best suits them fills their needs. For others, it could mean following what I have suggested in this work. Submit ourselves to that highest power by regularly meditating with the peace and serenity that lies deep within us, having no expectations other than allowing that Power to make us feel at One with It. After all this Power is the Peace we are searching for. Finally we need to commit ourselves to regularly updating and upgrading our moral conscience base with this Power deep within.

If it is an illness, sickness, debilitating or life threatening conditions that has us on the brink of despair, wishing it removed or gone will only bring us deeper into despair as our pleas go unanswered. Instead of treating this condition as an intrusion into our very pleasing life, or a punishment for something we had done or are doing, embrace it as an expression of the self. By embracing, accepting and take ownership of this illness or sickness, we are overcoming the fear that we associated with such conditions. We now know that though there are some cancers caused by viruses, most cancers are manifestations of something already within us. By accepting that this is a part of us, we are actually accepting its' cause, without necessarily knowing the specifics. Just as importantly, we are also accepting the possibility that we could be coming to the end of our physical time here in this particular life. In accepting it as part of our humanness means we become whole and at one with all aspects of our self and though it may not necessarily remove the cancer or tumour, it certainly makes it easier for us to deal with this particular condition.

As an example, a person with a deformity, accepting it as part of who they are, stands a better chance of living a balanced life than a similar person who compensates for that deformity. If cancer formed from within us, isn't it also a deformity, albeit a life threatening one?

It is hard to believe that at such a time there can be a bonus from such a diagnosis. However, having a more defined understanding of when our time on this mortal soil will end, and plenty of time to get our lives in order to meet the great friends waiting for us on the other side, it can be just that.

A Beginning

Death is not our enemy, it is our friend. Though it is an ending to this particular physical life, it is not the end of our soul's journey; it's just a new beginning. Of course when it is our friend, family member or someone special to us who is dying or heading into some serious illness, we feel so useless and helpless. All the well wishes under the sun can never express fully our helplessness. But there is something we as friends, relatives or concerned professionals can do.

We can turn within to our own belief system, and ask the source of true belief, the Power, Truth, or God, to assist this person. For those happy to follow this line of suggestion, the simplest way to do this is in the form of a short meditation where you place the person you care about into a cocoon of purity and serenity within your mind, and no matter what you may think of the person you wish them only good will. Put your goodwill thoughts in that cocoon as if you are talking to that person, and then wrap the whole lot up in God's Love and hand this cocoon over to this power, Truth, Creator. It will do the rest. Don't have expectations, nor put expectations in the cocoon. Simply submit your will to God's law to be done, along with your good wishes for that person, to the Creator force, and leave it with them.

Are We Of Our Own Making?

Something or somebody influences everything we do in our life, and often in such a way we don't even realise it is being done. We are spiritual beings born into physical bodies, one visible and animated, the other hidden and unknown to everyone but ourselves. When we look in the mirror, hear ourselves on a tape recorder or see ourselves on a video, we are seeing our outer self or our physical self. This is the part of us that others know us by, mannerisms, body language and physical appearance. If you are like most people, you will at

Chapter IV

least cringe when you face this outer part of yourself. All in all we are quite contented when we don't have to see, hear, or observe ourselves via any of these mediums available to us. There are many actors, entertainers, and radio personalities who claim they never review their performances. They do what they have to do and then move on. Why? What is it we know about ourselves that causes us to feel maybe we have been deceived when we hear or see ourselves externally?

It is not just that we are aware of a self that is different to the outer self that others know us by, the outer self we recognise in the mirror, see in a video or hear on a tape recording. It is how others perceive us, how they react, that determines the choices we make and how we tend to live our life.

This is the first step to self-discovery. The outer, physical self is what allows us to move around from place to place, to experience, feel and interact in a physical way. The inner self is our core being, the basics of who we are and what makes us different from other. When alone, sitting quietly somewhere and our physical body is still and almost in a sleep state, as if idling, does that mean this inner self, this breath, soul or spirit, is automatically controlled to do the same, or are our two bodies operating independently? Can we be fully conscious and alert to all the sounds around us, yet appear to an observer as if we are sound asleep? The answer of course is, yes we can.

Does the physical body need external stimuli in order that we use or create with our mind or our imagination? No, it doesn't. We can create wonderful images either in this state, or fully conscious in what we often call a daydream state.

The inner self we know better as our spirit, our child within, or our soul, lives within our knowing, our mind, or our spiritual centre. It is this psyche, derived from the Greek word psychos, which literally means of or pertaining to the breath, soul or spirit. It is therefore the psyche-psychic part of us that connects to the non-physical, spiritual world that exists deep within, yet separate from, us all. Unless we are made conscious of the differences, it is the physical world that overrides our spiritual or inner world. It acts as a limiter that prevents the inner soul from fully expressing itself, and therefore our inner self has to take a back seat while the outer determines how our life pans out.

Physical Distractions

There are the obvious distractions, which come under the heading of physical senses, seeing, hearing, tasting, touching and smelling. There is also the fact that the human body is in constant need of movement, if not for the obvious needs such as waste management, food and fluid intake, cleansing and sleeping, then for simple circulation needs. To sit in one place without moving for long periods of time, cause sores, poor circulation and other long-term problems associated with the physical body. There is also the intricate interaction or social system we have evolved, that has us having to pay our dues to our society. These include collective productivity, or work, procreation interaction for the continuance of our species, or sex, the difficulties we have created for ourselves in achieving this process, and the accepted interactions we use to make us a civilised society. This is our need to abide by our collective laws and protocols. At least these are what we are supposed to abide by.

Our physical form has major limitations. We can't fly without machines or add-ons. We can't stay in or under the water for long periods of time without tools to assistance us. We can't withstand temperatures outside of a very limited scale and are poorly built for survival in the variable weather conditions that can be found right across this planet on which we live.

Chapter IV

It has taken the collective psyche of the human race over many millions of years of evolving to allow us to overcome these limitations to the level we currently exist. When we look at the research of the human form, there is very little we don't know of the physical or outer persona. We have studies from food, diet, care and maintenance, sexual function, birth, childhood habits, adolescence, puberty, adulthood, childbearing and child raising, improvements in physical well being and performance, sports enhancement, through to mid life, older life and finally dying. Yet we know very little about the function of the human mind, particularly the psyche. In fact from my reading of a number of different articles on the Internet, it seems science does not accept there is a soul connection to an external, spiritual world, but that the psyche aspect of our brain is an exclusively internal organism, similar to a computer without Internet connection. Could it be that to even broach the subject within the scientific community, one must first override the strongly held scientific perception that we humans are born with only a storage system in our brains.

There have been attempts in the past where science has broached the receiver concept of the brain, such as by Carl Jung with his collective consciousness theories, and then the experiments in the US under the banner of telepathy or ESP, and in particular the case of the CIA and their remote viewing experiments. All of these attempts have had one common barrier imposed on them. None can prove or disprove that there is a source outside of the known; Whomever God is, he or she can't be proved, and therefore he or she doesn't exist. If therefore that area is basically blocked from serious research, then all other aspects that might exist in the sense of a parallel and spiritual based world cannot and will not be taken seriously.

It seems to me that we are living in a world more influenced by the ideals of science and humanism, rather than by a collective of spiritual truths, derived from the experimenting of the individual. To most of us our psychos or inner spiritual

power lies dormant because we have been discouraged from using the tools that will activate it. This leads to a very interesting question that I have yet to see science adequately answer. Why does science rarely even discuss matters pertaining to the inner self? For example, what does science say exactly is our imagination, imagery, thought creation and thinking? Is it something we create? Is it something created independent of our knowing or knowledge, our thoughts, our physical form, our psychos-soul, or is it a combination of all of these?
How many times have you heard intuitive obtained material dismissed with:

"Oh they must have read it somewhere, or seen it on TV or subconsciously heard someone talking about it."
Or "How powerful our subconscious mind is that it can cause us to believe something is a psychic phenomenon when it is nothing more than having a great imagination."

Are we only able to tap into our own thoughts, memories and feelings or are we capable of tapping into the thoughts of spirit and spiritual beings? Are they somehow able to superimpose their thoughts into our memory? If we accept these thoughts and emotions can either impose themselves or that we can encourage them, where do they come from? And if they are imposed on us, how can we control them, to accept or reject them? How do we know the difference, and how do we know when we are being imposed upon? When Carl Jung referred to the collective unconscious, what source was he referring to?

To put simply, when we have dreams, imaginings, and thoughts come to mind without our instigating them, did they come from us or from a spiritual source?

What if thought can be the creation of the individual, but also independent of that individual? What if the individual who believes they have created a specific thought, are simply receiving that thought from another source? This thought could have originated from the individual, their guides, lost souls, or from what I understand Jung believed, namely the collective of all thought that remains in the ether, which anyone can tap into, either consciously or unconsciously. Has science ever explained to us the differences, enough for us to determine when we are creating imagery personally, or when we are receiving imagery from another source?

100 Monkeys

When it comes to choices, we are more likely to be open to new and untried ideas at a younger age, than when we are mature adults. And, as a general rule, it is the young that tend to bring about changes and introduce new ideas into our society. I can remember my guides telling me at one time: "Responsibility, especially in leadership positions, leads to natural conservatism. Popes don't write rap songs and presidents don't take the risks they would if they weren't presidents."

And just as the youth may introduce the new, it is often they, in their senior years who not only discard it, but who also dismiss it as having been a whim of their youth. The established members of society prefer to stick to the tried and true. I can remember a young university student, back in the 80's, enthusiastically introducing me to the 100 Monkeys Theory, which was doing the rounds at that time.

Back in the fifties, so the story goes, scientists in Japan had isolated a group of monkeys on an island for research purposes, while the main group stayed on the mainland. The carers would go out in a boat to the island and feed the monkeys with sweet potato.

Some of this food would fall onto the sand and some would fall into the water. It was discovered that certain monkeys found that the sweet potato in the water was less gritty and more palatable, and so they would return regularly to pick up the potato in the water.

After some time, the scientists made sure there was no sweet potato in the water, ensuring that all the food was covered in gritty sand. It didn't take long before the monkeys that had first insisted on the sand free potatoes, began to take the sand covered sweet potato down to the water to wash them clean before eating them. It was further discovered that the first monkeys, the ones who had gone for the sweet potato thrown into the water, and the ones that actually took the sweet potato to the water to wash them, were the younger members of the group.

After awhile the older monkeys started to accept what the young monkeys were doing, and it wasn't long before all or most of the island monkeys were washing the sand off their sweet potatoes before they ate them. Then a most remarkable thing happened. Without any contact whatsoever, once the majority of the islander monkeys had got into the routine of washing their sweet potatoes, the mainland monkeys, without any coaching, started to wash their sweet potatoes. It was the younger monkeys on the island that had started this phenomenon, not the older, wiser ones.

In the field of science, as in all fields of our collective society, the peer group structure is very limiting. The scientific community must work within parameters and guidelines that prevent them from wandering into unproven theories or getting tangled up in religion, spiritual beliefs or myth. It is very difficult for them to even address the possibility that there just may be a whole life-after-death world that exists outside of their knowledge. The thought that souls, when they leave their physical body, just may continue on into some other continuum, and from within this continuum, may well be the source of at least some of what science refers to as telepathy, ESP or remote viewing, is an area rarely taken seriously by

Chapter IV

them. More concerning is the attitude taken by the scientific community, as well as other bodies, such as the humanist, alternative spiritual believers, religious and political, when they are put under the microscope in those grey areas no one really has answers for.

Such a grey area occurred during the early months of 2005 when the world was made aware of a very bitter battle that had been going on in the United States. For several years the parents of a clinically dead woman fought the courts to have her remain on life support while her ex husband, and her legal guardian, pushed for her life support machines to be shut down. The reason for his decision was his wife's expressed wish that in the event of a long-term coma her life be terminated. The 20 court hearings to that time, had all ruled this woman, Terri Schivo, as a result of a massive stroke, was considered clinically dead and only surviving as a consequence of artificial life support. Those supporting the opposite view claimed she was animated and cognisant. For ten emotion filled days, the world watched as this woman died.

It was a terrible and emotionally charged story that had her husband being accused of trying to terminate Terri's life so that he could get on with his new wife and their new relationship. There wasn't one body involved, or that had a point of view on the case, that didn't come under the questioning of a very concerned world community. No one it seemed, in any of the many camps, either for or against, had answers that satisfied that larger community. It was like the case actually showed up the weaknesses of all those who had a part to play or had an opinion on it.

The whole episode of life and death is one that is very controversial, and where, no matter what is said, people will strongly disagree. However it must be said that the day we prolonged life was the day we opened Pandora's Box on this very difficult subject. Similarly the day we discovered how to prevent pregnancy, we also opened up areas that will forever cause us angst and division. Not that I am suggesting for a moment that either prolonging life or preventing pregnancies is right or wrong. I am asserting that changes to any system, moral code or socially accepted norm should take into serious consider not just the long term consequences, or possible immediate moral dilemmas, but also the long term opposition that could well bring any such a good intention or notion to it's knees.

It is in so doing that we get a better understanding of why the Power gave us the option in the first place. Not the obvious advantages, such as longer life, or preventative measures for unwanted births, but how these changes affect our personal moral code, and position us in relation to our soul's journey this time round. The hard line approach that because she was breathing and her heart was pumping was an indication of human life got totally thrown out the window when the autopsy, after her death, showed there was absolutely no brain function, nor ability for her to have had any control over any self functioning. She was, as the doctors had said all along, a living vegetable with no cognitive functioning whatsoever.

So where was her soul? And more importantly, after so many thousands of years interacting with God, why had none of his ministers of religion not known this?

If US President George W Bush had God in his ear, as he had claimed on many occasions, why didn't God tell him about Terri's condition? Was it that God didn't know, or was the President following another, more materially centred god? The problem with all of these scenarios is the collective versus the individual. How much does the opinion of the collective control us individually? What would our opinion be individually had the collective not been so strong?

How popular would the Beatles have been had the collective not overridden the individual consciousness? Not that there was anything against this powerful collective's energy at that time, but considering how many supporters later developed a totally different point of view, how many had been taken up in the wash that we called Beatlemania? How many wars would we have been involved in had we not had such a strong anti war movement at the time? How many scientific discoveries would we have today had the individual been allowed to express an opinion different to the collective?

Where would the euthanasia and the abortion debates be today if the individual opinion overrode the collective? How much hypocrisy exists within the religious and spiritual collective we use as a base for our belief?

The Will of Choice

I started off this section asking Are We Of Our Own Making. I then showed that something or somebody influences everything we do in our life, and often in a way we don't even realise it is being done. I have gone on to show that much of what we choose in our life is not necessarily our own choice, so much as our following the choices of others. The collective is a very powerful influence on us all, and very difficult to ignore, especially when that collective pays our wages, runs our country or determines our social interests and media, and what it dictates to us.

Our choices must be informed choices. We must make wise decisions based, not on what the majority opinion may think, say or suggest, but on what we know to be right by our own personal discernment. With experience, even when there is uncertainty in the decision we make, we learn to trust that discernment and to make choices acceptable to our own circumstance. If we don't make fully informed choices, those choices will come back to bite us over and over again. Even after we have made an informed choice it can still return in need of re-addressing. At least we have the satisfaction of know that we chose as wisely as was possible at the time. Remember it is the choice of others that often starts these phenomena. However, their choices may not necessarily be in our best interest.

It is choice also that puts the concept of fate into a less definable place. Some believers in fate have us locked into a scenario where all choices are blind to us, and only seem like choice after we have passed the point where a decision was made. To explain further, this concept of fate claims we still travel the same path, even after we believe we have made choices that are seemingly to the contrary: No matter what choices we may make, it isn't choice at all, but a fated path we can't get away from.

Before we are born our soul has an understanding of what it is we are to learn and experience. These fated or predetermined areas are those things which after birth seem immutable such as parents, ethnicity, global location at the time of birth etc. In this sense we are fated. However the actual life path, the environment we live in, the places where we are educated, work, play or live in, and friends we choose, are not locked into a fated or predetermined. Neither we nor the source of all, God plan our life. Our guides, through the intervention of the power or God, help us choose a general path that will best serve us in the particular life we are about to live.

The choices of others and ourselves are never known. What would have been a scenario today may not be the case tomorrow. The original intention could have had us being born to certain parents, at a certain place in a certain country or area, to be raised within a specific socio economic environment. Our intended parents could have chosen not to continue on with our pregnancy, or chosen to give us up for adoption, or one parent may have chosen to take on the responsibility of raising us as a sole parent. Either person, at the time of conception, could have said no or taken precautions.

Choices by others could well have changed the original plan of how we were to live that particular life. The particular journey our soul needs to bring us onto the next level is therefore the decision that the power, in consultation with our guides, finally makes that best suits all aspects of our journey. Nothing is set in concrete; everything is fluid.
It is not that we have a planned life made for us before we are reborn, it is that we are put into a generic situation where choices further on down our life path are more conducive to the changes we need to make rather than if we were put into another, more restrictive one.

There are those that claim we have overridden God's will by inventing the pill, creating safe means of aborting foetuses and by inventing a safe and reliable form of euthanasia. When we consider the many millions of prayers prayed by Christians asking that such abortions, pregnancy preventions processes and euthanasia be stopped, why is it that he instead seems to give us more and more choices to undermine what Christians claim are His plans? Nothing comes to us that hasn't been allowed by that very same God. Such choices are given to us as a part of our personal learning. Put another way, such choices are part of our personal obstacle course in this particular life. We are the ones who have to make the specific choices for our own life. We cannot rely on the Church, parents, or society in general to decide the outcome of our life.

A slightly different facet on choice concerns where we choose to live. Couldn't it be said that anyone leaving their home country and who either invades or settles in a country other than where they were born is also breaking God's Law?

Many will say such a notion is preposterous bordering on the delusional. Yet aren't such people changing where God wanted them to be? Aren't they preventing life, their life, to exist as God planned it, in that particular place? In a sense this is what people are saying when they claim human intervention in any aspect of our life is opposing God's law. They are saying it is acceptable to change where we live, but not to change our offspring or our own life's plan by medical intervention?

To suggest that a God can create a being so intelligent as to outwit its Creator could have this person a candidate for this same accolade. God, the Creator, the power knows the intricacies of any of our particular incarnations and the long-term plan of our many lives long before we have even entered our first incarnation. It knows the consequences of our actions in a general sense. Because of this, the power is anything but judgemental of our actions or us in any one particular life. It knows our true feeling towards it from the many encounters it has had with us over a very long time. After all, we are extensions of that power and Love. So long as we as individuals make the choices we feel are in accordance with our understanding of what is right, Truth and good in that particular life, we are doing the will of that power, Creator or God.

To clarify what is meant when I say the power knows the intricacies of our particular incarnation. The word know is used in the same sense as a parent who knows that when their teenage son or daughter goes out for the evening or away with friends, they know in a general way what their young adult is up to, but not the specifics.

Returning to the main theme, the important part of choice is ensuring the decisions we make are informed ones. To make important choices without properly investigating all options first is not only dangerous, but one that could leave us feeling vulnerable, guilty and possibly perceived as stupid in the eyes of those we love and who support us. We should live each day as if we were living it for the second time.

Chapter IV

It is our responsibility to ensure we are fully informed when we make any choices. How we respect all aspects of the current life we've been given, and how we do the best with what we have, determines how harmoniously we will pass through this life. It is the way we live our life based on our moral conscience value that determines the quality of our spirituality, and which then determines the quality and level of our guides. We aren't invisible beings without a history; in fact we are more like snails, leaving a distinct trail of where we've been and how we've lived that life. Jesus said "You will know them by their fruit and what you sow, you reap."

When it comes to choice and psychics, what is it that determines who we choose? If we are the psychic, how do other people choose us as opposed to someone else? We perceive a person by the way they dress and present themselves, and no matter how much a person may argue against this, the fact remains that presentation can mean the difference between a client visiting that psychic, or choosing to try another. How we present ourselves influences how people perceive us.

I can recall visiting psychic fairs around the mid 1990's noting how the different readers presented themselves as a guide to what I should, or shouldn't do. Based on their presentation, I doubted any of them were good examples of psychic presentation. Most were middle aged or older, openly puffing on cigarettes, obviously over weight, hair that had been dyed far too many times and wearing the most unnatural of clothing. I mused if they were supposed to be representing a higher order wouldn't it appear therefore to potential clients that this highest order was also pretentious? If these representatives of spiritual knowing had high quality guides, wouldn't these guides work with them to improve their image and better their presentation? If their smoking and being overweight was health related wouldn't their highest Guides have shown them some doorways to better health?

And if a person, visiting such a psychic, were supposed to receive a message from their Guides to say they needed to give up smoking, or loose weight, would the psychic be capable of giving such a pure message without pangs of their own weaknesses interfering in such a reading?

Is it possible that a smoking psychic is capable of giving as good a quality reading as a non-smoking psychic? And if that psychic is in denial about the seriousness of the addiction, won't that attitude also be a part of that person's value, and won't that reflect in a person's readings? And what of the psychic, being a regular marijuana smoker, receiving a message indicating marijuana was not good for the client's health, would he or she pass on such a message?

It is not only smoking that can affect our quality of psychic channelling. How much of a person's own weaknesses can easily colour the pure essence of the message given by such a psychic to their client? If a psychic considers smoking either cigarettes or marijuana or both, to be acceptable, that their health and presentation is acceptable when human authorities say to the contrary, then they are not channelling quality guides. If they are not able to discern what their guides are suggesting for them, in relation to their health and living habits, they aren't going to be too clear when it comes to the same areas in someone else's life. I am not referring here to psychics who have an illness or medical condition and have tried to improve themselves or are under the care of a medical person. It can be that such a person is an extraordinary psychic.

Here is a personal experience of how certain foods can affect our psychic ability. I have Candida and am gluten intolerant, but I didn't find out I had this condition till 2001. Though my original psychic sessions were very good, I would tire easily and I felt there were more misses than I felt there should have been. Once I discovered what was causing my problems, and changed my diet I greatly improve physically. My psychic ability improved dramatically and continues to improve.

There is of course a difference between a food allergy and smoking. One is a part of our daily needs, the other is a choice we make, and not essential to our daily needs. Smoking is a curse for those who unfortunately have got caught up in the habit, as is trying to loose weight for those trying to control it. My comments aren't aimed at those who are genuinely trying to control either. I am aiming my comments at those who don't realise how much their own personal uncontrolled weaknesses are interfering with their psychic abilities, and the messages they are passing on.

Habits are choices

Let's use this tool and attitude with all our old habits; habits that may have, and may still be, causing damage to our self esteem, our self worth, our moral conscious values and therefore our ability to climb our particular spiritual mountain.

What is the quality of our memories when we look at our first sexual encounters? Memories may include masturbation, touching some one in a sexual manner (opposite or same sex) to full on intercourse. What deep memory do we hold of our feelings of these past encounters? Did we agree or disagree with what we did, or what was done to us at that time? Do we still carry any guilty feeling or regrets, either of ourselves or of others, and if so are they still having an effect on our actions and attitudes today? Is our attitude towards the opposite sex still influenced by what may have happened to us back in our early teens? Are we still coming to terms with our own naivety, our vulnerability, our unintended choices of the times that completely shaped our life, a life we wish we could somehow lived over with changes?

Some of us may say there was no damage done, and that may well be true, but it is a very good idea to search deep within our own psyche just to be sure, because even the slightest anomaly could affect our moral conscience base.

A bit like realizing the little bit of badly poured concrete in the foundations of a house we thought was good enough back then, has now caused the whole building to be torn down. Luckily we don't have to tear ourselves down; we just have to adjust the past memories to align with what we now know to be right for us. Our view of our sexual nature is important for it is connected to our creativity. Any blocks because of previous attitudes, hurts and misconceptions can interfere with our ability to receive messages from our guides.

Some of us may pass off our weaknesses as "oh well that's just me" or "well if you don't like my ways and my habits, too bad." Of course the more we improve ourselves by overcoming our weaknesses within, the better our presentation, the way others respect us, the way we feel about ourselves, the higher the quality of calibre of guides we draw and the better the network of friends, lovers or partners we will draw to us. We all make choices. Some are informed, some are made for us and some are choices that haunt us the rest of our days. We must be serious about the choices we make, ensuring we know the consequences of each and every decision we make. We must recognise that a choice instigated by others may be a projection out of their unconscious mind. Many choices are not like choosing a flavour of ice cream but stem from a combination of our consciousness and the directions of our guides and divine source.

Remember we all have many emotions and feelings to experience from lifetime to lifetime, before our many sessions of experiences here on earth are done. There are many who believe the world is heaven on a stick, but that of course, all depends on where the stick is placed in relation to us as individuals.

If we are sitting uncomfortably on that stick, we are enjoying anything but heaven.

"Live in the world, not off the world."

On the Light Path   Peter Lyons

Children Of God Are Butterflies

Children of God are like butterflies and moths
With delicate gossamer wings
They are drawn so easily to the flames
Of life and are so often burned

They are so sensitive to the winds
Of change that they can be easily blown off course
And yet these butterflies and these moths still find their way
To the path God has set out for them

You are this butterfly, this moth
With a part of God deep within you
And though you have been burnt
And have been blown off course many times

It is important to remember that it was not
You who blew you off course or burnt you
It was your sensitivity towards others
That has allowed this to happen.

If you remember this and keep this in your heart
You won't feel guilty for what you
Thought were your mistakes.
Who therefore was responsible?
Was it the elements? Were they to blame?
As God has made the elements, is God to blame?

And as We Guides are part of God
As God is part of us, are We to blame?
If We, God's representatives, and God
Feel no guilt, why should you?

It is just the path you are on.
Go now and enjoy your life
And be at one with God
Who has never left you
Because you have never left Us   1988

Chapter V

Children of God

I refer to the power, or God, in the plural as opposed to the standard singular person. I am NOT being disrespectful but, have found for me, the secret to the God being. Over many years my guides have taught that there is no difference between God, the Creator, the White Light Source, the Power, the Universe, the Holy Spirit or Guides. They are all part of the Whole we lovingly call God.

This is how my Guides explained it to me.

There is a core of pure spirit, from which all has derived. This core has a non-dense centre and therefore cannot be seen or felt in any way, because it is pure spirit, pure peace, tranquillity, serenity and love. This love can never be totally understood by us while we are in a physical form in this physical world and yet we all strive for it. We are drawn instinctively to it. Whenever we feel sad, depressed, irritable, uncomfortable or restless, it is because this entity of calmness we thirst for is missing.

This core has no beginning and has no end. It is so small as to be immeasurably tiny and yet so dense in content it is impossible to weigh. This core is where all souls come from. This core is what most people refer to as God. Its place of existence is what we call Heaven, although Jesus better described it as God's mansion, in which there are many rooms. Each room is the particular heaven where we originated from and will return to in time. We are manifestations of that core. It is us and we are it.

"In the beginning was the word, and the word was made flesh." If you translate that into, "a thought that is action is word," then this will make more sense. After all if there were no means of communicating this thought prior to the creation of a mouth how could thought be converted to word? The word is a concept of vibration. Scientifically all that exist is the atomic structure that vibrates. In the beginning was the word, the vibration and the vibration is God. Or in the beginning was the meaning (word) and the meaning (word) was/is the creator. Also as we think today so is our tomorrow.

Divine thought is thought that comes before any action, be it our own, or spirits. It is not easy for us to comprehend, from our very self-based humanness, a world where divine thought is the existence of all matter. It is important to understand that self-based human thought is much different than divine thought. Our thoughts form the perception of reality being created by the collective of souls of the spirit world. Nor are we somehow an independent representative on some creation forum while in spirit. We all have our own parts to play, based on what we know to be our absolute Truth, but we are only parts of the collective. It is Truth, from all souls as a collective that the creation then uses to create a perfect testing or experiencing ground where all creations can learn by experience.

There is no individuality at this core or at the expanding dimensions that many of us are from or heading toward. Pure love and peace has no need of self-protection, ownership, secrecy or individuality. Our personal connection to divine source prevents us from lying or deceiving and trust reigns supreme. No one is banned or barred from this place of peace. It is the individual's soul that knows whether they are worthy

Chapter V

of this core or final resting place. It is the individual's soul that will determine whether they will either have to opt for work in the lower guide-ship plane for awhile, or return for another spell here in a physical body.

This is where reincarnation comes in. The first time we were born into the physical world, we learned the basic rudiments of the physical body and plane into which we were born. We learnt the simple and basic aspects of life when we were born as human through the different levels of development until we evolved to where we are now. The soul developed differently. There is a very good possibility that in those early days in the evolution of human kind, that the breath, soul, spirit of the person was far more knowing psychically than we are today, and yet our physical or material ways would have been far more primitive. An existential existence seems to be important to development of our sense of understanding ourselves as more than just this body. We would have been more inclined to use our intuition, gut feeling, or psychic senses and less our collective or learned knowing in the way we live today.

In other words we would have been far closer to our guides, but those guides would have been far less spiritual, and more carnal; more into helping us survive physically as compared to today.

To observers looking back we would have seemed uncanny in our hunting, gathering, and understanding of seasons and at the same time seemingly cruel, basic, and primitive in the way we executed our many fundamental and uncomplicated functions. Not unlike animal or bird behaviour we might observe today. In earlier times our life span was thought to be short and yet major religious work talk about lives that were as long as 65 thousand years. It is thought that our emotions were far less sensitive. Illness, death and dying probably carried a different perspective than today. The dominant and overriding challenge would have been to survive. As we evolved we encouraged and nourished that unique human inventive and creativity side we have that other animals lacked. This led us to look more at what humans can do as individuals and as a collective. Spirit evolved as we were going through our intellectual and physical evolution.

A Prayer for Today

Go still and quiet within your mind with your understanding of God deeply in your thoughts, and your intentions. Remember this is your quiet and holy place; this is where the power dwells within all of us.

Remember this holy place is heaven deep within you, which we can only reach if we are pure of heart, and don't bring troubles or worries with us when we enter this holy place. Now become at one with what you know to be pure Truth, for this peace, this power is God within.

Next recognise just how much respect you have for this power who sustains you on a daily basis by reviewing what you have this day that you didn't necessarily have before. It's not necessarily what you wanted or thought you needed, but what you have that sustained you after the event.

Draw to mind what it would say to you concerning your weaknesses or guilt feeling, and any matters you may be harbouring deep within. It knows your thoughts before you even contemplated them, it knows your reasons for why you did what you did, and it is not holding you guilty, so then don't hold yourself in guilt.

Thank it for forgiving you your faults, assuming of course you make every effort not to do them again, having determined why you did them in the first place. Be mindful you will need to do the same to others as you are asking of It to do for you.

Remember this power will never take you anywhere you are not meant to go, if you allow it to guide you. Trust more and more in it and it will sustain your physical, emotional, and spiritual needs. Amen.

On The Light Path

In Gulgong NSW, not long before I came to Queensland, I had a visit from a woman for a psychic reading. At the end of the session, she told me she was caring for her brother who was dying and had less than a month to live. She said he was killing himself by continuing to smoke heavily and drink alcohol constantly. She asked if I might like to visit him, just to see if I could "Talk some sense into him." I called to see him just after my very good friend the local Catholic priest, had called to give him what used to be called the Last Rights.

This woman's brother was very sick. He was propped up in bed, oxygen mask in one hand and cigarette in the other. He chained smoked the entire time I was there. He had four empty cans by his side and was slugging on his fifth, and it wasn't even 10am. My personal feeling was, "what a waste of space this man is. What a complete disappointment he must have been to his family." I knew he had been ejected from almost every pub in the town, and everyone knew of his reputation. I introduced myself, explained that I was a psychic, and with his permission, slowly went into a trance state. I didn't feel comfortable with what I was sure they would say to him through me, such was my expectation, but I continued just the same.

It was a few moments before my guides started:

On the Light Path — Peter Lyons

"Bill, you know your time has come, in fact you should have been here with us weeks ago, but you are letting others convince you that you are not worthy of your place up here with us. What do they know? How could they possibly know the wonderful work you have been doing for us, while they assume you've been merrily drowning yourself?

We know what you did for your friend and how you helped him out when he had no money for his kid's birthday party. We know how you helped another friend when she couldn't get her car going and you repaired it for her free of charge. We know of the many hours you spent chatting with the pub owner at your regular watering hole as he emptied his heart out to you, thinking of you as a drunk who had no idea what he was talking about. Even when on occasions, you would surprise him with your seemingly wise and sober answered, telling him things no one else would dare tell him that he needed to hear. Often you returned to your growling incoherently at something on the floor.

You have been our most wonderful servant, allowing us to pass on our messages to those we could never contact through other means, such as through the good priest who has just left you. Those lost souls we could only get to through you. And for this, we will punish you? For this we will cast you into everlasting fires and damn you? No, for this you will be heartily welcomed and well rewarded, as you rightfully deserve.

God does not judge you for actions over which you had no control. God knows his own, and Bill you are his and he smiles on you. Well done good and faithful servant, your reward awaits you."

Bill started to cry, as did his sister, as I eased my way out of the trance, misty eyed myself. Bill then told us that he couldn't remember the incidents that I had said in trance, but he could remember other incidents earlier in his life, where he

Chapter V

had helped people in a similar way. His sister reminded him of the birthday, because she had baked the cake. He couldn't remember because he had been so drunk.

I knew nothing of any of the matters that had been said through me, but I knew they were true, simply because there was no way I would have thought his man capable of anything more than that of a dying drunk, and also because of the immense feeling of love and joy I felt from my guides as they tranced through me . It was one of a couple of cases where my guides lovingly showed me how easily it was for me to prejudge a person simply by the way they lived their life in public.

I didn't get to see him again, and I lost contact with his sister. I think it was the priest who let me know he had passed away peacefully a few weeks after that incident. Bill just needed to know he was worth something. His guides were able to show him he was more than worthy of God's love, and therefore worthy of his own love and respect. In so doing they also showed his sister how very special her brother had been, and I am sure this was intended as a means of helping her to see him in a better light, especially after he had passed over into God's place for him. Was Bill a saint, a sinner or somewhere in between?

A saint is not necessarily a person who spends two thirds of their time on their knees praying, or a person who has a 'holier than thou' attitude. A saintly person is one who has a great understanding for the weaknesses of others, but a very low tolerance of their own weaknesses in relation to their moral-conscience base.

A saintly person lives a thoughtful, mindful, and an aware life. Remember Jesus' story about the rich proud man up the front of the temple, praising his worth, while the beggar sat down the back, beating his chest "Lord I am not worthy, but only say the world and I shall be healed." How many times would Bill have said that prayer, never having it answered till the end of this life? Sainthood is not some unachievable level that only a few can master, or a prestigious award given out by a whimsical group of nobodies in Rome. We are all on the sainthood journey and eventually we will reach this status, even if it takes us thousands of lifetimes to do so. This is the Light Path of which I speak.

We are all Saints in the making. We are all sons and daughters of God. So long as we recognise our weaknesses, change the aspects of our life that we know need changing and that we know we can change, leave alone those aspects that we can't change, and hand those unchangeable and uncertainties over to our guides, then we are doing all we can be asked to do.

A Saintly journey is one where we continually work at rebuilding ourselves. As a jet needs to be stripped down, thoroughly checked, and rebuilt, so it is with us. If we can't get it working properly in this life, that's OK we have many, many more lives where we can but try, try-and-try again.

If we are a person, who has never deliberately or wilfully gone outside the boundaries and have always, or for a long time, followed what we know to be right, pure, true and good in accordance with our moral-conscience value, then we must be a few kilometres ahead on our soul's journey.

The question is what were the boundaries for Bill? And what are the boundaries for any particular person? From what I channelled for him, he was well and truly within the expectations his guides had for him, but no one, including Bill knew it.

Who knows what particular path a person is on, other than that person? What right do we have to judge and, in the case of Bill, interfere in God's plan for him? We can't always assume we are ahead of, or equal to others, any more than we can assume we are way back in the backfield waiting for someone to give us a tow, or so far back that we are past value to that power. We are all simple travellers on our own learning path, with enough on our plate to keep us going for at least this lifetime, without having to worry about someone else's shortcomings.

Reflective Consciousness

The most powerful tool we humans have is not love but Truth. Love is the calming, peaceful base we need to fully embrace before we can use Truth to its fullest. In order that we fully embrace love, we must continually broaden what I will call our combination. This combination consists of our understanding, patience, kindness, and tolerance with respect of the other person and the power within us all. To this we must add total honesty. We can in no way be dishonest, no matter how justified the reason, to ourselves or to others, because to do so, weakens our interaction with that Power within.

When we have fully embraced this combination, we are ready to embrace, and then to become, the Truth. You can't just try and be patient, kind, tolerant, etc. You have to dwell or meditate, with your guides, on each one of these worlds to get a deeper understanding of what they mean to you; a dictionary was a great tool for me here. As you go through each word, assuming you ask for that honesty you will need to keep you on track, each of those individual combination words will become manifested beyond your understanding of them as mere words.

This Truth, which will be the culmination of all of these combinations, is the power that can move mountains; bring down the most powerful, uplift the most humble, uncover the most putrid and heal the worst of illnesses. Having only part of any of these is like trying to use an out of alignment Laser to cut through the hardest of metals; it won't work.

On the Light Path — Peter Lyons

It has been my experience that those most critical of others trying to do their best, are those that choose excuses to justify their own shortcuts. A judgement is when no matter how much the proof to the contrary, we still remain unmoved on our original opinion, and refuse to change our stance. A judge in a court of law, irrespective of the findings after the decision, never changes his or her mind. The case has to go to another, usually higher, court.

199

On the Light Path — Peter Lyons

Hebrew 1:14 = Are not all angels ministering spirits sent to serve those who will inherit salvation?

Spirit Friends

Spirit Friends follow me, patiently teaching me,
Leading me to this special place

Loving, They're guiding me, showing me where to be
Till finally They showed me Your face

Arm in arm in God's White Light, hand in hand together
We will walk a million miles,
Their Light and Love will Guard and Guide us

Spirit friends helping us, there's no stress, there's no fuss.
We are one, walking down God's road

Sharing life's love and pain, there's no loss and there's no gain
All are one sharing out the load

Arm in arm in God's White Light, hand in hand together
We will walk a million miles,
Their Light and Love will guard and guide us

Spirit Friend are with us patiently Guiding us
Leading us to that special place, to that special place.

2002

Chapter VI

Guides and Guardian Angels

In reading back over what I have already written, I notice that, unintentionally, I have skipped over some areas, or have only touched on them lightly. I mentioned our duel personality, the outer being the face and features others know us by, and the inner the one we know ourselves by, but I did so in a way that may have left more questions than answers. To expand on this think of the computer as a comparison, because we humans are very similar to this man-made intelligence.

Our mind is like a computer, where we can create imagery, not unlike the different graphics programs available for our computers. We absorb knowledge from schooling, university, and general knowledge. Our day-to-day interaction with other people, places and things acts as our scanner, CD driver, or any other external input device other than the modem.

We have a Random Access Memory that permits us to hold certain information at any one time but that we usually don't remember later. These include our daily activities, people we pass, or places we visit. Usually the information in this RAM gets wiped out pretty quickly, and most of the content gets forgotten, with only a reference note remaining.

We also have a hard drive, which is split into two sections. The first is like a longer term version of a RAM where we accumulate the past information, such as remembering what we had for lunch two or three weeks ago, or what we were doing at work or home before we went to that lunch, even though it may take some effort to recall it fully. This information often gets forgotten in time.

The conscious is what is currently in the mind at any one time. We have a recognition system where we either recall by choice, or if some information just "comes into our heads." We know if it is safe to present to the RAM for it to be thoroughly understood, or thought through before moving on from it to some other matter. Such matters could be a painful event that, to recall fully, only brings sadness and tears. This is our virus scanner.

In receiving psychic matters we need to pay attention to how to we properly use our sixth sense. Our sixth sense is our Internet, and the process by which we receive psychic matters. We have to discern what spiritual aspects we should tap into. Just because it comes from spirit doesn't mean its necessarily wholesome, good for us, or can be trusted. If we can't identify those thoughts or images that come to mind, or their source, then we could be getting seriously damaging input, just like a virus to a computer. These could take a long time to clear away or repair.

We need to firewall ourselves, and to do this we need to have a base that we know is True to us. This firewall is our moral conscience base. We must know what is right and wrong for us, according to Truth and we must upgrade this moral conscience base regularly.

Now we need to install the virus scanner. This is when we are constantly vigilant to what we are thinking, so that we are not subconsciously letting viruses sneak in to our hard drive, or our operation systems, and undermining our equilibrium. The near enough is good enough syndrome when processing matters in our mind is the doorway to serious interference.

Chapter VI

It is important to be conscious of how our thoughts make us feel. Are they negative thoughts causing us to constantly worry and has that become part of our personality? These with other tolerated imperfections are the signs we need to be conscious of, as they could very well be doorways to viruses.

Next we need a discerning selector that allows us to only interact with that which is safe for us, a body or unit, which knows the spirit world better than we ever could, and that we know we can trust. A body we know can help us to differentiate between our own thought, negative thought and those thoughts that are from a high, pure, and truthful, source.

So where do we find such a body or discerning selector? How hard is it to find?

The answer is that they have been with you since the day you were born. They are there in your mind, in your thoughts, quietly minding their own business, waiting for you to recognise them and to give them permission to work for you. In the same way we draw negative guidance, so we can draw the positive. In one instance we take whatever is available, in the other we only take the highest, best and purest.

These are your Guides, Guardian Angels, and God's personal Messengers to you. God's connection to you is as an individual and an independent part of your soul. It is often seen as spirit, child within, or higher self. To most of us they seem to stay silent. They often act in a way we assume is an action or impulse from ourselves. How many times have we believed something to be our imagination, a hunch, something we just thought of, or covered under the term it just happened?

How many times have we had an impulse that has lead us to a good or a not so good situation? How many times have we gone to say one thing, and something totally different has come out of our mouth, and not necessarily something bad?

On the Light Path — Peter Lyons

Nothing happens by chance, and as I indirectly stated earlier, everything is created by something. If we didn't instigate or create or plan or make a matter happen, who did?

Just because you didn't know this, doesn't mean that you haven't been guided, that you have been left unprotected. There isn't a day that they aren't with you, just waiting for you to recognise them. But don't expect to hear a stranger's voice in your head; they will simply use your voice or thoughts. This is why we often think it is our own thoughts we feel or hear.

In the movie Ghost, when Whoopee Goldberg's character recognises Patrick Swayze's character for the first time, Patrick's character is stunned to think he could actually be heard. This is the same with our guides, who are so used to giving, but rarely being recognised as an entity in their own right. The more we recognise them the more active they become within us. Using a computer analogy, it is like a person that only uses one part of their computer constantly, suddenly getting the computer to work in areas otherwise never used. It will take a few attempts before the computer works properly in those areas, without a malfunction.

Our guides are a collective rather than individuals. That is we don't have one or two guides, but billions and billions of highly evolved souls. They are on call for us at any one time in relation to our needs according to spirit law. These guides act on what is right for us at that time, not necessarily what we may think we want or need. Though they are many, they speak as one voice and present themselves as one image.

So how do we tell the difference between our own thoughts, our imaginings, and our guides? By regularly meditating in a way that spiritually up-lift us to that level where we know, without doubt, we are in the company of that which is Truth.

Chapter VI

An Exercise

Here is an exercise that may better explain this. Assuming you're relaxed and in a quiet environment, breathe in a long, slow, deep breath, hold the breath without straining yourself, and slowly let out the breath. Repeat this exercise, while at the same time, checking to ensure you are relaxed and comfortable physically. Now relax your mind to the best of your ability. Remove all thoughts, feeling, emotions, worries or concerns, so that your mind is still. A good way to tell if you are in a state of peace is to give a sigh and at the same time smile while slumping into the chair, like you are melted butter. This should bring about a noticeable improvement in the way you are feeling.

Next, I want you to think of a place that either you have been to, or that you know of that you would like to go to, a place that brings a feeling of serenity, peace and calmness to mind. For example, you may be in a tropical rain forest, or taking a misty mountain walk, or lazing around a mountain pool in a pine forest, or snug inside a log cabin with a blazing wood fire keeping you warm as you look out at a snow capped Alpine mountain. Whatever the image is OK so long as it does not hold any sad or regretful memories. It must be completely calming.

Imagine you are actually in this place right now, there in your mind. From the ground you are standing on to the distant horizon, the trees, the grass, the animals, the buildings, the sky and time of day. Is it morning or night, what season is it? What sounds would you hear in this special image? Birds, wind, waves lapping on the shore, water rushing over a waterfall, whatever sound best suits your image.

What is the taste that is in your mouth right now in this beautiful image? Is it salt-water spray, or fresh mountain water

On the Light Path — Peter Lyons

spray, moisture from the trees? What taste would best suit this place?

Reach out in your imagination and touch something in this image. Maybe you are running your hand through the waterfall, or your feet may be splashing in the lake. You may be holding onto the bark of a tree, or holding a flower, or vine in your hand. You may have birds landing on your shoulders.

Now what fragrance would you smell in you special place? Nectar, honey, blossoms, or smoke from an open fire. Musty decaying undergrowth you would associate with a rain forest, whatever fragrance you feel best suits this place you have created.

OK so now to do a quick review. You have slipped quietly away from distractions, and the world in which you were active before this exercise. You have closed off your physical self to the best of your ability, so that if anyone were to be observing you, they would assume you were asleep.

Your physical body is just ticking over, like a car motor idling. The psychos, that soul, breath, spiritual part of you, is aware of what is going on in the physical world around you, but is more concentrated on enjoying this beautiful place you have created. Not only have you successfully shown yourself the difference between your outer and your inner self, you have also created an image based on what I gave you as a prompt. Even though my input was specific in a sense, you controlled the final outcome of what was 'put' into your conscious mind.

This is true imagination, the art of creating thoughts, images and sounds in your mind from your own input. So then what do we call those images, thoughts, feelings and knowing that come to mind that we didn't deliberately or knowingly create? Dreams, flashes of thought, gut feelings, premonitions, intuition. Where did they come from if we didn't consciously create them?

If we deliberately and consciously create an image, then we can claim it as our creation. If the image comes to us without us consciously being responsible for it, then there must be another source outside of ourselves.

I believe that the individual is a receiver of information and that the information can come from a number of sources, including the spiritual realm as well as the physical. It also suggests that there is a peaceful, joyful, non-invasive source as well as a fearful, worrying, undermining source, each running counter to the other that we can tap into. It suggests that we have available a direct link to both those sources. The higher or peaceful Source is the one that isn't easy for us to readily tune to and takes discipline and focused concentration in order that we don't unintentionally receive the less peaceful source.

Getting To Know Our Spirit Friends

It is my understanding that our guides are the representatives to us of this higher source. It is they who help us in all instances of our life without restrictions, limitations, or boundaries. There is no area they can't help us with, if we are willing to totally trust them. The difficulty is, what we want and what they know is in our best interest isn't necessarily the same. They won't interfere in our choices, nor will they override our will, but they won't necessarily clean up our mess if our choice gets us into trouble either.

A good example here is the child and the fire. The parent tells the child not to touch the hot article but the child insists on having its way, then somewhere along the line, when the parent is not watching, the child finds out the hard way why the parent tried to stop them. Part of our learning is that what we sew we reap. It takes a little time to get into the practice of accepting our guides, but consistency is what brings it about.

In my case, I would have wonderful conversations in my mind with what I thought were my own thoughts and my own creative thinking. I can recall many a time having a joke or humorous conversations with my crazy mind. However, as the thoughts became more independent of my own, I began to realise there was another source creating these humorous little one-liners. It was, as the good Catholic, saying my morning and evening prayers, which brought me closer to the realisation that the source of the humour and the source of the prayer replies were one in the same.

Somewhere down that road, I began to change my prayers from the one-way pleading that we all were taught was the way to commune with God, to a two-way interaction.

I can recall thinking of a particular circumstance that I was having difficulty with, putting it up in the pleading prayer form, with all the justified reasons why that particular unpleasant circumstance should be changed. And then in the ensuing silence wondered what God would say in reply. It was from this that I started to believe I was double guessing God's reply, and in so doing, not only ended up with answers to my prayers, but also aware of the replies coming from a different place in my own thoughts. Take for example the time when I was pleading in my prayers for enough money to complete the holiday hostel I helped to build back in the early 1980's. My standard prayer back then went something like this:

Father God, through your son Jesus, I ask that you give us the resources, support and finances to complete this hostel that I believe is for your work, of your will and for your glory. I pray for this in Jesus' name. Amen.

Chapter VI

As time went by and the project hit harder times, I asked myself was I of pure heart, was God listening and if in both cases the answer was negative. What was I doing wrong? It was, while sitting quietly alone in my rather dilapidated shed that I started to ponder if there were other reasons why the project was having such a difficult time.

While walking around the property, I came across my wonderful donkeys grazing in the lower paddock, and I asked my favourite donkey, the one I called Mum, what does God really want of this project? Is it God's project or mine? Am I wasting my time? Had the donkey answered, I wouldn't be writing this work from the many beautiful places up and down the Queensland east coast. Instead I would be under heavy medication in some group home or institution wondering what is sanity?

As it eventuated I had a revelation of importance to me at that time. What if my being there was not so much for the original intentions of the hostel, but for a personal learning curve where I would help individuals to learn more about them selves.

Later, as I became more aware of guides and how they work, I realised it wasn't me who opened up this new vision in my mind, via my lovely donkey, but my guides speaking to me. They were helping me to find my own solutions. And there was nothing I could do but to trust that they knew my needs. It was from this basic process of asking myself what God would say to me that I began to get answers that I knew weren't from my own knowing.

It is pretty rare for the power to pick us up off our track and put us onto a better one. It usually waits till the next set of points come up and gently moves us across to where we are meant to be. It will move us from our difficult situation with the least amount of shaking and destabilising, but not necessarily when or as we may perceive it will happen.

If however we stubbornly expect the Creator to do things our way, and are not willing to compromise our needs or values, we may never get an answer that will please us. Remember to "Let go and let God…"

Naming Our Guides

A question many people ask is what are the names of our guides and specifically, what are my Guide's names? Well my guides don't have a particular name, any more than anyone has guides with a specific name. If you want to use a name for your collective guides, you can use your own name. After all they are a part of you as you are a part of them. They reflect their uniqueness through you, and that, combined with your breath, soul or spirit and your physical persona, is why you are so uniquely special. There will never be another being on this planet as unique as you, so expand and express yourself to your fullness, and see what mountain you can bowl over.

Although it has been fashionable to have a name for this guidance conglomerate, as we move more and more into this new Age of Aquarius, spirit will be tending to use individual names for themselves less and less.

In the Aries Age, it was common for angels to be referred to with individual named, as in the Old Testament. In the Pisces Age, from the time of Jesus until just recently, there were less new angels, but much reference made to past ones. Now that we have entered the Age of Aquarius, a time of brother-sister hood, collectives, humanism, science and communities, a time different to any other Age, our guides will be more know by their actions, rather than their particular names. This is primarily because names tend to distract from the message

Chapter VI

and encourage glorification of the messenger and also feed the egos of those through whom the message is delivered.

Our guides interacts with our soul, our spirit, our child-within, or our higher self, and because of this they can't be seen physically because they are pure spirit, without density. Our guides are made up of varying densities of spirit. This so they may interact with us here in the dense, physical world. Those closest to us can be sensed either by a good psychic, or appear in an Aura photograph in different energy forms. The higher the guides we have around us, the purer their guidance, and the harder they are to photograph or see because they are pure spirit.

I can remember back in my little Hervey Bay home while being in a very deep trance-induced meditation, my guides showed me this huge vortex. It was broad at the top and narrow at the bottom. Descending down the vortex I realized it was made up of billions and billions of highly evolved souls of pure spirit. All of whom had given themselves over to the highest good, with no individuality as such, but willing to serve the greatest good. They were stacked out wide in circular rows, the top or outer rows were the learners and the bottom or inner, were the pure pristine non dense spirit centre of the person's guides.

The very high pristine guides at the bottom look like they were on a platform or stage. They couldn't be seen individually because they were so brilliant. Yet there was an awareness there were many in number and presenting as a glow of golden white Light. They were actually superimposed onto the physical person, and connected to the core and serenity that is God.

Imagine this physical person and from deep within them is this brilliant blinding light that emanates out to about the elbow of an outstretched arm. This energy is a blinding light spreading outward from this person. The brightness became more recognisable in varying colours, not as a band of light, but a spectrum from the core, and expanding outward about 4/5 blocks.

Those pure souls of the very highest calibre were the core of God as expressed within that person. The blindness they caused was not because of the abundance of light, but because of the lack of dense matter, which makes them pure ether. This is unbearable for us to tolerate in the physical world unless we are totally in-tune with them. This is usually only when we are in spirit ourselves. A very difficult task considering we are living in a dense, physical body.

The lesser pure, but still very high souls, are the ones those of us who are psychically sensitive may pick see or sense in the ether around the person. It is usually further out from this that we may have colour showing up in an aura photograph. The quality and quantity of guides depends on the need we have in relation to our level of spiritual experience and learning.

This vortex of energy that acts as a conduit or channel between us here in the physical world, and the core we know as the Creator or God, is called angelus in Latin and is the root of the word angel. This angelus cannot intrude into our life process. Hence, we know them to guide us and why the word guides is also used to describe them. As they transfer messages to and from us they are also known as messengers.

When the human person tunes in deeply to their guides the energy is intensified. This protects the pure ones from contamination. It also assists those outer, but still highly evolved souls, who were learning from this intense and pure download.

This explanation may not rest well with those who are looking for a personal one-on-one or supportive spiritual being

Chapter VI

such as a relative that has passed over. Guides do all of this, but it is the person's needs wherein lies the difference. If a person cannot move to an understanding in their mind that they are as much a part of the guide-ship as the spirit energy guiding them, there will be very little forward growth. This particularly applies to those doing psychic work and who claim they have the wisdom of some long departed icons as their guides.

Aura Photography

Aura photography is a wonderful way of determining where we are in relation to our guides. Have an aura photo taken and then another one taken after you have attuned yourself (for a period of 4-5 months) to your guides. Call on your guides to be with you when you sit for the second photo. Then compare the two photos and note the differences. This is to show you what they want for you to see, rather than your own expectations.

If you have been to an aura photographer and they have said they can't get any colour, it could well be because you have such a huge quantity of high-level spirit energy around your etheric body. Obviously if they are pure spirit, nothing of that calibre of purity in your aura will show up in such a photograph. If you have a concentration of colour, either mixed or in blotches close around you, this can be an indication of where your guides are currently working.

Where the colour is centralized could indicate the need for clearing. It may be they are working on clearing blockages in you spiritual vision, an area that you many not see needing work. The variation of colours usually indicates your guides are working with you to re align you in those particular areas. The stronger the colour close to your core, the more likely you are to have lesser quality guides assisting you. This doesn't mean you are not worthy of guidance. It can mean that you are possibly holding on to, or are working through, something at a lower vibrational level, such as prolonged hurts and anger. A lower vibration level of guides, though still very high, are able to get close to you without being contaminated by other energies that may be around you at that time.

There is no right or wrong, greater or lesser guides out there waiting to infiltrate you and overrun your designated guides. Guides will always be in alignment with your understanding of Truth.

Chakras and Guides

When we are interacting with our guides, without contamination of any kind our vibration is literally humming. It is then that we have all five horizontal energy centres or Chakras in alignment. It becomes a pure feed or interaction with no blockages from the first or Base Chakra to the seventh or Crown Chakra. If we have blockages in any of our five horizontal chakras, this can throw out our energy balance, similar to an unbalanced washing machine in spin cycle.

If the third eye is out of alignment, if we are not interacting properly with our guides, and we are not up grading our moral conscience value or are harbouring negative thoughts, then Sight (sixth) Chakra will be out of alignment. When our communication is out of control, or that we find we have been offensive to others, or others claim we display negative, unfriendly, or rude body language, then it could be our Throat (fifth) Chakra is out of alignment.

If the personal relationship part of our life is one in need of constant attention in some way, we feel our life is only partially functioning unless we have someone else in our life, then our Heart (fourth) Chakra could be out of alignment.

If the material aspect of our life determines our happiness; if we must have material wealth before we feel safe, driven by the material world and having little trust of how safely our guides provide for us, then our Solar Plexus (third) Charka is likely to be out of alignment.

If we have poor self esteem, letting the criticism determine how we feel about ourselves, depressed and need medications, alcohol or other stimulus to make us feel good, then our Sacral (second) Chakra could be in need of repair.

If any or all of these chakras are out of alignment, then the interaction of earth or material energies passing from the base or Root (first) Chakra will be too strong within us, and the golden pure essence of power entering the Crown (seventh) Chakra will be blocked or limited.

When all of the chakras properly aligned, the pure golden power from the Crown (seventh) Chakra superimposes over the energy from the (Root) first Chakra, so that both energies interact perfectly within that person. Visually it looks very similar to the Star of David, which my guides inform me, was where the symbol originated.

From our perspective, the effect is perfect interaction with our guides and our higher self, Soul, Breath, and Spirit. I put these words in capitals because when this happens we are no longer human in the traditional sense, but intimate with the golden power.

We become at one with that greatness as it becomes at one with us. This isn't for our glorification, ego, or personal gain. But that we become a fully functioning channel of that power. This allows a complete cycle of trust to flow between us and our core being.

When you are at one with your guides and God only you and God will know.

I Had a Dream

I had a dream last night; you were here with me.
We were heading back from the Mountains; you had your
Thermos of tea.
We stopped and shared a cuppa, and as you kept guard
I filled a Hessian bag with sandy loam.

The bitter winds were blowing. The sleet and the snow
Would soon start falling, we had to go.
But you just sat there smiling without a care
Brushing the sleet from your soft gray hair

It's almost fifteen years since you passed away
But it only seems like yesterday.
You were far more to me that my mother's dad,
You were the best friend I ever had.

You're in your special someplace way up there,
Gently rocking in your old easy chair.
No doubt with two shillelaghs (Irish walking sticks) at your
feet
And your hat crushed underneath you seat

2002

Chapter VII

Family Members as Guides

An earlier reference I must address concerns family members as guides. When I asked my guides they jokingly exclaimed, "can you imagine the captain of a Jumbo Jet announcing, 'Good evening ladies and gentlemen. I am you captain, your co-pilot, your navigator, and your host and general runabout. As soon as I get a minute, I will be back there to serve coffee and tea, just as soon as I work out where the hell we are, and how to get over this mountain.

Spiritual guidance is a much bigger job than running a super-size aircraft. It takes many dedicated and specialised souls to help each one of us personally, for nothing we do in any particular life is preordained; everything is a changeable based on multiple choices. Family members may be assisting in your spiritual guidance team, as well as known icons that have that particular expertise, but it is a team effort.

When a person passes over into God's wonderful Kingdom, the last thing they want or need is some energy drawing them back to the physical plane, because of unfinished business or because a relative misses them. They need to be completely free of all material emotions and feelings relating to the physical world altogether. They need to heal when transitioning from the physical world to the spiritual one.

Though we are feeling sadness as part of the natural grieving process, we have to recognise that the family member in spirit can pick up on our sadness. They can feel helpless and confused at not being able to put our mind and heart at rest. Hence why, even though it is natural to feel sad, it is important to know and feel in our heart that our loved one is safe and in God's care. Two wonderful prayers come to mind that may illustrate better what I am trying to say:

"It's holy and wholesome to think well of the dearly departed that they may be freed from their restriction."

And the other comes from a Requiem prayer,

"May Eternal Light shine upon them and may they rest in peace, for ever and ever".

There can be a problem if we want an instant reply from a loved one in spirit, or to chatter with them whenever we want to. That is not to say that personal contact with a loved one in spirit is wrong, It is who, how and why that person is making the contact that is of concern. The person who didn't get to say good-bye to their relative before they passed over, and is trying to make amends for the guilt they feel is one kind of concern. Another is the person looking for a reason why the recently departed never completed a matter or made peace with the one left behind. A third is a person who never thought a day would come when they would be separated from that dearly loved departed one. If a person tries to link up with the recently departed, without knowing how to protect themselves properly, or how to differentiate between genuine family member in spirit and a lost soul, they could very likely draw in a low entity. The more the intensity in our query, without protection, the more likely we are to draw severe interference.

Spirit doesn't see us as we see others here in the physical world; they are drawn to feelings, energies and emotions.

Chapter VII

They may think they are being drawn to someone they loved in their physical life, because they sense in us similarities to their friend. Because we don't always know if the person in spirit is the family member we seek, we can easily be attracted towards lost souls, or they can be attracted towards us. Just like we can easily mistake the identity of someone we may encounter in a darkened familiar place.

I have had sessions when someone has asks for confirmation that a deceased family member is their personal guide. When they find out that this is not what is given me they become quite emotionally disturbed and break into tears. Others have reacted as soon as their loved one's name was mentioned. This is usually a sign this person is experiencing a connection with lost souls and not their real relative at all. Of course not all results of releases are necessarily unhappy ones.

Within days of my visiting a friend in country Queensland, just as I had started to review this work, we had a friend of hers come to visit. Immediately on meeting this woman, I felt a mild discomfort, but nothing to cause me to isolate myself. In the general conversation it was mentioned that I am a psychic and this woman revealed she had her father as her guide. The opportunity was such that the best I could do at that time was for me to show her how to do the release meditation and leave it up to her guides as to what happened next.

A few days later this woman again visited interested in enquiring about different aspects of her life from a spiritual perspective. In the course of the conversation, I suggested she again do the release meditation, only this time I suggested she call her father to her and that she ask him specifically to leave her and go to where he was meant to be in accordance with spirit law. I then got her to stay deep within her meditation till she felt ready to return to the physical world. It took her a much longer time to return this time, but it was obvious from the moment she opened he eyes, that there had been a change.

She noted that she felt far calmer and peaceful, but that she missed her dad not being there. I suggested she return quickly to that peaceful place in her mind, and then that she asked her guides for any information concerning her real father. The result was almost instant. Within seconds of her returning to her peaceful place, she said she could feel her father's presence, only this time he was far more at peace than had been the case when last she encountered him. The entity that she thought was her father previously, was in fact a lost soul who she had released and had encouraged to go to the peaceful place it sought.

Lost souls can easily mimic our loved ones to the point where they even take on the loved ones imagery, not that these mimics are necessarily bad and evil. They may be well-intentioned souls not necessarily knowing why they are feeling such a sad connection, and assume it is coming from a loved one in the physical world who is drawing them back.

They can easily be drawn to someone with similar feelings, without knowing they've been drawn to a stranger. This is how some souls become lost. Then there are those souls that are so totally confused with their own weaknesses that they desperately cling to any sadness, longing, or emptiness that may be around a particular living person.

It is the physical person, so desperately wanting to contact their loved one, who assumes any spirit energy is the right spirit energy. They don't for a moment realize they may have attached the spirit of a complete stranger. When there is a lost soul interfering in a person's personal life, as opposed to that person's real relative or friend, the interference will be inclined to isolate, sadden and generally change the nature and manner of the person who is still living in the physical world.

Chapter VII

Contacting Loved Ones

If you feel there is someone around you who has passed over and you have been happily interacting with this person then there is a good chance your spirit friend or family member with you in accordance with God's law. It is the state of mind of a person that determines if that person has a contented, peaceful soul around them or not.

I have had so many people adamantly state that the energy around them is their loved one in spirit. When they do a simple release exercise, as was used by the woman in the example above, the difference stuns the person. They can't believe they have been so convincingly fooled, and usually express how free they feel as a result of the release.

The best way for us to contact our family member in spirit is to go though the switchboard of our guides, as it is they who act as the conduit between our loved ones and us. Don't try making any contact with your loves ones, even through your guides, especially if you are very emotionally connected to that person in spirit. Chances are your needs will over ride your guidance, and you will end up with a lost soul. It is best if you leave your thoughts, love, and feelings for your loved one with your guides and they will pass on your message to your loved one for you.

In time when you least expect it, and when you are best able to accept it, you could have a sensation, like a perfume, or a feeling of peace and contentment relating to your loved one come to you. You're guides, acting as a protective buffer zone between you and your loved ones are allowing them to come to you the safe way. This way prevents psychic interference, and leaves you feeling very peaceful with a knowing and loving calmness as your dearly departed loved one seem to descend toward you in your mind or your thoughts.

Lost Souls

Some people have asked me how it is they have lost souls around them, even though they did nothing to encourage these entities. They may feel very much at ease with an entity, feeling or emotion that reminds them of their deceased loved one. If this is the case, they need simply to ask their guides for clearance. If these souls or ghosts seem to be less present after guidance intervention, then they are most likely lost souls. If you still have some concerns about whether you are interacting with your family member in spirit or a lost soul, you simply need to ask your guides to check for you, and They will take care of any souls that shouldn't be there.

For those of you that want something a little more reassuring, try this simple meditation process. This is the release meditation I have made reference to preciously.

In your mind, after initially relaxing and then doing the simple breathing exercise, call on all in spirit that may be around you at this time. This includes you guides and any entity you feel may be with you, good or bad, including deceased family members, Saints, animal spirits or others.

Thank them sincerely in your thoughts for what they have done for you over the past years. Even if you don't know if they have done anything at all, thank them anyway. Ask them to leave you and to go to where they are meant to be in accordance with God's will or spirit law.

It is important that you don't try holding one or other soul or spirit energy back. Your guides, those that are meant to stay with you, will stay. All the dismissing under the sun won't send them away. After you've done this, just thank those that remain, and ask that they fill the gap created by those souls that may have moved on.

Chapter VII

If there had been any lost souls, entities or interference around you before the exercise you are likely to feel a noticeable change within your mind or thoughts afterwards. Some say they feel like a slight freeing up, a sensation of something letting go, followed by a feeling of calmness.

It is usually a good idea to forget about the particular family member in spirit for awhile after a release has been done. This allows the doorway that lets the negative entities in to become permanently closed. Don't feel sad at the family members passing and therefore your loss, but instead leave good thoughts towards them in your mind. Don't expect a miraculous, first time cure, it may take a few attempts before you are completely clear of the negative energy. Your guides will link you to your departed friends or family members when they know it is safe to do so.

When someone comes to me for a full session, before giving them information, my guides through me do a psychic check of that person and their guides. This is to check to make sure there are not lost souls who would interfere with the session. Using a similar process to the one I have just shown you, the guides get the person to remove whatever interference may be around them. They monitor through me as the release is taking place. Often these sweet and loving people can be so embedded with lost souls thought to be their loving family members or friends in spirit that it may take a few releases before they are totally free of this negative or lost soul energy.

If you want to seriously put your house in order, by wanting release from lost souls, changing or upgrading your spiritual moral or conscience base, simply be constant in this wish, and trust your guide's.

I had a young girl visit me for information concerning a relative who had passed over many years before. This very sweet and gentle young person was more than happy with the session. She was happy until I said her uncle, of whom she was enquiring, was now happy in spirit, but was concerned for her welfare. She angrily revealed that this uncle had molested her as a child and she wanted him to rot in hell, not go to heaven. These kinds of encounters can stop me from doing psychic work. They can be so very difficult to deal with. She wanted revenge. It took almost two hours explaining through our guides that the memory, not the uncle, was bringing her down. She sobbed how unfair that sounded, and my guides said, but you don't know what kind of life he will have to live next time to pay off his karmic debt for what he did to you. I was finally able to get her to agree to a release.

A few months later she visited me and said she couldn't believe how free and relaxed she felt. She said she couldn't believe how the memory of such painful events in her life had almost crippled her, even after the person responsible had passed over many years before.

Passing Over

What I mean when I refer to a physical person and their spirit. Normally when a person passes over or dies it is their physical form that remains here in this dimension. The physical form breaks down into dust and dirt. Their spirit or soul, which continues on into a spiritual world and never dies. It is like they are in a dream from which they never wake. A dream that is so beautiful that they don't want to wake from it.

When we pass over at the end of a particular life, the imaginary place we created in meditations becomes a real place. As we move along in this beautiful place any unfinished matters we may have left behind back here in the physical world will bug us until we feel we must take action. These discontented feelings eventually lead us to deciding on our return or to reincarnate. I am not referring to the early stages of our passing over, when we may have felt the tug of family members we left behind, but the longer and deeper need for something to be sorted out before we can feel we are ready for eternal peace.

Time in spirit is not the same as time in our physical world. What might seem like eighteen months to us physically could seem like moments to those in spirit. The sadness they feel from us may not be very long to them. I am, of course, describing a person who passes over with the least amount of fears, concerns, worries, uncertainties or apprehensions. The emotions and intents we hold as we die are carried with us. In spirit or in the physical world, matters of concern and fear can be a distraction for us from the state of peace we need. Only in a state of peace can we look properly and calmly at the causes of the apprehension.

A person, who passes over with worry on their mind, especially worries that have built up over a long period of time, won't just suddenly stop their worrying. They will continue to worry as they have always done. The difference is that there won't be an external world feeding or encouraging worry. Eventually they will stop and realize they are open to much joy, peace and serenity. It just means they stayed a little longer than necessary in that place some call Limbo. Again it may only be a little time to them, but in earth time it can be possibly hundreds or years.

A person who has very strong convictions in their life will carry them with them when they pass over. A strong willed person could hold onto those convictions till they realize they are no longer of value. Those souls who pass over peacefully and without incumbencies get a free pass to continue on their soul's journey.

Possession and Mind State

There has been a definite decline in the numbers of people who follow specific religious beliefs. The fundamentalists of both the Christian, and non-Christian beliefs are far outnumbered in the world by those who no longer hold to a specific faith or religion. Many now actually follow a potpourri of ideals.

In an instance back in the Health food store in Maryborough some years ago, I saw first hand how a possessed person could challenge a person's right. I had visited the store on a day other than when I would normally do my sessions, because on my session days I didn't always get to chat with either of the owners. Usually when holding sessions, my A frame sign would be out the front of the shop. I would sit in an obvious section so people could see me. This day I deliberately sat myself at a table hidden from the shop front by the protruding counter, so people wouldn't approach me for a "just wondering if you can help me."

The owners of the shop, Len and his wife Nola, had just sat down to have lunch when we heard this commotion in the street. Someone was very loudly shouting abusing about a block or two away, the sound of the abuse was coming closer. Finally the abuser was standing out the front of their store. She was a middle-aged woman, whom Len and Nola knew as having a serious mental illness. I could see this woman as she stood at the shop front, a dazed look on her face, but it would have been almost impossible for her to see me.

The owners ignored her and kept on with their meal. Suddenly the woman stopped her raging and took two steps closer to the shop. "You," she called, "yes you." She wasn't actually looking at anyone in particular, but I felt strongly she was addressing me.

"You can never touch me," she said, "your holy ways will never remove me from this woman." The couple looked up from their lunch and stared at me. It was obvious her comments were directed at me. Because neither of them had ever claimed to remove lost souls, nor had anyone else that worked

Chapter VII

there. They were certainly aware that I had done so in many of my sessions.

"You have no right to impose your sanctimonious piety on others, you worshipper of the underworld, you devil of the cloth, you fraud, you viper, you false prophet." Nola and Len were smiling by now, but I was just stunned.

"I know you're there psychic, I can smell you. Your stench is filling the street. I detest priests and churches, but your evil far outweighs any of them. You will be destroyed this very day. You will face me on my terms. You are nothing without your protection, and I will drain it from you, like water from a tank."

And the abuse went on for quite some time, before finally two police officers bundled her into a waiting police car and, we assumed, whisked her off to the mental health wing of the district hospital.

I rarely see anything psychically in the way of souls or spirits, but I certainly notice physical changes in people. From the moment she appeared at the door till she was removed she had changed in appearance at least fifteen times and looking distinctly different each time.

As we sat in the aftermath of her tirade, I could feel a definite sapping of my strength, both physically and emotionally. I was starting to feel quite ill literally and slipping into a state of depression. Thankfully, having had similar experiences, though not quite as powerful as this, I was able to recognise the symptoms of the attack. I immediately excused myself and sat in the reading room at the back of the shop. There I did the release meditation, calling on my guides to remove the interference, till I felt I was safe enough to continue on. I drank copious quantities of water, which eventually settled the stomach.

Some months later, the same woman, who had been fully treated and now back to her normal self entered the shop while I was waiting for my next session to begin.. There was absolutely no recognition of me by her whatsoever, nor was there any of the possessed energy around her that had been present previously.

There is nothing wrong with possession if that possessor is a benevolent entity. If we are at one with our guides, are constantly upgrading our moral conscience value, and honouring constantly Truth. St. Frances of Assisi was a good example of a benevolent possession. He lived his life understanding of God in a way that endeared him to those he served and the Power that possessed him, the core Creator.

It is negative possession most people associate with the word and of course this kind of possession is anything but benevolent. If our mind is under the control of anything other than the power of serenity, peace, or contentment, then we run the risk of being out of control. Under such circumstance we can easily do something that endangers our or another's life. This can happen without us having any idea what, why or how it happened. And what of those possessed persons who have a psychic ability, but who don't necessarily know they are possessed? Those who have so much contradictory information in their mind that the person tries to do physical damage to themselves to stop the mind numbing pain?

These days, such a person could be classed as having multiple personal disorders and put into the mentally ill category. In the pre-psychology psychiatry days, people showing such symptoms were classed as possessed and sadly locked away into institutions.

The days of locking up the mentally ill person, even for a short period of time, applies only to those diagnosed as a serious physical danger to themselves, or others.

Chapter VII

A person with interference from low level spirits, or lost souls, will respond well to medication, which blocks out their conscious for a little while and allows their guides to bring the much needed peace they crave.

It is my understand based on what psychiatrists have shown me, and confirmed by Spirit, that a person with mental illness can feel compelled to overly use the thinking process in searching for answers, when there are really no genuine questions. When the person properly uses the prescribed medication, the spinning mind slows down or stops.

From Spirit's perspective, when the person seeks out answered to non-existent or non-genuine question, they are actually reliving the anxieties of those souls lost in the ethers.

By combining appropriate medication with meditation and rebuilding daily routines, the person not only becomes familiar with these changes but also comfortable with the outcomes these changes bring. From a spiritual side, the person's mind is more inclined to a state of peace, and therefore more inclined to accept guidance.

Not all negative possessions reflect as mental illness. A person falls under this category when they have a poor to non existent moral conscience base, live a more self-based life, little mindfulness and harbour deep resentment for perceived wrongs.

How many Judges, lawyers, and police officers, even when the evidence is so blatantly obvious, have heard accused murderers, molesters, or criminals say "But I tell you I didn't do it. I am innocent."

Where a person's use of alcohol or other social drugs is so serious that they can't fully recollect their actions, they are allowing a power to possess them to do what the rational person wouldn't do. It is highly unlikely that such a possession would happen to someone with a decent morals basis. In my many trance and guided sessions, I have been shown by my guides that if the convicted person were possessed at the time of the crime then they wouldn't recall it happening.

So in Earth, So in Spirit

If you can imagine all the complexities of thinking and thought processes we go through here in the physical world, being duplicated in spirit, then you'll get a better understanding of what souls can and can't do.

These lower level individuals, now in spirit, still want to continue with the world they created in the physical world, but they need physical elements through which to work in order that they can continue this work. They can't see that what they are doing is wrong because they see themselves as victims or wrongly accused. In a sense they are victims, because the evil entities that were guiding them when they were in the physical world are now the gang of low-level entities they feel forced to belong to now that they are in spirit. Individuals here in the earth plane who have little or no moral conscience value and whose mind is so strongly affected by intense low-level thoughts, are sitting ducks for this kind of spiritual gang.

It is not just the criminally minded that they target. Anyone who has not got a proper understanding of right and wrong, and who is not drawing higher Guidance, are potential victims to this energy.

Seeing the habits and weaknesses in others, but totally unwilling to even address the same or similar habits of themselves, is also a very good indicator that a person is open to interference. But remember, this statement is to be used by you for you, not by you to determine or accuse someone else. Their weaknesses are their business. It could be assumed by some that such a person is suffering a mental illness, considering the similarities of the symptoms, and this could well be the case. The question is what came first? Did the person suffer from some mental disability first, or did the mental disability come after?

So an obvious question is going to be, what does a person's Guides do when that person refuses them or doesn't know they are being guided by wayward souls? It is hard for us living in a world where we know we physically terminate after so many years, to understand how the timelessness of the soul's journey fits in. Spirit works with both the souls and the physical person that has been mislead. Their intention is not just to save, or redirect the physical person who is under the control of the way-wards, but to also redirect the way-wards themselves.

As you can well imagine, this takes a lot of patience, understanding, tolerance, kindness and respect for the person they are guiding and the way-wards. It also explains why we, on our road to our perfect place, must also be tested in these areas. After all we will most certainly spend some of our time doing our share of guiding, and in order that we become decent guides, the more we get tested in our mundane lives, the higher the guides and the higher we function when we have our turn in spirit.

On the Light Path — Peter Lyons

Oh God

There is a God I'd proudly say,
But now he feels so far away.
Not like before when He was near,
When He'd whisper His Words in my ear.

When He'd give me strength
'Gainst the strain,
Of the evil world, and its hate and pain.
Where are you Lord, why aren't you near
In my time of woe, in my time of fear.

Oh Child, My Child so deep in pain
From all that hurt,
What have you gained?
Oh Child, My Child my Special One,
There's ne'er a time that you're alone.

Oh Lord I ask that you be kind
To my wretched soul and
My tortured mind.
What can I do to find release,
To bring me to Your state of Peace?

My Son there is a special way
That I will show to you this day.
Find yourself a pleasant spot,
That's quiet and calm,
Where fear is not.

Where nature's music's playing near
And nature's incense fills the air.
Where you may come
Both morn and night
That you may bath in this Pure Light.

Continued on page 245

Chapter VIII

Appropriate Meditations

My first awareness of meditation was a statement my dad had learned in his days as a lay-brother with the Missionaries of the Sacred Heart, a Catholic working order that provided food for priests and teaching brothers at that time. This was before he met and married my mum.

He would often say we should "meditate and supplicate oft." Supplicate is to pray or ask in a humble fashion. I can recall my days as an alter boy, watching the Mercy Nuns at Waitara saying their morning Office before Mass. They would take a certain part of the morning prayers or Office and would quietly meditate on this section, before moving onto another section, doing the same thing. There was one exception to this ritual, and that was the morning I accidentally extinguished the Sanctuary lamp that burnt constantly as a reminder to Catholics of the Blessed Sacrament ever present in the church. The nun's choir of 'tsk, tsk, tsk' made things worse. I can also remember our family saying the Rosary and the repetitive litany to Our Lady, which, my parents informed us, were devices for meditating on the life of Jesus and his Mother. It wasn't till the 70's that I heard there was a different form of meditation practised by Buddhists, Hindus, and adopted at that time by the New Age and hippy cults and groups.

My first involvement with a non-Catholic meditation was when I visited the Enmore Spiritualist Church back in the

70's. My real commitment to meditations of the Spiritual kind didn't start till my days at Peacefields. I would lay quietly before going to sleep, and allow God, as I understood God to be, to come over me and speak to me in my thoughts.

As a means of identifying my thoughts from those of God, I would speak out quietly my thoughts, feelings, and requests, and then allowing God to reply. Most of the time I assumed it was my imagination, and didn't see much harm in it. Occasionally, when a visiting friend and Catholic priest would visit, I would tell him of my practice, and he would advise caution. Considering this was the same priest that I had told of my psychic episodes, and who had sent me to the Pentecostalists for advice, I can understand his reactions. I made sure it was something I practiced as a private action, not making it commonly known what I was doing.

I had to stop this process when my wife-to-be found out. Because of her concerns, her increasing mental illness and my not being totally convinced that it was the right thing to do, I stopped. Later, after she left me in the early 90's, I started to increase my personal method of meditation, initially to help me deal with the deep loss I felt when she left. As I became more settled in my new solo status, I started to get other information, much of which set the foundation for this book you are now reading.

I slowly and cautiously started to interact more with alternative spiritual people and groups in Mudgee and Gulgong, and later in South East Queensland. From these early contacts I revisited that which I had learned year ago at the Enmore Spiritualist Church's learning circles: The fundamental understanding of how to meditate, the standard breathing exercise, how to visualise spiritual objects, such as significant flowers or crystals and how to identify colours in a person's aura. There was that same expectation with these groups that some kind of hidden wisdom or imagery from the Universe

Chapter VIII

would soon be installed within the practitioner. This didn't happen with me, nor was I any closer to psychically seeing anything in the way of coloured auras.

These were always very long and drawn out sessions, especially the meditation groups in Queensland. Most of the participants would end up going to sleep, for which they were seriously reprimanded by the teacher. It was explained in no uncertain terms that to go to sleep during a meditation left you wide open to invaders or low-level walk-in entities.

I didn't go to sleep, but I would find my mind peacefully wandering off to the activities of the day or another time. I certainly didn't see or feel anything remotely like what the others were getting in their meditations. In fact the recall of arrogance I had felt in my youth, concerning a special calling, returned stronger than ever.

I was convinced that there was a power, light or energy source that I could tap into, and that was all I needed. The less I made things happen and the more I trusted this light, or energy source to do what It knew was right for me, the more peaceful I became.

In private home meditations I began to shorten the process and started to receive from them my own breathing and centring exercise. This process allowed my mind to be still and open, yet highly alert to their peace. Still using the system that had been taught in those original groups, I would pull the light towards myself from outside rather than from my own centre. A number of years later my friend, Sharon, said she saw the light coming from within. She saw it as a part of us and not external to us.

The epiphany I experiences was stunning. The Light was within and not floating around out there in the Universe. This light was from the Creator, and we were all part of that light. We were not separated from the light but a part of that Creator. And rather than dragging this Light into our being every time we had a crisis, we simply had to recognize it, waiting inside us.

From then on I started doing my meditations based on this premise. I began accepting that the light was already within. I reached out and touched the physical world around me as if I was the lighthouse but not the light.

The first major effect from this was an awesome feeling of worth. I felt that everyone is worthy of this Power within. We are part of it as it is part of us. I knew it has need of us to spread itself as much as we have need of its peace.

It changed my mind set from dependency on a fleeting power I once called God that only came if I remembered the proper phrase, code, sitting position or ritual. These rule were the assumption inferred from previous meditation styles. The awareness came to me that God was always there, never fleeting or leaving and always loving.

All we need to do is to accept and recognise it as the source of the serene peace. To accept it has always been with us as we honour it. To become more at one with its power in order that this gift increases within.

This is now the basic form of the meditation I now use for personal lost soul releases, house cleanses, Chakra alignment, and healing sessions. I use it as a protection for those who may be grieving or in mourning after the death of a loved one, or those going through a personal trauma. It is also what I recommend as a base for anyone wishing to improve their spirituality. I do nothing without first checking that they and I are properly attuned, via a two minute version of this meditation.

A Simple Attuning Meditation

Chapter VIII

Inner Child

There is a sweet place far away,
It's clearly in my mind.
I'd love to take you there someday,
If you can find the time.

It's in another hemisphere; it's in another world.
There is no hate, no pain no fear,
It's the place of the inner child

Way deep down inside us all
Lays this tranquil and peaceful pool.
It's our link to Creation's love,
Our connection to God

You need no pass no member's fee,
You need no special skills.
You need no Church or special place,
All you need's the will.

Once you've been there you'll want to stay,
How clear your mind will see.
You'll break those bonds that hold you back,
Yes you'll break free.   1985

Earlier I asked you to join me in a little experiment, which is actually the beginning of the meditation. I have included it here in its fullness. I always suggest for beginners that they include the part marked by an asterisk for at least the first few times until they feel confident of the routine. Enjoy!

First find yourself a quiet place; take the phone off the hook and keep away from kids and distractions of all kind. Some people like soft meditation music or the use of incense. There is no need to sit in any particular posture or pose. There is no need to sit in any particular posture or pose, other than to make sure you avoiding circulation or cramping problems.

Start breathing in a long, slow, deep breath. Hold the breath without straining yourself and then slowly release the breath. Repeat this breathing process as many times as you wish. Check your physical being to make sure you are relaxed. Check all over by moving your neck, shoulders, arms, and main trunk of your body. Clear your mind of all thoughts, emotions, expectations, and apprehensions. Relax yourself as close as you can into a sleep state without actually going to sleep.

*For those that know or have been told who their guides are, or for those starting their own spiritual journey for the first time, this part is important.

In your mind, call on your guides, angels, or any entity you feel has been watching over you including valued family members, special people, and sacred icons such as Jesus or specific saints. Thank them sincerely in your thoughts for what they have done for you over the past years. Now ask them to leave you, and to go to where they are meant to be at this time in accordance with spirit law.

Don't try holding onto them in any way. If they are meant to stay with you, all the dismissing under the sun won't send them away. You may have been holding onto guides who have been preventing your spiritual growth, especially if you have been lead to believe you have a particular saint, angel or family member as your one and only guide. In letting go of those that you feel are special to you, you will be allowing them the freedom, contentment and peace they seek. At the same time you will receive the guidance you're meant to have for your soul's journey during this lifetime.

Chapter VIII

Now in that complete stillness and emptiness of mind, know you are worthy of the Creator's best for you. You have the best team of guides helping you to do the will of that power for this particular life path in accordance with Truth-based moral conscience centre.

Allow this power, this energy of total peace to expand out from deep within enveloping you as it soaks through into every part of your spiritual, and physical being. Allow it to expand from you filling your energy field, to expand out into the very room you are in right now, and out as far as it will spread.

As a helpful tool, you might like to extend your arms as you envisage this expansion of energy. I used to do this in my early days of meditation, and the tingling sensation that passed through my whole body has to be experienced to be believed. It may not happen the first or second time, but if you feel you are actually spreading this energy from deep within you, it won't be long before you experience a similar phenomenon.

Now just allow this very beautiful Peace to ebb and flow through you, so that nothing in the world matters to you. You are totally free in this Serenity. In your mind hand over to this peace any matters of concern, confusion, sadness, and anything that disturbs you. If you try to itemise each concern, you may unintentionally fire off the very worry, pain or sadness the meditation is intended to prevent. Instead imagine your burdens as a huge bundle, like a Santa Claus sack, and hand this over to your guides. Leave it with them and trust them. They won't take this bundle away and bury it somewhere in the back yard of your mind. Instead they will start unravelling it with you over a period of time, sorting out each piece in a more manageable way. It will take time, but you will get a better result than if you were to worry and soul search as you tried to churn it over in your mind.

Remember, if you started a particular ball rolling in your life, or instigated any action without first asking your guides, it's a little unfair to ask them to un-tangle it for you. They will assist you the best they can, but there is only so much they can do.

Their job is not to live your life for you, only to assist you on your particular path. Like a good parent they may stay silent when they know your request to is something you should be trying to deal with yourself.

That doesn't mean they will leave you in the lurch with those things you have messed up. It simply means you can't expect them to solve your deliberately created problems, only to allow them to find a way through the maze. Best scenario here is to seek their guidance before you make a decision, or take an action, not after.

*For those that have had a change of guides, or are new to this, remember the responsibility is no longer yours but that of your guides, once you start willing the will of the Creator into your life. So there is no need for you to try and make things happen, or to doubt what may or may not be occurring. Building a mutual trust is the first part of this new Journey.

The more you feel you can trust this process the closer you are brought to peace by the Creator via your guides. A good sign your guides are at work around you during the meditation, is when you feel more relaxed and at peace than you previously felt.

When you've finished, thank them sincerely, then slowly open your eyes. Don't rush the returning or awakening process, but slowly allow yourself to slip back into this material world, which we all must live. Remembering they are still with you and never leave you. When we open our eyes, we are open to

Chapter VIII

the physical world, and when we close our eyes, we are open to the spiritual one. Both worlds coexist in harmony, within and without.

If we ever feel we see our guides or any spirit formation when we have our eyes open, there is a good possibility we are seeing dense or lower evolving souls. Pure spirit can't be seen. Density is what makes matter visible in the physical world. Don't worry or concern yourself as to whether you are protected or not. If you exercise the meditation regularly, your guides will take care of those souls you should or shouldn't be entertaining.

Never be fearful. Trust in your guides, the Creator that you are a part of, and therefore yourself. Believe that you are worthy, and a special one-of-a-kind creation of the perfect Creator. How can, and why would, a perfect Creator create imperfections?

Always call them to mind the moment you have any uncertainties or apprehensions, as you would a friend. Remember, when in doubt, call on them.

Don't feel you have to visualise them, or to identify either your guides or God specifically, They know your needs before you even think of them. They know you better than you could possibly ever know yourself. They were with you when you were born, wrapped around your soul. They ensured your soul was not damaged in the birth process, as you descended from that place of purity into this place we call the physical world. And they will be with you when you pass over at the end of this life, to protect you from pain as they guide you onto the light.

As a beginner it is advised you try doing this meditation at least once a week. Then as you become more familiar with the process, you will get a better understanding of your own specific meditation, and how regularly you will need to do it. Your guides will be helping you determine this.

After awhile, you will know the meditation so well that you will feel quite comfortable shortening it to about two to three minutes till, with regular usage, it can take but a few moments. I do a very quick version before I drive, work, walk, make a phone call, or any action I plan. I use this meditation for chakra alignments and lost soul release and the results can be quite amazing.

In one case I can recall a woman entered the room as if she had just come from a funeral, so deeply embedded were the lost souls around her. She admitted to being a worrier, and that she lost sleep because of this worry. When I asked her what was causing her worries, she could only reply in confused generalities. My guide, through me, showed her how to do a shorter version while I was in a trance state, and I could feel the interference around her being pealed off in layers as she went deeper into the release state.

After she returned from the exercise, which seemed to take ages, I asked about her well being, to which she replied yes in a voice I didn't recognise. I opened my eye and it was like I was looking at a totally different person.

She was laughing, more like a chuckle, and said she couldn't help it. When the session was finished and she went to get up from the chair, she said she was feeling very dizzy and very light headed. The owner and staff in the shop knew her well and couldn't believe she was the same person.

In another reaction a person said her mouth was all rubbery, like she had just come from having an anaesthetic injection and found it difficult to talk. In a sense that isn't such a bad description of what happens. It is very much like a person has been operated on and all the unnecessary, useless parts,

Chapter VIII

no longer needed within the person's psyche, have been removed.

The most common comment after a full release is the contentment the person feels. This can be just a nice peaceful feeling through to a feeling of lightness, as if a weight has been removed. I often feel it would be helpful if I had a pair of diver's boots to give people to stop them floating away. In fact one woman joked that if I gave her a paintbrush and a bucked of paint, she would paint the ceiling on her way out.

I had another case where a person had a similar release, but it wasn't till after she had gone home the surprises started. She had a neighbour whose dog always barked and acted savagely every time this woman entered her own back yard. After the release, the woman noticed that when she entered her back yard, the dog's barking and growling eased off, till finally it stopped.

A few days later the dog escaped from its yard into her yard. She was taking the washing out to put on the line, when she spotted the dog in her back yard and froze. A flash of thought reminded her of her morning meditation, and she immediately handed the situation over to her guides. The dog didn't react; in fact it was as if she wasn't even there. After hanging out her wash she slowly returned to the house and called the neighbour who came and removed the dog.

A few days later she tried moving slowly closer to the dividing fence to see if the changes in the dog were permanent or temporary. The dog acted in the same friendly manner as it had when it was in her yard. It wasn't long before she was patting and playing with it as if they had been friends for years. The last I heard of her, she regularly baby-sat the dog when the owner had to go away on business trips.

A more recent story was when I first met a woman friend of my mate Dave back in 2001. The moment I saw her I felt uncomfortable and wanted to move from her company. Dave was shocked when I told him how I felt. He had known her for many years to be a very caring, friendly, genuine and kind person. I just assumed I got it wrong and thought no more of it.

In 2008, a month prior to Dave marrying his very special lady, this person was visiting as part of the preparation for the wedding. She and Dave, who is extremely gifted psychically, were chatting away in the lounge room. Dave quietly asked me would I like to join them in the house. It was then they told me of how this woman was experiencing some very disturbing events in her life. With her permission we did a release meditation. At this point Dave rejoined the main group. The moment I opened my eyes, after the meditation, I could see in the woman what Dave had seen for years. She was beautiful. Not a skerrick of what I had previously seen, only brilliant reflective peace and tranquillity.

There had been a man in her life for almost 20 years who had an embedded and serious psychic infection so powerful that anything or anyone close to him was controlled by it. This entity was not the man himself. I felt he was a good-hearted man, but had a very powerfully imposed emotion over which he seemingly had no control. This woman is in the process of removing herself from his company, and looking for ways to get him healed via an absent meditative healing circle.

I mention this particular circumstance because it caused me to realise that I had made an opinion of her, not based on who she was, but on how an entity, over which she had no power controlled her. How many people do we know that we simply say "I don't know why but that person makes me so angry," or "I just don't like that person." And yet when questioned as to why we are uncomfortable with them, we can't honestly answer, instead putting it down to a gut feeling. I know in my early life, I had a very serious energy from someone else overpower me, causing others to see me as someone I was not, and it was anything but pleasant.

Continued from page 232

> First relax and clear your head of
> Thoughts that fill your soul with dread,
> Then breathing slowly, fill your mind
> With My Pure Thoughts,
> My Light Divine.
>
> And as It swirls around inside,
> Searching out the harms that hide,
> You'll feel the pressure peel away,
> Leaving you to face the day.
>
> And first thing 'fore you start your day,
> Turn your thoughts inward and pray
> That We may Cloak your soul in Gold,
> So hell will ne'er again take hold.
>
> There is a God I proudly say
> A God no longer far away
> That speaks to me, so strong and clear,
> When It speaks Its Words in my ear.

1994

Northern Waters

Someone's fishing in the moonlight out on the bay,
The tides slowly ebbing.
Sitting solo 'gainst the back light,
Summer breezes gently calling.

He hears the call of northern waters,
As he fishes the bay.
He tells his friend he'll get there some day.
She smiles her smile; she tags along.
But like his dreams, she knows he'll soon be gone.

There's a young man in the moonlight,
Out in the bay, the tides slowly rising.
He's always felt it's calling,
Like a past life having its way.

He heard the call of northern waters,
As that life slipped away.
His vow from then is why he's here today
He knew as time slowly slipped away,
His dreams and hopes would all come true some day.

2001

Chapter IX

Reincarnation

When I first started hearing about reincarnation, it was mostly from Christians and family members who knew very little about it. The thought that I would come back as a bug, only to be splattered on the car window screen of someone I had wronged in a past life, did not impress me. Therefore I was not a believer.

Of course I was reminded by my good Christian council that Jesus had given us the example of the rich man up the front of the Temple extolling what he had done for God. The poor man sat up the back, beating his chest saying, "I am a sinner, have mercy on me." The inference being that in our one and only life, there are going to be those who have it all and those who have not. Those who live a good Christian life will make it through the Pearly Gates, while the ones who squander away their gifts, get sent down to stoke the boilers for the heaters of heaven. Though it was never said, the inference was that people with hardships constantly in their life were not following God's way.

I had a problem with this, because I knew of people who had lived by this rule and yet had been dealt a miserable life. I wondered how God could give one person a life of luxury, and another a life or poverty. One person having everything fall into place for them, while the other, who had tried just as hard, had nothing but obstacles, hardships and misery. This did not seem like the actions of a fair and understanding God to me. I stayed with the one life belief primarily because it was part of the faith I followed at that time. The alternative was something I wasn't quite ready to embrace.

Reincarnation became a major stumbling block for me, especially when I finally accepted my psychic gift and started to do psychometry sessions. I can clearly remember telling my guides I would be happy to do psychic work as long as there were no past life or reincarnation stories involved. All seemed to go well.

Then in the late nineteen nineties, and as part of a session, I visualised this young girl wearing an old laced bow peep bonnet and wearing a hoop style dress, with long socks and white shoes. She was being encouraged to get into a boat by her older brother, who I could see had knee length short trousers, long socks, leather shoes, a shirt and tie and a cap, all from the eighteen hundreds era. The girl was obviously very frightened and unsure about the safety of the boat, but trusted her brother's instructions. As I was passing this information onto the woman she said, "Oh I'm getting goose bumps and I feel quite emotional'.

I continued to see this young woman clumsily trying to get into the boat. She was further out from the jetty than her brother could reach. As she tried to right herself, she lost balance and fell overboard. In her panic she somehow got the bonnet caught on something under the boat. This trapped her under the water and she subsequently drowned.

I wondered what this story could mean, and asked the woman if it could have something to do with a past relative of hers who may have died that way. The woman said no and immediately started to cry. She told me how she was terrified about getting into small rowboats, and how, as a child, she

Chapter IX

got into serious trouble when she refused to join her family in boat journeys.

She recalled how a well-planned family picnic had to be abandoned, because the picnic site was across a lake and only accessible by small boat. Just before she left the session, she thanked me sincerely for the very helpful past life reading. I didn't respond to her comments, nor did I accept its premise.

My reasoning and deductions convinced me this person had lost souls around her that had passed over in a similar, tragic way, or I had somehow tapped into a dream laying in her subconscious, which had been preventing her getting on with her life.

The problem with this scenario was that if it was lost soul interference, then the all clear message I got from my guides, after the initial release, was wrong. And if it was a dream, to what did it relate? Dreams don't stay constantly with a person for that long without relating to something of importance.

I saw her again, possibly two or three months later, where she asked me to join her for a cup of coffee. She said at first she was dubious when she had first heard the past life story, yet somehow there was something frighteningly familiar about it. She said it wasn't till she had returned home and listened to the tape recording of the session, that she realised a huge weight had been removed from her.

The reason she had come to see me and to share a cup of coffee was to tell me of the thrilling weekend she had with her husband. For the first time ever she had gone on a boat ride with her husband. She said at first she was very nervous and mildly panicky as the boat shifted to their weight, but once they got going, it was like she had discovered a whole new world. They had travelled from the local marina to a friend's yacht moored at one of the isolated buoys.

On the Light Path — Peter Lyons

I am not sure if this woman was responsible, or if it was just coincidence, however I started to get more people coming to me, asking for past life readings. This only caused me more confusion. Particularly as the stories were relating to times, places and circumstances totally different to the person's current situations.

The more I tried to rationalise each case that came to me, the more I became convinced about reincarnation. My guides assisted me when some people came to me with stories that could well have been a past life. After the initial release, they were able to show me the difference between a lost soul's interference and a past life. I was soon differentiating between the feelings of the lost soul and past life stories.

I knew I could no longer straddle both ideologies; I had to follow what was now a very obvious truth to me. My difficulty was how to deal with my Catholic faith, my Catholic friends and my family.

What I did next was probably instigated as a means of proving to my Catholic collective and myself, that reincarnation was not my imagination influencing the imagination of those that visited me. As a means of checking myself, I would firstly write down what I felt was the past life of the person, or the place where the past life had occurred. I'd then ask non leading question to the person so as to confirm if what I had got was correct.

One of my past life sessions, using this method, was of a person having lived in the Middle East, particularly around Egypt in the time of the Pharaohs. She had been very poor and either disabled or very ill, as I didn't see her living past her fifteenth birthday.

I felt she loved to sing and possibly performed in that life begging for money. As the illness became more severe, it affected

Chapter IX

their vocal chords and throat. Eventually it prevented them from earning a meagre income; this caused a very rapid decline in her health. I wrote this information down and then I asked the person:

"Of the following four countries, which one if any meant the most to you when you were a child, Germany, USA, Egypt or Australia?" Because the person was born in Australia, it would be normal to assume she would have chosen Australia, but she didn't. Instead she said she had always had a thing about the Nile and Egypt, especially when she was very young.

She said that her father had fought in the Second World War in and around the Pyramids. She just assumed she had picked up bits and pieces from what her father had shared with her. I then asked if she could recall her feelings back when she was a child, particularly if she could recall anything emotionally relating to that time in her life. She replied that she loved to do little concerts when she was quite young. She would dress up in grown-ups clothes and sing songs, but that she would become quite horse and breathless without explanation. Her parents had sent her off to a number of specialists, but none could find anything wrong with her.

She said she could also recall her parents telling her that when she did her little shows, she wouldn't dance or move. She said they considered this strange because when she wasn't singing, she would become quite animated when doing any dancing.

She simply didn't combine the two till she was in her early teens. Then she said as a passing remark she had a premonition, when quite young, she was going to choke to death at around fourteen or fifteen. She had even stopped eating small things, such as nuts or lollies, for fear they may get stuck in her throat. But thankfully it didn't happen. I asked, in view of her comment, about having been taken to see specialist for her throat, could she recall if she was a reasonably healthy girl back then. She replied up until puberty she was always getting sick with chest infections. If she got a cold, she would likely get pneumonia; no half measures she laughed. I asked could she recall if her health improved noticeably at any particular time in her life. She said that at about fifteen or sixteen she started to have a whole change of life, like she had become a new person. She put it down to the natural physical changes that came with puberty.

When I told her I got her in a past life as I have described above, and handed her what I had written, she was noticeably shocked, like she had been hit with a revelation. It was like a wall between her subconscious and conscious mind, relating to this matter had suddenly disappeared. She was particularly surprising she hadn't connected all the events herself; so obvious were they to her now.

I continued to get more and more past life stories in my sessions, with each case showing me a little more of the differences between past lives and lost soul interference; each case having a specific and justified purpose for a person to know of their past life experience; each case giving cause for those held back by deeply embedded fears from past life events, to move on with their lives.

The effects of this very steep learning curve were immense. I had to jettison many of my preconceived and rigid ideals and start to look at life from the perspective of a soul living in multiple physical forms. It gave me a totally different attitude to and respect for how God really loves us.

It made more sense to me now why some people seemed to have great lives, while others, no matter how much they tried, still seemed to end up on the bottom rung of the ladder. With reincarnation, everyone eventually gets to climb to the top of his or her ladder, after experiencing all aspect of what the physical world has to offer in a fair and loving way. As we individually achieve this, we expand the love of the Creator in a way no one life could ever achieve.

Assuming I have put a convincing case in favour of reincarnation, who then determines what our next life will be after we pass over? Who determines who will go on to the light and who will be sent back to suffer more ice cream, sun burn, pizzas, puberty blues, romps in the hay, acne, million dollar bank accounts and childbirth?

The answer is not a bearded Deity sitting on a white cloud with one hand pointed threateningly at us, while the other hand pulls the lever that dislodges the trapdoor under us, and sends us "back down." Nor is there a panel of saints, or lawyers, or other auspicious souls just itching to take advantage of us in some way.

There are numerous books, tapes and videos available on the subject of personal improvement, particularly on the subject of creating our own reality. The belief is, whatever happens to us is of our own making, and in a general sense that is correct. I don't believe we create every little aspect right down to kicking our toe for the first time.

I believe while in spirit and in conjunction with our guides we develop a template or draft outline of what it is we need to experience in that next particular life. This template centers on those important areas we know we need to experience. Experience in order that we satisfy any desires that will delay us from our long-term goal.

Once I started to feel comfortable with reincarnation, I began my own personal review relating to what may have been reincarnation connected. To say the awareness and awakening came thick and fast is an understatement.

Karma and Karmic Lessons

There are some very interesting notions I have heard relating to Karma and Karmic lessons that beg mention here. The principle of Karma is when a person passes over and then returns into their next life, those areas where they have wronged someone, will be metered our against them in equal measure.

For example, Bob was a rotten male, cruel father, and a deceitful vengeful, husband. His wife on the other hand, was a loving, subservient, and socially controlled prisoner of his aggressions. His children were also gravely affected in many ways so that their lives, and subsequent lives, were greatly influenced by his serious wrong doings.

According to the popularly believed form of Karma, this man would be born back into a life where the wife would have her way with him, as would the children, so that he would receive back from them what he gave in that past life.

The problem with this scenario is that there would be no growth. He dominated in one life, she then dominated in the next life and he retaliated in the following. Then of course the children would also be included in this merry-go-round, and there would be no end to this tit-for-tat experience. What would be gained, other than revenge?

If a person hits you in the eye this life, the Karma couldn't possibly be equated simply by your having the opportunity to hit that person back in the next life. The matter is far more complex that a straight out transfer of one action for another. What caused this person to strike you in the first place? Did you instigate it or did it come out of the blue? What caused their anger, uncontrolled aggression and purposeful disregard for you? How were they able to commit such an act and get away with it?

Chapter IX

The Karmic lesson would be such that the person, originally aggressing, would not want to travel that road again as a means of expressing their frustrations. They would have to experience the effect this action had on the one they aggressed, as well as the long and short-term implications of that action. There is no way the aggressed could metre out to the aggressor the full implications of the original action. To start with, the aggressed person wouldn't get away with it; no matter what society they both lived in that next time. The aggressor would need to undergo a number of painful life experiences, to fully realise the effects of their actions. They may have to live a number of painful life experiences. This may entail a number of experiences where the original aggressor is unfairly set upon, or imposed upon, by complete strangers.

This applies to us all. What we sow in this life, we reap. If not in this life, then certainly in the next, and usually in a way we couldn't possibly or fully comprehend. Another good reason why we should recall what Jesus said to this matter:

"What you do to the least of God's children, you do to me."
As we are both God's children and part of God, whatever we do to others will comes back at us in a different way in another life.

So basically we are all going around in ever increasing circles, spiralling upwards towards perfection, life after life. From our first time on this physical world, to where we currently are, and eventually to a point where we will never want anything other than what we have at that time, pure bliss and pure contentment.

Fragment or Whole Soul Theory

There are many alternative theories within the Church of reincarnation. One that holds a particular fascination for me is the fragmented soul theory.

On the Light Path

Peter Lyons

I originally got sippets of this theory from spirit in the late nineteen eighties. Since then I have heard similar theories discussed by others, including a version my friend Sharon told me about.

The basic theory is that when we pass over into spirit at the end of a particular life, we spend time in this heavenly place till we decide to return to the physical world. We do this in order that we burn off karma, or negative aspects, as we head towards perfecting our soul. I find it less confronting to use this model of reincarnation when talking to those still influenced by the Christian teaching of one life per soul.

The split soul theory suggests that when some souls pass over at the end of a physical life, they split into many parts, like a seedpod exploding. The individual parts are determined by what they have achieved and what they haven't achieved thus far in that soul's continuing journey. Those parts that still need to learn in certain areas are drawn to a cluster of similar particles with similar learning needs, to form a new soul, while those parts that have learned and experienced as much as they can, move onto that place in spirit that brings contentment to them. I guess you could call this place Heaven.

Using that seedpod analogy, it is like the seedpod opens up, the ripe seeds move on to a place of fulfilment, while the green or immature seeds gather with other immature seeds and start all over again.

Imagine a person who has exercised patience, kindness, understanding and all things that a righteous soul should exercise in a particular life, except for one. This person, for some strange reason, whenever they were anywhere near a cat, wanted to strangle it. Now I'm obviously being light hearted here and am not intending to upset cat lovers. The point being made is that the element within this person, namely a certain need for a tolerance, didn't get sorted out this particular life.

Chapter IX

According to the traditional reincarnationist, this soul would have to return fully back into the physical plane, to almost re-do that life all over again, simply because of one weakness.

In the case of the split soul theory, after this person passed over, all aspects of the soul would continue on to the light, except that part or cell that could not tolerate cats. So that cell needs to reincarnate, but it is not dense enough to reincarnate alone. It must wait for other (parts of souls) elements needing to learn in certain areas, but not necessarily patient with cats.

Now what if there are other cells belonging to other departed persons who loved cats, and these cells are drawn back to the earth plane purely in a teaching roll, so as to help those with a particular cat problem? Neither collection of cells would be able to reincarnate alone, nor would they survive as two halves or a whole soul, so they get shuffled in with other souls who also have some learning to do and zap, with the whack of a doctors hand, they are breathing life into the newly born baby, totally unaware of what other parts they are living with.

What interests me about this theory is that in spirit, soul cells are more inclined to coexist with other soul cells without much difficulty. This happens because they don't have physical bodies to limit or restrict them, or to cause others to see their faults or failings. But once they, as cells, come into the physical world as a part of a collective, they are locked in, with other unknown cells, for that life. In this way they feel the pain as well as the praise, as a collective of not only their actions, but of the actions of the other cells making up this new soul.

An obvious question therefore is what happens to the term "my soul?" Is there a true soul, or are we all made up of soul cells? Does the soul only exist while there is human form, and then after passing over into spirit, only cells?

On the Light Path
Peter Lyons

I believe we are a combination of both. From when we originally started way back before the physical universe. We were a complete soul made up of imperfect or raw cells. This original complete soul or mother ship has within it, other evolving souls or ships. As each cell evolved from one life form to another, even if they have incarnated in combination with other cells from other ships, as they separated after that incarnation. They return back home to the original ship or soul. It is this soul-ship that holds the memory of all past lives of each of its' individual cells. And it is this soul-ship that determines what incarnation the next cell collective and new soul should take.

As clarification, these individual cells are not necessarily locked into their soul-ship exclusively. But can become a part of another soul-ship structure for a period of time. This happens after release of the cell during what most see as death. At the end of the cycle of that particular cell, which may consist of billions of life cycles, or more, it will reunite with the original soul-ship from whence it came.

There is the possibility that certain cells may not necessarily have a direct say in that particular soul's physical person's life. They may be a part of the person's guidance team, and restricted or limited in some way in their assistance. These particular cells may be imprisoned within this person's aura as a means for leaning some aspects of stillness, discipline, and tolerance till that time when they have experienced what their soul-ship knew they needed to experience.

On the other hand there could be juvenile or immature cells having to learn cause and effect. This could be a result of their carelessness with the physical person they are supposed to be guiding. This could explain why a young person might be totally reckless as a teenager, due to these immature cells having more of a say than they should at that time. Then as the juvenile cells mature, the physical person, who was embedded with these juvenile cells, also becomes more mature.

Chapter IX

The now mature cells, see what adverse affect they have had on the physical person they've supposed to be guiding. They see the difficulties this physical person now has to deal with. They quickly learn to act in unison with other cells of that soul rather than out of self will.

Within our physical being are our soul and spirit forms. These two forms can coexist with the minimal amount of cooperation. When these two forms embrace and lovingly accept each other, it is like the two copulate, with the resulting baby being a positive and focused thought. The quality of the thought produced depends and is determined by the more powerful of the two parents. If the person is more inclined to trust the physical world's teachings and ideas, as opposed to their own spiritual-soul combination, then that person's thought will be more materially based. If the person relies on the soul, without the spiritual input, then unrealistic expectations will dominate that person. In this second scenario, the person may talk on a lot of esoteric matters, but their life shows there is very little of it happening in reality. The closer the equality and respect the two inner forms have for each other within the individual, the higher the quality, and better balanced, is the thinking this combination produces.

When two physical bodies interact, as in a physical, personal relationship, the quality of each of these individual people's combined soul-spirit forms, will determine the quality and effect each persons will have on the other. The more the two become at one with their own individual soul-spirit energy, the more likely they are of staying together as a couple. Of course there are degrees of this and in most cases the interaction between the two soon causes each individual's soul-spirit combination to develop and improve, or alternatively give grounds for one or other to separate. I call this interaction between the two persons the sandpaper effect. We don't like thinking we aren't perfect, but in actual fact it is our imperfections that have us here in the first place.

On the Light Path

Peter Lyons

I can recall spirit telling me a story many years ago, while I was preparing metal for welding. I had a rusty old tow bar hooked onto the trailer we used at the hostel and it needed replacing. We had bought a brand new galvanised unit to fit onto the old metal, and I was in the process of grinding back the rust to make a perfect weld.

In my mind, as if I was hearing the brand new galvanised metal talking, I heard, "look at him over there", indicating the rusty piece, "he thinks he's so pretty and perfect. Just wait till he finds out he has to have his rusty outside grounded back before he can come anywhere near me." Then when the rusty piece was finished, I took hold of the galvanised piece and started to cut it back to bare metal.

"How dare you," I could hear it saying in my mind. "I am perfection. I don't need the same treatment as that rusty old piece over there." Of course both the rusty and the galvanised surfaces have to be cleaned back to bare metal in order that a weld can take hold.

My guides, via my rather furtive imagination, were pointing out to me that the shiny presentation we build on our outside is mostly contrived. Unless we accept our faults, and then are willing to make self-corrections, the joining we try to make with another person may not withstand the bumps and bruises the world inevitably throws at us. We may separate from that person, but the need for a relationship invariably leads us to another person, where we again have to face the grinding-back-to-bare-metal scenario.

The day after talking with my guides, I discussed this information I received on the joining of the souls-spirit forms, with my psychic mate Mike, of Sharon and Mike fame. During the discussion, we started to look into what particularly separated couples. We got onto the subject of a person being self-based and another being selfless based. We have tradi-

Chapter IX

tionally been taught that the self-based or self-centred person is wrong. Spirit said that there is nothing wrong with a self-based person.

They then explained what they meant by self-based.

Most people come under the self-based model and have self-survival or self-safety as their core. People need to feel their personal needs and wants are attended to first before they are able to focus on the needs and wants of others. Of course this would include that person's chosen partner, children and blood family.

On the other hand the selfless person is one who, though they to have self-needs are able to adapt and exist fully whether their needs and wants are being met or not.

Traditionally this was the lifestyle of priests, nuns and religious missionaries who successfully lived in environments, totally alienated from the environment from which they had come. That is not to say all missionaries, or religious persons were selfless. In fact, the horrific stories of native peoples being maltreated would more likely be as a result of self-based persons trying to live a selfless life and failing miserably unable to admit it.

From a higher spiritual base, the person who is able to live more the selfless life, as opposed to those that live a self-based life, are more capable of taking an independent role in serving spirit than the person who has needs of self and family over riding their progress.

A very simple example here is what happens when we are trusting. Take a person who has complete faith and trust in God, or their understanding of that power, but yet still locks up their house, even when they are inside. Society supports this person's actions. Insurance companies support this person's actions. Police and lawmakers too support this person's actions. But does the teaching of Jesus support this?

Then there is the person who also has complete faith and trusts in God, but they assume their property will be safe, and so don't bother locking or protecting their goods, even when they are away for a period of time.
Who is right? Who is wrong?

Let's assume both persons are robbed, the first person can claim the loss of property from their insurance company, and may stand a chance of receiving some compensation for that which was stolen. The second person can also make claim to their insurance company, assuming they too are insured, but their reimbursement may be far less.

After such an event, which person will remain as true to their faith as before? Jesus said we can't serve two masters, we learn to love one and despise the other.

If we have total faith in our belief, then we not only leave our goods and property open to theft, we don't insure it either. Nor, however, can we consider it our property. It is the property of God, and its taking is not ours to question. In this instance, the value of the property stolen should not have a serious monetary value, because as it is God given, it will suffice our needs without necessarily holding true monetary value.

Again as Jesus would say, let those who have ears hear, and eyes see. Put simply, it is from within your oneness with what you believe that such a true and correct action for you will be discerned. Not everyone is called to live such a selfless life this time round.

Animal Reincarnation

Another question often asked of reincarnationists is do animals, insects and living creatures, simply have a physical life only? Does the collective cell theory have any application for

Chapter IX

them? If so, do they also evolve from their collective cells and move onto other species, beings, and possibly humans? And what of the many animal appearances psychics see, after the animal has died, surely this must be a sign that animals have a soul?

There are to many animals both domestic and wild that show too high an intelligence, just to simply die and get buried in the ground never to be seen or heard of again.

There is every possibility that we experienced a life as an insect or animal from that cell perspective I have already mentioned. And does it really matter if, as a cell, we were actually learning and experiencing as a frog or a lizard or even an ant, leech, grub, maggot or any other life form? The rules that apply to the cell shouldn't be any different simply because that collective of cells is in one physical body form or another.

I had a wonderful female dog called Paddy. She lived to the ripe old age of 14 before cancer caused me to have her put down. By now I had married and we were living in Gulgong NSW. We both took Paddy to the vet where we said our farewells the evening she was to be put down.

The next day we both got up early and started doing yard work to keep ourselves occupied. My wife mowed the lawn and I trimmed the edges. I was in the shed putting more cord into the machine, when I saw with my peripheral vision, Paddy round the garage door. Nestling herself into the corner as she always did when it was starting to get hot.

At first I didn't twig, but then suddenly in shock I looked up from what I was doing and glanced over at the corner where I thought I had seen Paddy. She wasn't there. At that precise moment, my wife came racing into the shed, in total astonishment telling me she had just seen Paddy scratching herself under the lone Kurrajong tree under where she often laid.

Later that day the vet told us he had an emergency the night before and decided to put Paddy down the following morning, around the same time we both had seen her at our home. If animals have no soul or spirit, or one that only lasts while the animal is alive, then what did my wife and I see, or at least sense, independently of each other?

I believe animals have a soul, just like we humans. As to which soul is the superior, I won't even hazard a guess. It suffices to say animals, such as dogs show remarkable loyalty to their owners. This is often more the spirit of what makes a guide than some humans I have had the displeasure of knowing. That is not to say I believe our guides were dogs, or other animals in their past life. Instead I suggest you the reader, in your quiet time with your particular team of guides, ask them for an answer to this conundrum.

What if we, who inherit human form, are the lower down on the evolutionary scale? What if we are not at the end of the evolutionary chain, from a spiritual learning perspective, but at the beginning of it? In other words, what if animals, birds and insects are what we, as souls, will eventually become before we finish our final time on this planet.

A variant to this theory that makes a lot of sense to me is that there may be no standard process, that the soul-ship determines the type of physical form that particular cell will take in that particular life. In other words some may evolve from bug to human, while others may evolve from human to bug.

We may incarnate as a single cell, or as a collection of cells presenting as a soul, or all possibilities in between, depending on what physical life form we incarnate into.

I don't have an answer to these theories, and if I did, I wouldn't have a need to return for another time on this mortal coil.

Chapter IX

Maybe in my next few lives, I can write a continuum to this current works, with information I gain in between times.

On the Light Path   Peter Lyons

The Return Of The Wirinum

The old black man sat in the shade on this hot and dusty day
His bark and wattle humpy meant that for a while he'd stay
It was the early seventies and a change of special note
Meant the aboriginal people for the first time now could vote

He'd come from deep inside the land once called Wirradjuri
He'd been sent by his elders that the cursed land be set free.
This man they sent was special, he knew the sacred ways
And what he said determine if the cure would go or stay

In the latter eighteen eighties there had been a massacre
Forty thousand natives killed by the English settlers.
The elders were defenceless against this brutal force
All they had was sacred magic, and its use, their only course

Towns built on sacred land were touched by this great curse
English settlers and their offspring felt the curse the worst
Until the country recognised that slaughter had been done
Not a single town would grow, until forgiveness had begun

One night while he was sleeping, two men with evil minds
With courage from a six-pack and a racially prejudiced blind,
Drove into the old man's humpy in a stolen rusty truck
Killed the elder and the chance of peace
This old man could have struck.

The Central West of NSW began its slow decline
With loss of precious business
As the companies closed their mines
Towns reduced to villages and villages into dust
And homes once prized in those past times,
Reduced to rubble and rust
Still no one said I'm sorry, for what they knew was done
So the cures remained to plague the folks
The old man's death begun
Then in the early 80's someone special was sent back,
A white man sent by Spirit to heal the singing track.

He didn't know of Spirit ways, nor that he had been called,
Till one night in his dreaming, the Elders showed him all.
They showed him Secret Knowing
That had once been lost to time
And how to use them wisely, and where to draw the line

He travels through from town to town,
And no one knows he's there
Except the wise old elders who know they need not fear
He sets the wheels in motion of this ancient sacred plan
That only wise folk in the know will fully understand.

2000

Peppermint Tea

We are living in a time of the miracle cure.
Take a pill or a potion and you're cured in the hour.
For some it's the answer but it's not for me,
I fix all my problems with a Peppermint Tea.

My girlfriend's cooking is a fright to see.
I eat what she gives me cause she's bigger than me.
It grows and grumbles in my rummy tummy
Till I fix it in the morning with a Peppermint Tea.

My car is old and the motor is poor,
Accelerator permanently flat to the floor
When you want to get it started,
You don't need a key,
You just hit it in the carbie with a Peppermint Tea.

Now some sniff coke and some smoke pot,
While others again like to try the lot
But if you're into organic and natural like me,
You'll fix yourself a strong bong of Peppermint Tea.

1984

Chapter X

The New Age

"From age to age you gather a people to yourself"
(Taken From the Consecration Of The Catholic Mass)

Most commentators now believe and accept we are currently in the early stages of a new age, the Age of Aquarius, the Age of the Christus, the time of the anointing, or commonly known as the time of the Christ Consciousness. The Greek word for anointed is Christus.

This doesn't mean we will have Jesus descending on a cloud from somewhere up in Alfa Centauri, but rather have an ability to tap into the higher Spiritual knowing and knowledge once exclusive to early pioneers such as Jesus and other well-known shamans.

This new Age is best described with the word, choice.

We have never had as much choice as we are currently enjoying. We will continue to enjoy this ability to choose from now till the next age, around 2,000 years hence. Yet with more choice we have more complexity, alienation, confusion, and distress, which makes us all more unpredictable. It is understandable that most of us will follow the easy options in the first few incarnations to this New Age. Eventually our soul will learn that we won't grow until we take the salmon journey and fight against the popular mainstream ideas.

It is a time when it will seem the saint walks amongst the seemingly unredeemable. It will be a time where there seems to be no absolute in what is right and wrong and no particular religions, spiritual beliefs or principles.

Using the chakra centres as an example, we, as a collective, evolved from the very first Age or base chakra, through the various other ages or chakras, to this current Christus Age or crown chakra. We began our journey back in that lower chakra time. The individual practices were developed for the specific needs of that culture or country. Within those tribes, individuals were chosen who were considered to have some special traits above those of the other tribal members.

This process involved the imposing of rigorous, and sometimes cruel and degrading disciplines, on the chosen ones, by means of ceremonial rituals that were determined by a powerful but unseen few.

The claimed intentions of these ceremonies and rituals were to help the selected ones increase their receptiveness to a perceived higher level of spirituality, while at the same time gaining them a position of higher worthiness within their community. The true aim of this elite few however, was to steer the collective monoculture to their particular way of thinking using these selected few as a puppeteer would use a puppet. When these specially selected males, it being a male dominated society, were deemed to be at the point of receivership of this higher learning, the graduate was said to have received the anointing of God. The Greek word for anointed is Christus.

I recall the words of a very forthright priest who recently said to me:

Chapter X

We seekers of truth make very little difference to those with stone hearts and brick ears. I have no doubt the American political earthquake, which is about to shake us all, will devastate those Christians Churches built on poor foundations. Of course there will always be the great survivors, the spiritual cockroaches, who will continue on long after these religions have gone, but all things including cockroaches serve a purpose in God's great plan.

Spirituality will not die. As long as there is humanity, the Holy Spirit will assist in spreading the real good news among the worlds populous, whether Islamic or Christian, Hindu or Buddhist or any of the many other religions or sects. Even among the followers of your area, of the New Age ideologies, there is still the true spiritual message being spread.

The most interesting of phenomena is the ability of the Holy Spirit to convert and use the most destructive of human forces for long term good. The catch is to remember that our physical life is a terminal one and that God has a whole new, vastly better one, just waiting for us.

Another wise comment came to me from this soul in Spirit, via my guides:

Don't waste time correcting or criticising the beliefs of other who may attack you and your beliefs. Accept that they have another, different journey to the one you are on.
Be willing to share your spiritual beliefs with those receptive to your sharing. If they uncover weaknesses in your spiritual base, ask them for a solution. Take their point of view home to your meditations and ask us for guidance.

If you find people criticising your beliefs but unwilling to show you a clear path to follow, don't be critical of them. Their criticism could be caused by their own personal fears, rigidity to their own belief, or a lack of spiritual knowledge.

Respect what they have to say always mindful they could well be there to teach you something that only their encounter with you can do. Ask that the great light of the Creator be sent in love to them, as you accept it is being sent to you and that they and you may continue on your respective spiritual journeys. Have faith in the Creator's universal purpose.

Finally if you are considering becoming a disciple of The Holy Peddle Of The Rotating Tumbler Of The Virgin Monastery Movement, or such sect, ask yourself; what is my purpose for joining such an organization? What are they offering that I don't have within my own oneness? How strong is my spirituality, particularly my understanding of God, right now?

And finally another quotable quote from Spirit while walking along the ocean in Hervey Bay:

If a boat were to be encrusted in barnacles to the degree that the Christian Church is entrenched in myths, lies and legends, as it is now, the boat would have sunk long ago. The difficulty for any reformer within the Christian Church is to know where the barnacles stop and the boat starts. Sadly the barnacles, so damaging to the Church, are now considered part of the boat. It will take an enormous amount of effort to even attempt to differentiate the two, let alone to try and remove this destructive aspect.

This Aquarian Age we are now entering is the age of freedom, originality, humanism, altruism, detachment, open mindedness and logical thinking. This is the age most likely to threaten religious belief like no other age, and therefore the age we are most likely to see religious wars like never before.

On the Light Path — Peter Lyons

Fear Not

When I look out at the forest and see mighty trees
I'm aware a branch could fall from one
And wipe me out with ease
So does this stop me walking out
through these mighty towers
To sit protected by their shade
among the native flowers?

And when I fly in foreign skies with murderers all round
Do I sit catatonic, until I reach the ground?
What would it be that I most feared if my answer were 'yes'?
I'd have to say the fear of dying, would that be your guess?

I see a woman smiling, a young child at her breast
Protective, caring, loving, a mother at her best
Does she hide, ever mindful her soul constantly crying?
Aware that soon she and her child could be struck down –
Left dying?

There's nothing safe about this place that we all
share and love
With it's core of molten lave, and meteors above
But blissfully we wallow in our own complacency
Until that day that Hell breaks loose, and
then we pray our plea

Yet deep inside each one of us a Perfect Power dwells
There is no force or power that this Pure Peace can't quell
It's where our Guides or Angels live, as does our Inner Child
This Peaceful place is Heaven that dwells inside us all

2001

Chapter XI

How to Survive This New Age

During the cusp time we are currently living in, between the old Pisces and the new Aquarian age, and beyond, the trick will be to keep alive the comparatively new things learnt from humanism and science, as well as continuing to accept the old pagan, mystic and traditional native beliefs, while keeping a healthy recollection of the core truths of Christianity, Islam and Judaism. It is from the blending of all these beliefs and ideologies that we will evolve a new and robust spirituality, one that will be choice based as opposed to rigid rulings, as we establish ourselves into this New Age.

The strength of purpose, with the least resistance from any of the players, will determine just how smoothly we move into this New Age of choice. The stronger the resistance of the old, the more likely we are to discard that which the old held dear, and the harder it will be for us to meld that old learning into this New Age. Or put another way, if the resistance from the old ways is less, the more likely it has of having a part to play in this new spirituality.

From what my guides have told me, there is only one way to transcend to the spiritual world from the physical world, and that is by separating the soul or psychos from the earthly body, in order that the soul can enter into this alternate world or spiritual realm. We call that process, passing over, passing away, or dying.

It may have seemed feasible, logical and attainable in the time of Jesus, and up to recent times, for souls simply to drift skywards in order that we reached Heaven, but learning and experience over the past 2,000 years has shown us that this is impossibility. It is understandable in this Age of Aquarius, an air sign in astrology, that we would be drawn to 'airy' and simplistic solutions. In time we will realize these air answers or imaginings created from another air aspect, that is an uncontrolled and undisciplined use of the mind, cannot sustain us in the longer term. They will only leave us floundering as we try to find the purity amongst the polluted. On the other hand, those who discern and choose wisely, when searching for the pure water from high-up the stream, are the ones who will have their Spiritual thirsts quenched.

There are no longer clearly defined parameters or guidelines for us, as was the case in previous ages, especially under the banner of psyche related practices. There is much vagueness and uncertainty as to whether a person is psychic, religious, spiritual, pagan, occult or an alternative health practitioner. It is common for any of the above to claim psychic status. Not only does this cause uncertainty for those genuine seekers of the truly gifted psychic, it also raises doubts and offers more confusion for those genuinely gifted individuals searching for their own psychic identity. One can only imagine the diverse array of options being offered by so-called psychics.

Amongst well meaning people dabbling in the psychic realm, are some that are using hypnosis. I am not referring to those that use hypnosis with people trying to give up smoking, or where stress and nervous conditions are helped by such method. I am referring to those that use the practice for past life regressions or to encourage trancing. To teach that any

Chapter XI

message or information coming from a person is from this person's subconscious or conscious and is untainted, or that "anything tranced is good enough," is down right dangerous. From what I have already stated, if there isn't any understanding of lost souls, low level interference, or understanding of high or low level guides, then the unprotected seeker can be left wide open to psychic interference.

Commonly, the psychics most people relate to or visit are tarot card, crystal ball or palm reading psychics. From the ones I had encountered there is a need to re-evaluating of the system style and technique being used. It wasn't uncommon for the ones I encountered, to scatter their sessions with words such as, "don't, you should or you shouldn't, never, and no," and many other negative comments without offering an alternative or practical assistance to the person seeking their help.

Very few of the tarot card, crystal ball, palm reading psychics I have encountered seem to have a clear and open understanding as to the spiritual system they use. Most rarely question their source, if they believe they have a source. Many have stated to me, "you should never question your guides or the information they give."

This flies in the face of what I was taught by my guides. The very first thing spirit insisted on with me was not to assume you are a mountain unto yourself. I was told that questioning the source of my guidance simply meant I was affirming my true guides. They knew my hearts intentions better than I did. All my dismissing and commanding would never send them away if within my heart my will was to do the will of the Creator.

I have had more than my share of psychics whom I have not known to be practising psychics at the time, coming to me for a session. As with any person needing release my guides point out when they sense serious interference around that person. They then show that person how to attune to their guides so as to release the interfering energies. Most walk out angry that I'd dared to tell them how to be a psychic, which is not what was said to them at all. Some have even told others of my blatant arrogance and egocentricity, as they perceive it, which only intensifies the negative energy around them. This can make their readings for others even more off base than before. I know of one such person who lost her gift completely and moved away from the area. Another had a serious breakdown, as my guides said would happen, if she didn't start following her guides.

Though there will be those who say a false medium can do no harm, I totally disagree. The charlatan mediums and psychics make it very difficult for the genuine psychic medium to help those people who are serious seekers, because the seeker can't differentiate, which psychic is genuine and which one is not.

In this new Age, because of the lack of guidelines or parameters relating to psychics, it makes it so very confusing for a person who has tried everything and everybody when they are in genuine need concerning some serious matter.

One such person asked me if I was able to do a psychic cleansing of her apartment for her, as everything else that had been suggested for her to try had failed. This young woman had major difficulties with a psychic energy that was causing more than mischief with not only herself, but other members of her family as well.

When I arrived it was obvious from the moment I set foot in the house that there was a major infestation. I asked if she had tried to remove this infestation herself, or if anyone else had tried because it seemed to me that whatever was being used was not only failing her; it was actually intensifying the interference. This is a humorous condensed interpretation of what she said.

Chapter XI

"I have these rose quarts and other crystals here by the window and all through the house, and I cleanse them individually every week by taking them down to the sea and once a month I put them out into the moonlight for further purification. I have cloves of garlic hanging outside all windows and doors and I have drawn a pentagram of salt here in the room where I keep seeing the ghosts. I sprinkle holy water liberally around the house every ½ hour and recite three incantations to St. Jude, followed by this affirmation Mantra I got from a Sia Baba article in a magazine. I have holy pictures of Jesus, St. Germain and Michael the Archangel in each of the bedrooms, and this picture here of John Edwards. I burn sage leaves and regularly dance a sacred dance taught to me by a Balinese Mystic, but I can't use the feather with the sage, as I was supposed to, because I'm allergic to bird feathers. I have had a friend do an aboriginal smoking ceremony three times, and another friend who channels a Hopi Indian, temporarily turned my house into a sweat lodge. Oh! And I say three decades of the Rosary every other Wednesday."

I asked her had there been any noticeable and sustainable changes for the better as a result of all this activity. At first she vaguely answered yes, but when I repeated 'noticeable and sustainable' she said no. She followed this 'no' with apologies for her not having done something right. In other words, this whole scenario had left her feeling very guilty that she somehow was increasing the problem.

Not helping her at all was the advice of her Wicca friend, who had recommended books, spells and potions that became ever increasing as each previous suggestion failed. I asked if her Wicca friend had ever visited her house and she said once or twice, but that the Wicca friend had inferred that this young woman was somehow off track or doing 'it' wrong. This had left her with a very stinky house, soggy carpets, a serious guilt complex, increasing pesky spirit energies and the possibility of eviction from her rented apartment.

On the Light Path   Peter Lyons

We both did the attuning meditation, where she handed the apartment and all its contents over to the power or God, as my Guides through me affirmed and witnessed all that was happening. Then we had a cup of tea. It was during this cuppa time that I noticed how more relaxed and animated she had become.

I checked up on her about six months later to see if there had been any changes and it was as if I was speaking to another person. The house had a fresh new feeling about it and she looked like she had just returned from a holiday.

In the case of another woman who asked me to do a release on her house, she said that the place was usually wonderful and peaceful, until her daughter returned from her 'happy times' away with a particular boy friend. The woman contacted me two weeks after the daughter had returned, and, on my arrival, the first thing I noticed was that the place reeked of garlic. She explained that she had visited a New Age bookstore and had been told by the Gothic lady serving behind the counter that garlic would ward off evil spirits. I showed her how to do the release and then waited for the daughter to return home from work.

I met the daughter and asked if I could talk to her privately. I said I was picking up drug use by her and her boy friend. She strenuously denied this. I said that because of the mindset they must have had when using the drug, they had encouraged low-level spirits into her mother's house. I explained that the drug use in itself was not the issue here but the state of mind they were in when using it. I said that her mother's guides had dedicated the house to goodness and that if she or her boyfriend continued their dope use with that particular mind attitude, there would be a serious incident happening to her.

Chapter XI

I explained this wasn't a threat, but a prediction from her guides. I said I could see her involved in a big argument or fight within the next six weeks, the result of which would force her to leave. Three or four weeks later, she and her boyfriend, who had been smoking dope and drinking heavily, ran over the neighbour's dog and smashed the front fence. This resulted in a very big fight and the police had been called. They were both arrested for the damage to the fence and killing the dog and for a large quantity of marijuana found hidden in the boot (trunk) of his car.

He got a jail term, while she got a suspended sentence. She moved out of her mother's house and closer to where the boyfriend was jailed. The house is now spotless and the mother has told the daughter never to return till she has dried out, straightened up and stops her lying and thieving.

It is important to note here there is nothing wrong with crystals or incense burning any more than having fresh cut flowers, room deodorants, wind chimes, dream catchers or meditational mood music. When it comes to psychic healing and psychic readings, it must be remembered the source of this energy is not these inanimate objects, but is the power that dwells within us.

Some people have said they are psychics and proceed to explain astrology or numerology to me as their psychic tools. Though there are many astrologers and numerologists who are psychic in their own right, the actual study of these techniques is not in itself psychic. For those that don't know, numerology teaches that the name we are given, and the date and time of our birth, creates a vibration that affect the soul's journey and that some numbers and names have more power than others. While I agree generally with this, I note for example, that certain persons with certain names have a similarity in their actions or personality, it can be said that this is not the case in all instances.

Astrology relates to the time of our birth and how the vibration of certain planets affects us physically at various times throughout our life. It shows a road map and the interaction we have with the places (planets).

If you accept the fractured soul theory I mentioned in the reincarnation section, it could be they are a comparatively new soul made up of a compilation of new learning cells. When a soul has already had some experiences there is no need for that soul to undergo that learning again. In such a case, our guides move us through that particular area with the least amount of interference from delays or obstacles. In this case, the astrology reading can seem more miss than hit, because the predictions, having already been experienced in another life, won't occur this time round, or if they do, they will occur in a milder, less noticeable way.

The astrologer or numerologist gifted with a psychic sense can give an even better interpretation of a person and their chart, without having to incorporate the need for a person's historical record. They can do this because they are seeing the physical path via the chart, while psychically receiving the spiritual aspects from the person's own guides.

There is another element that affects our soul's journey and what path we may have to live physically. Because we may not have necessarily achieved what we were meant to achieve in a particular incarnation, we may have slowed down the overall blueprint planned for a particular time.

Every action of a human person, and the subsequent reaction, creates a tapestry or blueprint that future generations use for their particular learning or journeying. If that blueprint or tapestry is not there, or is delayed, then the process or learning, experiencing and therefore expanding, is slowed down.

Chapter XI

This is where the volunteers come in. These souls are rarely heard of or recognised in the earth plane, but are the kings and queens in the spirit world. They are the true saints. These are the ones that choose to return to the earth plane to assist the overall growth of humankind by taking on unnecessary adversity in order that the growth continues at a determined level, in accordance with the higher will. If you're wondering who they are, look among those who live in intolerable situation, are treated inhumanely, unkindly, and unfairly and yet still seem to have a wonderful attitude despite their appalling conditions.

In our society they are the ones who give us hope, who give us a reason to fight for peace and to want to make the world a better place for all.

In other cultures however, and I believe this is the case in some beliefs in India, these people are considered to be of a lower casts and not to be assisted out of their miserable circumstances. From the guides' perspective, to not assist these persons, is the very reason there will be future need for such souls to have to volunteer again and again, so as to rectify that which such thinking creates.

The more we assist and are touched by the lives of these people I have described, as opposed to those that deliberately get themselves into a selfish state of attention seeking, the more likely we are to quicken the evolving, or manifesting of the collective soul's journey. Sadly, the latter gains our attention far more than the former. Hollywood nobodies, poorly nourished models, drug taking pop stars and self absorbing celebrities fill the pages of most magazines, TV talk shows and even news reports.

An area of particular vagueness, loosely gathered under the new age umbrella, is that of spiritual healing and alternative health practices.

A number of these self-made healers base their diagnosis on what they claimed they've read in books by such authors as Louise Hayes, Deepak Chapra, Wayne Dyer and others. I must stress here that I am not refuting what these authors have said, written, or teach because I have not read any of them. I am referring to those that have chosen to take what suits them from these authors' works to support their own egos. I am a good psychic because I am a very good sceptic. I discern all things against Truth and if it doesn't ring true, it usually isn't, at least not for me.

The original Reiki technique was definitely handed down by spirit to a particular community at a particular time, for that time and those people. Spiritually based healing or these kind of healing techniques, are not things you can buy, nor is the process exclusive to any particular system. The power, and therefore spirit, speaks through anyone willing to be a channel, and gives whatever is needed to whoever is in need. If a genuine Reiki practitioner listens to their inner guidance, they will definitely be directed to an appropriate healing method. This will come from their guides working within them, not from an old process that no longer applies for today's needs. Computers software programs have system upgrades from time-to-time. Wouldn't that also apply for a spiritually based healing process as well?

There are many people who are naturally empathic, that is, they can pick up the feelings, emotions or pains of other people. If someone is doing a healing on them and they haven't been shown how to properly protect himself or herself or the person they are working on, the healer can actually transfer emotions to that empathic person. White washing with white light is not enough. The healer has to call on their guides from deep within, and the empathic person doing the same, to prevent the transfer of these lost emotions or feelings.

Chapter XI

Nothing has energy in itself, but it acts as a focal point for a psychic. When two psychics, or persons concentrating on a psychic based matter, interact in any way, they create a focal point. For example, when a person comes to a healer, the intention in that person's mind is that the healer has an answer to their particular ailment or problem. The healer, on the other hand, wants to achieve whatever good he or she can, relating to the patients needs.

However, the person on the table may either be blocking the necessary changes needed for a physical healing, or not even know that their ailment is not physically based. The energy now swirling around both the healer and the patient is totally confusing to say the least. This becomes more intense when the healer is less knowledgeable to a matter than the person on the table, such as is the case when a psychic, in good faith, allows a healer to work on them.

If a doctor were to visit other doctors, in a collective environment, and those other doctors were less knowledgeable than he, they could still override him and his judgement, even thought he is perceived as an authority. This same situation occurs in spirit. Even though the patient may be far more aware of a particular ailment they have then the healer, the healer, and the healer's guides, will have the control.

The patient's guides can only watch, hope and pray that the guides of the healer are at least hearing some of what they try to pass on.

A serious weakness with these healers and their practices, as with many psychics, and much of New Age practitioners in general, is the lack of encouragement for self-empowerment given to the client. Instead of encouraging the person to self-help, these practitioners lean more towards encouraging dependency on the practitioners and their practices. This is done by encouraging that person to continually and repeatedly return to the practitioner for ongoing healing, or in the case of clairvoyants; psychic readings. This simply entrenches this person's problem by creating a reliance on the healer or psychic, which in turn, causing the person to doubt their own inner healing skill; a skill we all have if we wish to use it.

The best healers are not without, but within. We don't need to rely on someone outside of ourselves to administer healing to us. Our guides are our healers and the more we encourage people to interact with their guides, the less there is the need for external healers.

That is not to say there isn't the initial need, possibly over a couple of sessions, for some people to have external help, either in the form of spiritual healing, physical manipulation, or manipulative massages. So long as the healer is aware that the patient has personal healing guidance, and therefore encouraging the patient to utilise this personal guidance, there shouldn't be a problem.

I must stress here that the kind of healing I am referring to here is that which comes under the heading of alternative healing practices: Practices that incorporate spiritual or psychic interaction as part of the healing.

A method of spiritually based healing I was shown back in the late eighties is spiritually guided healing. It was this early form of healing which was the cause of me being banned from the psychic research centre in Mudgee NSW.

It consists of the healers, or persons willing to participate, acting as witnesses. While the person being healed, with the aid of their guides, is lead to do their own healing. It works best when the person lies on a table or flat surface, so that the witnesses can stand around them freely, moving to where they feel their own guides wish them to be. After an attuning meditation, the person goes into a deep state of relaxation, close to trance status.

Back in 1997, not long after I first met Mike, who had just become Sharon's partner, they invited me to move in with them till I could find a place of my own. Though Sharon had seen me work and knew of my gift, Mike had no idea, other than what we had told him. For this reason I pretty much kept my skills and gifts to myself, till one remarkable night.

He has a very serious back ailment and he was constantly in severe pain. Sharon suggested to a very sceptical Mike that we do a spiritually guided healing with him. After much reassurance, Mike gave us the OK to try. We got him to lie on the lounge and to do the attuning meditation. Sharon and I were directed by our guides to stand, one at his head and the other at his feet. Mike's guides then started to work on the physical, emotional and spiritual areas deep within Mike that could have been causing the illness.

As Sharon or I felt different things going on within Mike, we would voice the specifics out loud, as did Mike, if he felt, heard or saw anything happening. I clearly recall, when I had been standing at his head, seeing a series of triangles in place of Mike's backbone, moving in time with his breathing, like they were floating on a gentle wave. Sharon had visions of intense light concentrated around his lower back, where his ailment was at its worst. Mike also had visions of light and imagery around the areas where he had experienced the most pain.

After about a half hour or so, with Mike sounding more likes he was sleeping than healing, Sharon and I both quietly adjourned to the kitchen for a cuppa. Another 20 minutes or so, we heard a stirring in the lounge room, followed by a noticeably loud thud, and then hysterical laughter a few seconds after that. We rushed back into the lounge room to find Mike had rolled off the lounge and was lying on the floor, giggling like a drunk-man.

He awoke and reached for his smokes lost his balance and fell off the lounge. He described feeling like he had been anaesthetised. The session didn't get rid of his condition, it certainly gave him the best sleep he'd had in a very long time. Mike was so impressed with the changes that had come over him that he asked us to show him more of this psychic process.

The three of us began holding regular psychic circles, based on the relaxing meditation. Mike quickly showed signs of being a trance medium. He began experiencing tingling sensations around the back of his neck, a feeling of euphoria, and an overpowering light headedness. Assurance by both Sharon and myself that all was well and that he had no need to be frightened, he started to allow his guides to expand this gift for him.

It was during one of these sessions that Mike had his first full trance. We had been meditating as per usual, and not really expecting anything to happen. I was feeling quite bored with the proceedings, as nothing much had happened for quite a few of the previous meditation sessions.
Suddenly Mike started to act in a restless manner. Sharon and I both looked to find him with his eyes closed, and his hand up at his neck. We immediately felt, from what our guides were telling us, that Mike was in trance. Both of us, in turn, asked Mike questions, till finally we had a story of the character that had entered Mike.

The period was the 1940's in Fascist Italy, and the scene was a dark cobblestone alleyway, winding between old stone or brick buildings. I could see, in my imagination, a young man, possibly in his mid twenties, sitting in a small corner of these buildings, holding his hand to his right shoulder, near his neck. He kept telling us he was OK, that he just needed to get

Chapter XII

his breath back. He knew he had been shot, but that he would be OK as soon as he had rested.

It seemed, from what we gleaned from conversations with him, speaking through Mick, that he had been an active Fascist, working for Mussolini. After realising how wrong that was, he changed camps. He had been working for the underground, till someone recognised him, and assuming he was still with the Fascists, took him to this spot and shot him. He still believed he was alive, and that he could reconcile himself with the underground, just as soon as he got his energy back. My guides told me he had refused to move onto the light till he had put things right with the underground members, as he didn't consider himself worthy of serenity, and therefore the light offered, till that had happened.

It took quite a time to convince him he was in spirit, and that the war had ended more than fifty years earlier. Finally, and this would have been because Mike's own guides would have reassured him what we were saying was the truth, his soul was released from his locked-in status, and we saw him heading towards the light. Mike returned to his physical form, and, like anyone who has tranced for the first time, experienced the unique emotional aftermath of such an awesome occurrence. It was the one and only time Mike has had such a trance session. He has had many encounters with lost souls, but not coming to him in such a manner.

This was the beginning of a very steady spiritual growing experience for Mike, who today is probably one of the best psychics I have seen..

Song Of Madness

I've been writing a song of madness, the words
I can't explain.
My mind starts rushing backwards. Am I totally insane?
And her eyes keep coming to me as she passes
through the door.
She's asking for an answer for the one's that came before.

She passes right on through me, but part of her remains.
I can't control my actions and I know she's in my brain.
I can feel my body reaching and I know I'm up to high.
But I know that I must follow the ones that never die.

I'm spiralling above her like a mist that can't be seen.
I have no fear of falling cause I know she's in between.
And I see a body lying and I realise it's me.
So empty still and lifeless, my mind's completely free.

I've been writing a song of madness, the words
I can't explain.
And my mind starts rushing backwards, am I totally insane.

1976

Chapter XII

Remote Viewing Experiments

Around the time I first started to seriously compile this book, at the time where I mentioned I bought the original laptop, I went looking for material that I could use as a starting point. I happened to mention what I was looking for to the owner of the bookshop where I did my weekly psychic session. He suggested a number of books one of them was the Psychic Warrior by David Morehouse, written by one of the psychics that had worked on a project with the CIA from its earliest times.

David clearly explained how the CIA had recruited a number of military personnel who had shown an interest or signs of psychic abilities, of which he was one. The initial aim was to see how far the CIA could take this psychic ability as a tool for military purposes. It wasn't long before they had some of these recruits psychically going to places that were otherwise impossible to enter physically.

He explained how they had successfully gone behind enemy lines to find missing US military personnel, spied on secret Russian bases and installations, and even took a peek at the outer planets, including the moon and Mars.

Because he came from a Christian perspective, the difficulties he faced personally as he grappled with this procedure were enormous. His primary obstacle was the similarity of the project's objective to the occult practices his Church would have strongly taught against.

I could fully understand how he'd felt, especially while he used remote viewing to find a friend who had been killed in a South American country some years earlier. It was from that time onward, after sensing a dark presence around him as he searched for his friend that his journey into his own self-described personal hell began.

I was totally shocked and concerned at the thought such experiments were going on with little or no protection being offered to the participants. Also that such a project had existed with very few boundaries or limitations, and that the greater part of the experiments' details are still top secret today.

It wasn't just the Americans who were experimenting with this psychic Pandora's Box. The Russians had also been doing similar research. I have been unable to find much detail on their experiences.

The name Joseph McMoneagle kept popping up in David's work, as part of the CIA project, so I went looking for any books he may have published. I found, and subsequently read, three of his works. They were the Stargate Chronicles, Remote Viewing Secrets, and The Ultimate Time Machine.

The Remote Viewing project was a science based project and therefore based on those scientific norms. McMoneagle and his science-based team believed remote viewing was something of the human mind's creation, and totally within the individual's control.

If this were the case, then there would be little or no restrictions as to what, where, or when a person got information. Even in the many examples given of the successes of the Remote Viewing program, there were as many misses as there

Chapter XII

were hits. Why wasn't this enough for the researchers to at least look at the possibility of influence outside the individual's control, such as a collective consciousness or similar bodies, power or entities?

It could be said that indeed there was a belief that other psychics could intercommunicate psychically, hence why they set up very stringent rules and protocols. The whole purpose of the protocols was based on the assumption that psychics are mind readers. But, there is a tendency for psychics, clairvoyants, mystics and the like, who don't believe they are linked to guides, to work from shortcuts of this protocol, if from any protocols at all.

McMoneagle and the SRI group, along with the scientific community generally, accept the paranormal in terms of provable and repeatable in their experimentations and that the remote viewers or psychics are the source of this phenomenon alone.

In the Remote Viewing Handbook, he explains in more detail the disciplines and guidelines that should be observed and those areas that should be avoided. Anyone reading McMoneagle's material will see the similarities to what I am saying, as I have received it from my guides and what he is saying is from a scientifically gained method. The difference however is that the system they use works without an inner protection, because they don't accept or understand the existence of this inner protection. The system I am recommending as an alternative, works totally with the inner protection of guides or the work doesn't begin.

Though this remote viewing team doesn't know it, nor seem willing to accept it, they have been lead to those places they visit, by guides. The question is who is guiding them and how safe is that guidance.

Even looking at the guidelines McMoneagle highlighted in his book, such as the remote viewer being conscious of his or her moods, status and emotions before doing the remote viewing? What if, unbeknown to the viewer or their employers, the target was a place, known to the person's spiritual guides, to be seriously dangerous for them to visit psychically? What choice does the operative have when their guides' message opposes the command given by their employer? Assuming the viewer doesn't know he or she has guides, they will sense a confusing push-pull sensation.

Under normal circumstances the person will assume this to be some natural human trait, and will therefore override their guides.

Where then does this leave the person's guides? Do they continue feeding that person information, knowing it will continue to cause a conflict within that individual? No, they will instead draw back and leave the person to their own means. If this person continues to draw in towards the target, there is a good chance negative energy will replace that person's guides, leaving that remote viewer very vulnerable to whatever awaits them.

This explains to me why, not only remote viewers such as David Morehouse had trouble of a mental nature, but also why others, dabbling in similar forms of psychic practices, such as astral travel, could well end up in difficulties of a similar nature.

For me as a psychic to do any work without oneness with my guides, is equal to a soldier going into battle naked, with no idea of the enemy or their capabilities. Remote viewing can be a very dangerous experiment, as this above example shows. It is no wonder that more than a few of the participants lived difficult personal lives after leaving the project.

Chapter XII

In a number of the remote viewers experiments there had been attempts to change the thinking, or mind set of certain bodies. This was done in order that good outcomes prevail from whatever decision these bodies may have intended. There is a very clear possibility such a remote viewing group could affect an individual, and that is when they tap into the lowest of spirit energy. To do this the remote viewing operative would have to have next to no moral scruples, as would be the status of the subject they were working on.

Again however, this process would be thwarted, as even the most dastardly of these operatives would have high-level guides. A final point relating to the McMoneagle remote viewing books is his belief that astral travel and remote viewing are not the same, and I have to agree with him. Remote viewers know they are still in the room, but that they are viewing and sensing, as if looking into the places they visit, whereas an astral traveller believes they are actually at the place they are viewing, and are a part of the scenario.

When the remote viewers looked in on a particular place, person or situation, they were able to have this confirmed by another psychic or viewer who had not in any way been contaminated, prompted, or interfered with by what the first person had received. Astral travel has not, to my knowledge, been scientifically verified, and in most of the cases I have seen, has most definitely been contaminated.

It is my belief that most people with even the most basic development of psychic abilities have experiences of astral travel, remote viewing, dream travel, energy interaction or feelings in either their conscious or their sleep state. It is our Guides that imprint these situations, places or memories on our mind and so real are they, we actually feel it is physically happening to us. We know from experiments that the mind can trigger all kind of physical responses.

On the Light Path

Peter Lyons

When we deliberately try to do any of this form of travelling, be it either astral or remote, without proper precautions, we leave ourselves wide open for any entity to superimpose whatever place, person or circumstance they wish, for whatever reason they may have. A simple asking permission and connecting to our guides in a state of oneness precludes any problems of other energy implanting us with their wishes.

I have had numerous dreams where I have visited places that I have never physically been to before, and though I don't recall most of these, I have enough of a memory of the event to feel certain that they were more than just imaginings.

In one recent dream visit I was a young man of about 19. I was either in El Salvador or a similar country. I was walking down a narrow dead end driveway or loading dock alley. On the left was the back of a restaurant and beyond, further into the alley, was a storage area directly behind the restaurant. I can recall someone approaching me, an older, more mature person, who was either smoking a cigar or thick cigarette with a cigar like perfume. I recall this person talking to me as I walked down this driveway, and he was in no way threatening, even though I did have a feeling of uncertainty and of mildly being unsafe. I don't recall much more of the event other than being very much alone, frightened and lying on the ground with a feeling of total helplessness. Then my feelings changed, and I wasn't fearful anymore. I had a sensation like I was drifting away from the scene, not with any vision, but simply feeling light, floating, contented and totally peaceful.

The next day I asked my Guides what that was all about. They explained that the young man had been killed, but his soul had not been released. So while my body was asleep they sent me, that is my soul, to him as their representatives. It was as if I, my guides and his guides became as one producing the strength for him to move on. When the work had been done they returned me to my sleeping body.

Some may say this is not unlike when they have astral travelled, and this could well be the case for some. The difference with this scenario to astral travelling is in this instance, I had no control, or pre planned idea of where I was going, nor that I was actually going to go anywhere, whereas astral travellers believe they pre determine their destination before entering a sleep state.

Also there is a need for the person having such experiences, such as I had, to know it is our guides, and not some other entity doing the moving to and from different destinations. The best way to know who is doing the guiding is evident in how you feel after you have woken up. No matter how scary the circumstance of what is recalled, you should first and foremost always feel safe. In my case it wasn't unlike being in an interactive movie. You will also experience a feeling that you have achieved something good even if you aren't fully aware of what it is you have achieved.

Spirit often uses people who are less affected emotionally to assist those souls having difficulties passing over. Even in this dream state we must be as trusting of our guides. If there is no trust we could panic, cause this soul to panic, and thereby cut off the assistance our guides are offering them. Spirit therefore will only use us if they know we fully trust them, and our regular meditation with them is how we achieve this.

There was another sleep case that occurred where I should have felt very frightened and in a state of shock. I was an observer standing behind someone who was sitting on a bench between two people. On the other side, across from where I was observing, was another person. A fourth person who seemed to have come from a toilet block to my left stood behind the person sitting opposite. This fourth person handed what he claimed was an unloaded pistol to this person sitting opposite, and got him to aim the gun across the table towards the person sitting in front of me. Just as this person aimed the gun, the fourth man pulled out another gun, quickly placed it behind this person's ear and fired. This caused the now dead person holding this supposedly unloaded gun to involuntarily pull the trigger, and his gun went off.

The next thing I know, I had become this person I had previously been standing behind. My concerns were for the dead person opposite and for someone to apprehend the person who was now fleeing from the scene. I went to get up to see if I could help. It was then I noted something soaking my shirt around my shoulder. As I looking I could see blood pumping out through my shirt and I realised I had been shot. The next scene had me running through what looked like a pathway in a long row of sugar cane or wheat. The sky was becoming overbearingly white, and the sugar cane colour also started to fade into a brilliant and painful white. I was lying on the ground and fading in and out of consciousness when the dream ended.

It was weeks later that I remembered the dream and I asked my guides what it meant. They told me I had helped another soul pass over. I asked why had no one used a mobile phone to call for help, as someone must have had a phone? They told me this event had happened back in the nineteen fifties in an Italian community. When I asked was it in Italy or possibly Queensland amongst the Italian migrants, they just smiled and said Thank you for your help. They didn't need me to know.

It is most important I reiterate that of all the work I have spoken about in this book, be it psychic sessions, releases, or dream state work none was instigated or create by me. They occurred without my knowing. I had neither control nor intention of creating any of them. To an outsider it would seem they just happened. Yet they weren't committed against my will. So trusting am I of my guides, that I have given them total permission to do so anytime I can be so used.

Chapter XIII

I would not be having these events occurring if I didn't know and trust my guides, or that they didn't trust me. I say this because there have been those who have asked me to help them develop their psychic skill for the wrong reasons. It may have been to get information for selfish reasons, or to psychically visit a relative in another country, or to frivolously interact with a deceased relative. Others just wanted to make money or have it as a material source of income. This is a sure way of guaranteeing nothing psychically will eventuate, or if it does, that it won't last for very long.

We are meant to be channels of this power of pure peace. To be used properly we must learn to trust this power so that it can actively use us without us balking every time it starts working. To develop this trust is a lifelong exercise for the psychic. It is a sign of love to us from that power within.

On the Light Path

Peter Lyons

It All Depends On How You Plan Your Day

How many times have we thought we've
found the mystery to life
Only to find when the testing comes,
those answers disappear
One thing searching shows up, that always stands out clear
When you think you've found the answer,
there's a challenge very near

We folks have made time savers, from when time first began
Yet the more devises we create, the less time seems at hand
Maybe as we all grow old, the more our mind will see that
The best way we can spend our life is under an old gum tree

Yeah life can be wonderful, and life can be a pain
It can lift you up like an eagle or drop you down again
Yeah life can bring sunshine, or it can bring you rain
It all depends on how you face your day

We constantly walk tight ropes, and have our share of falls
If we only see our bruises, then we don't learn much at all
We can blame the other fellow or claim our lot's unfair
But who's going to cry with us; who else really cares

1979

Chapter XIII

Channelling

Rosedale And My Koumala Home

Mike, Sharon and I have often receive channelled information. This is the full scenario of a case where channelled information we received set a change to my future path at a time when my future seemed settled. It is interesting to note how some of the information we received ran parallel to what were later to become actual events.

For quite some time, over a period of at least a year, Mike, Sharon and I kept getting that I would be moving from my very comfortable little home in Hervey Bay to an unknown destination. Sometimes we'd get north and other times we'd get south.

In early 2002, after a very successful run with a psychic column in a local Maryborough newspaper, I was told the paper was to close down. Within a very short time my regular bookings had dwindled to almost nothing, so that by July 2002 I was applying for unemployment benefits. As part of the deal, I had to register with an unemployment agency, and openly search for work. I was asked what work I had done to that time, and I informed the woman that I was a psychic medium, explaining about the column in the now-defunct newspaper. Though still professional in her attitude, there was a noticeable coolness in her attitude toward me. As part of the deal, she explained that within three months, if I wasn't successful in getting a job that I would have to join a retraining programme. Without my control my mouth said, "I won't be on unemployment benefits in three months time."

Again, spirit had overpowered me, because obviously they knew more about where I was heading than I did. In late September, I received a phone call from my brother to let me know our mother was very ill and that the cancer, which had taken both her breasts a few years earlier, had returned with a vengeance. I flew to Sydney where it was confirmed that mum indeed had cancer and only had a few months to live. As I was the only member of the family who had time available, it was suggested by my mum's doctor, and supported by the family members, that I become mums care-giver. On the 23rd of October 2002, three months to the day from when I had started on the dole, I was transferred from the unemployment benefits to sickness benefits so as to care for my mum. Mum passed away on the fourth of November 2002 at age 81.

On my return to Hervey Bay, I revisited the employment agency to find out when the carers' pension ceased and when unemployment benefits restarted. I was informed that the carer's pension would continue being paid till early February 2003. When my file was opened she found a note she had written to herself about what I had claimed concerning my three months claim. It was then she informed me she was a member of a fundamentalist Christian church and her church had told her what I, and other psychics, was doing was evil. As if I hadn't heard this before. She said she had made a bet with other girls in the office on the outcome of what I had said and she lost. With her permission, I gave her a free session.

Chapter XIII

So impressed was she that she left the church and further recommended me to her friends to visit for sessions prior to my leaving the Bay.

On the third of February 2003, three days before my birthday, the carers' pension ceased. My brother John, who was the executor of the will, phoned me on my birthday to inform me that my share of mum's inheritance would arrive on the 10th of February 2003.

The overall outcome of this meant I was provided with three months unemployment benefits, cared for with the carers' pension that allowed me to see my mother, and be with my family, both before and after she died, and kept financial till mums inheritance money had come through, all thanks to spirit.

Added to this, of course, was the spreading of more good news concerning spirit's work to the staff of the unemployment agency. But the story doesn't end there.

It was in the February-March period of 2003 that Mike and Sharon got news from spirit, indicating that I would be moving soon from Harvey Bay. In mid-March, Mike phoned me to say he had seen listed in a real estate agent's booklet, a house and post office for sale at a place called Rosedale not far north of Bundaberg.

A week or so later, Mike, Sharon and I drove up to Rosedale to take a look at both the town and the property. As we sat in the park opposite the house waiting for the real estate agent, we started to get relevant information from spirit. There were two buildings at the place, one the Post Office building in cream and mission brown colouring, while a very old house stood to the right and slightly back. Mike kept saying that there was something about the Post Office building itself, which reminded him of an old church. Sharon said maybe we were picking up that it would be turned into some sort of spiritual centre. When we focused on the old house, the three of us strongly sensed a very evil feeling concerning one or possibly two rooms in the house. Mike felt it could be a bedroom, while Sharon thought it was the lounge area. As to the town, I was picking up changes concerning the motor garage on the right-hand side coming in and a feeling that the police station should not be there. We were all getting strange feelings concerning structures within the town, that we felt either should not been there, or were in some way different. We were unanimous however; in believing this was to be my new home.

The inspection surprised us because we had envisaged things to be in the house and the post office that weren't there, such as the smelly and dirty lounge room or bedroom. After inspecting both the old post office building and the house, I put forward an offer, which was about $5,000 less than what the owner was asking.

We were absolutely positive I would get the place at this price, so you can imagine our surprise when, a month later, we received news that the place had been sold. What was spirit on about? Why had they given us all this information?

Separate to Mike and Sharon's searching for me, I had found a shed on a small block of land at a village on the beach at Clairview, about halfway between Mackay and Rockhampton at a price I felt was within my budget. Because of the very strong information Mike, Sharon and I had got from spirit, I had delayed making contact with the sellers of the Clairview property.

It was now late May and I had just been informed by the owner of the property at Hervey Bay that he was planning to put the property on the market, that he had had an interested buyer, but that they had wanted the house unoccupied.

Chapter XIII

My very good friend Dave had moved in with me for a few months till he could find somewhere to live after he and his previous lady friend had split up. Not only did we have to find a new place for me to live, we had to find Dave and his beautiful dog Duke a place also. Duke was no normal dog; he was a cross between a Doberman, a Rottweiler and a Great Dane. He was taller and broader than me when he stood on his back legs and considered himself a third person.

Dave, who worked as a mechanic, had been offered an old Nissan bus, and as it was too small for him and Duke. He suggested it might work for me. With the assistance of our neighbour Jeff, he converted the old 1980's model bus into a mobile home. At the same time Dave and I started working on building a small room in his workshop, enough for a bedroom till he could find somewhere else to live.

I finally got notification from the owner saying we had to be out by the end of July. With my newly out fitted Nissan Urvan bus I headed north to check out the shack at Clairview. I called in to Mike and Sharon's, who were now living at South Kolan, just north of Bundaberg, where we got further information from spirit concerning where I would be living next. Mike kept seeing a church and wondered if I may still get the old Post Office at Rosedale.

It was Sunday when I arrived at Clairview and it had taken me two days to get there from Mike and Sharon's. I drove up and down the only street in Clairview and couldn't find a for-sale sign anywhere. On a final pass before heading up to Sarina, I came across the shed. I asked the people living next door if they knew anything about the place, and they told me it had been sold in the January or February.

There had been three other places I had visited at Clairview, still listed at the real estate's WebPages on the Internet, which had been sold at least two or three months before. It goes without saying that I drove to Sarina in a rage. I stayed overnight at the caravan park in Sarina, preparing my double barrel blast for the real estate company for the next day.

On arriving at the real estate agent's office the next morning, I was greeted by an older, scatterbrained woman whose replies to my many questions gave me no confidence in her or the company at all. She disappeared behind a false wall flushed and red-faced and returned a few moments later, with a younger, pleasant faced person. It was my first meeting with Tracey who, along with her husband Ian, and their sons, have become among my very few close friends.

She apologised profusely for her company's stuff up and offered to take me around to visit various places in the area. The difficulty was that in the past four months, real estate prices had almost doubled, and in some cases, trebled their original price. She told me straight out that it was going to be difficult to find something within the price range that I was asking, but that she would try her best for me anyway.

She drove me to Clairview via Koumala, where she had been asked to reappraise a house that was on the market. We had already seen a few houses in the area, and I was quite disheartened. Why had spirit led me on what seemed a wild goose chase?

As we arrived in Koumala, I started to get a tingling feeling. I had already told Tracey that I was a psychic that I had been led by spirit to visit Clairview and was very disappointed with the result. She made no comment at the time, but has since told me that she and other workers at the estate agent thought I was a mental case.

As she drove me up the road to the house that she was to inspect, I started to get a very vague and sleepy feeling coming over me. I know this feeling enough to know that it is spirit taking control. When we arrived, Tracey explained she

Chapter XIII

wouldn't be long, and she got out of the car and was greeted by the woman owner. After having been inside for quite some time, Tracey mentioned to the woman, in my hearing, that I was very interested in buying a house and that this one would be ideal. However, the price was far too unrealistic. The woman said she had had the place on the market for two years or more, and said she needed the money urgently and therefore couldn't reduce the price further.

Tracey asked permission from the woman to take me through the house for an inspection, which the woman agreed to. The woman explained that she was not prepared for visitors, even though Tracey had indicated she would be visiting this day, though not intending to inspect the house.

It was then that Tracey told me the building had originally been a church and had been converted into a 2 1/2-bedroom house with a large living and dining area at one end and bedroom at the other about 15 years earlier.

We entered via the dining area, and slowly inspected the house through to the last bedroom. Even with most of the windows open and a sheet of glass missing from every one, there was still a noticeable unpleasant smell throughout.

Halfway up the hallway on the right-hand side was a guinea pig cage. As we passed, I noticed guinea pig droppings mounted high in the centre of the cage, through the wire base, and stuck to the carpet. I assumed this was where the smell was coming from.

As we came to the last bedroom, Tracey entered slowly, suddenly began to gag and then ran at speed to the front door. Having no idea why, I innocently entered the room. The stench was overpowering. The room was filled with the distinct smell of stale blood and urine, mixed with stale cigarette and marijuana smoke. I too made a hasty retreat.

Tracey took a few deep breaths before returning to the woman to explain the price she was asking was overpriced by at least $20,000. She explained that I had the money in cash, so a settlement would be quick, and gave her the price I was willing to pay. The woman said she would think about it.

Negotiations went on for the next few days, with me bartering a better price and she resisting every offer. Finally, Tracey indicated that I was losing interest, and that she would have major difficulty selling the house at the price this woman wanted.

I finally agreed to pay a little more than my original offer, on condition that the stove was replaced, the painting was completed, and the windows were repaired.

On the 23rd of July 2003, six years to the day of my moving from the rented home with Mike and Sharon at Bundaberg port, I packed up my belongings from the house in Hervey Bay, and with Mike's help, moved into the old church at Koumala.

It was some time later that we discovered the original land grant, prior to the formation of the community of Koumala, had been called Rosedale.
There is not, and has never been, a police station at Koumala that I am aware of.

The change of ownership, we psychically received concerning the pub at Rosedale, had just happened at Koumala prior to our arrival.

The details of changes to the caravan park ownership at Rosedale also applied to the changes that occurred at Koumala, as did the details of the high school, general store, and town's expansion.

On the Light Path — Peter Lyons

Eagle

Fly, fly away. Fly, you are free. Fly, fly up high. You are free.

I envy you with wings so huge, effortless, you fly so smooth.
I'd give my life to fly like you.
Soaring high on thermal waves, mountain tops mere earthly slaves.
Eagle, there's so much you can do.

Fly, fly away. Fly, you are free. Fly, fly up high. You are free.

When you touch ground you're earthly bound: No more the aerobatic's crown.
And that's when you become like me.
In the air you are the king, on earth it's man who holds the strings,
But eagle have no fear of me.

So fly, fly away. Fly, you are free. Fly, fly up high. Yes you're free.

So take your leave majestic one, you've not much time; you've not much sun.
Time to spread your wings my friend and leave.
I'm giving what's not mine to give, another chance for you to live.
So go to the place where you were meant to be.

Fly, fly away. Fly, you are free. Fly, fly up high. You are free.

1979

Chapter XIV

In Conclusion

Much has changed since I first started writing this book. I was living in a converted old church at Koumala, about twenty minutes south of Mackay in Queensland and my very good friends Mike and Sharon were living about three kilometres away. I had a 1980 Nissan Urvan bus, converted into a small mobile home, which I would drive to Mackay Friday mornings and do psychic readings at a crystal shop for the day. In the evening I would drive a further two hours to a caravan park on the O'Connell River, about twenty minutes south of Proserpine, where I would stay overnight. The next morning I would drive about an hour to Airlie Beach where I would do psychic readings at a book shop till 3.00 pm.

I would then return to the caravan park in the afternoon where I might get a customer or two, before packing down for another overnight stay. Sunday morning I would drive back down to Mackay where I would do promotional readings at the crystal shop till lunchtime, before returning home to Koumala.

At the end of 2005 Mike and Sharon sold their Koumala home and moved to Elliott Heads, near Bundaberg in Queensland. At about this time we kept getting messages that I too would be moving on. I found this hard to believe, because I was quite happy with where I was living, and the places where I was doing my sessions.

About two or three months after Mike and Sharon moved, I had a financial crisis. The council rates were due and I had no money. It had been my intention to pay the rates in quarterly instalments, but this council didn't allow for such a system, as most other councils did.

Tracy, my very good friend the real estate agent, who had sold me the ex church in the first place, came to my rescue and paid the rates for me. She was and is a very gifted psychic, who had no idea of her talent before meeting me, and she, and her also gifted husband, got a very strong message from their guides that it was right and proper to lend me this money.

I was now, for the first time in my life, in debt and unable to repay. The work had surprisingly and coincidently fallen off almost to the day the rates notice came in. I had no choice, I had to sell the church and move on. I had no idea where or with what the move would occur.

Tracy told me there was a real boom in the real estate market in Mackay and surrounding areas due to the huge mining expansion happening west of the city, and that I should take advantage of it. Spirit seemed to be pushing this option. They certainly weren't sending any cautious messages to the contrary through anyone. I went with Tracy's suggestion.
She put the place on the market at a bit over three times that which I had paid for it, expecting a buyer to bring it down to a fairer price. Within a short time, a young Sydney couple looked over the place and decided to buy at the price stated.

Around the Easter of 2006 a cyclone formed up off the coast of Queensland and started heading towards Mackay. It eventually twisted north and hit Innisfail south of Cairns. It shook quite a few people on the coast from Airlie Beach upwards. So shaken were the couple that they pulled out of the contract and returned to Sydney.

Chapter XIV

In the meantime on my many trips to Airlie Beach, I had come across a converted 1986 Toyota Coaster bus for sale at a camping and caravan shop. Because the contract had been signed for the sale of the house, and the bus was in such good condition and at a reasonable price, I put down a holding deposit.

I must stress that I didn't make any of these actions without first checking with Spirit. After all, and for a long time, I have considered all my possessions as actually being spirit's property. When the sale fell through at Easter I had no choice but to contact the bus owner to tell him I had to cancel the deal, as I had no money. He told me he was willing to hold on till I sold the house, as something kept telling him I was meant to buy it.

My immediate reaction was that either he was psychic, and therefore this was spirit's intervention, or he was selling me a lemon, and saw me as a gullible fool.

All went quiet after the cyclone hit. The weeks passed by with little or no interest taken for my house. A few months later, in a strange twist of circumstances, Tracy, who was taking a client to look at a house further down the coast, called in to my place to meet another person wanting to look at my home. Bryan, the person Tracy had with her, took one look at my home and promptly told the browser that either he commits to buying my house that night or he would.

Tracy signed up Bryan the next morning and the house was marked as under contract. The selling price was just under four times my original buying price. It was around late June or early July when I finally received the money for the house sale. I phoned Leo, the bus owner; about the twentieth phone call I had made to him since first committing to buying the bus. He greeted with a distinctly despondent tone. I told him the money had come through and his tone changed immediately. Later he said he was offered a better price by another person, and had planned to take it if I hadn't come up with the money this time.

I stayed with Tracy and Ian till the September, where I refurbished the bus to my liking, including installing solar voltaic cells, which have almost made me electrically independent. It was then time to hit the road.

I travelled south to Sharon and Mike's new home at Elliott Heads where I stayed till Christmas that year. I then travelled to Hervey Bay to stay with another very close friend David, and his new wife Glenda.

I now live in the mobile home, travelling northern Queensland for winter and southern Queensland for summer. I have enough money left from the sale of the house and after the purchase of the bus to live independently till at least retirement age, and possibly longer.

None of this was my doing. I didn't want to sell the house, move from Koumala, loose my friends, firstly to Elliott Heads and now to Victoria, give up my psychic reading places, or necessarily live in a mobile home.

The fact that it has happened, and in a way that I couldn't have imagined the consequences, is just one more sign to me that my Guides know me and my needs better that I ever could.

What would have happened to me, where would I be, if I had followed the normal human way? I would probably have borrowed money from some lending institution, and in so doing, been forced to go looking for regular paying work, especially with the sub prime crash and the effect it has had on borrowings across the world.

Chapter XIV

This book would no doubt have had to be put on hold, and all psychic work would become secondary to my primary need to make a living.

In view of the chain of events that have lead me here to where I am now, I think it is obvious to a blind man that spirit wanted me to continue my spiritual work as a priority, hence why they intervened to ensure that the work continues.

What of the future? With Mike and Sharon now living in northern Victoria, a good five hours flying time away, Tracy and Ian having to move over the next few months from their current rental property, to where yet is an unknown, my future is a complete unknown. I still have places to stay, with Mike's family at Bundaberg, and Dave and Glenda at Hervey Bay, but only spirit knows which direction they intend to take me next.

On re reading what I had written, prior to sending it to the publisher, I was totally stunned at the continuity, contents and phrasing of this work. It removed any thoughts I had concerning possible, though unintentional, interference to the work on my part. I knew, without even having to ask where the material had come from. Spirit had been working through me even when I had thought I had put them aside. You may recall this was during my time in Gulgong where I had decided not to antagonise my then wife with matters psychic.

So to say this is Spirit's project is an understatement. Though there are parts I found on rereading, especially when dealing with issues of which I am very passionate, I wondered whether I might have unintentionally allowed a little more of me to dominate their input.

Then came the mind blowing 'direct-from-the-Cuckoo's-nest' stuff, assuming my guides don't mind being called Cuckoo's.

These were not just the instances I mentioned where I gained astonishing information on my many walks with them. There were other such instances including the information on aborigines, reincarnation, meditation and most importantly, recollections of stories I had long forgotten. It was these that sealed it for me.

I am now very confidant that what is written is a fair representation of the material they wanted me to passed on, though that is not to say I fully comprehended it all at the time, or even fully understand it and the implications. Yet I know the more I listen to their inspiring voice, as I mull over the writings, the more I'll understand the fullness of their message.

And so now I come to the end of what has been a wonderful journey, not only that which I have shared with you, the reader, but what this information has made of me, and hopefully of you.

For those of you who may find this work heavy to comprehend I suggest you sit quietly with your guides and allow them to mull over it with you. After all your guides have as much knowledge to share with you as my guides have with me.

This returns us to the original theme I stated in the very beginning. This book was never intended to be a primary spiritual blueprint for someone to blindly follow. If it were, then I would be just another new age guru, selling yet another do as I do and not as I say book.

No one knows the particular Spiritual path a person is travelling, only God's Guides and that person have that knowledge, so therefore no one had a right to insist on which particular belief system another person can or should follow, because not everyone who preaches, teaches, or offers a particular belief, is necessarily the right one for us as an individual.

Chapter XIV

Such a person can only offer an alternative belief, guidance or religious point of view. We have a right to challenge all aspects of that which is offered in relation to our own spiritual path and the truth which we seek.

I add this because there will be some who will believe, by its very existence, this work of spirit and myself, encourages a particular stance, or point of view. After all aren't we claiming this work as coming from the highest of highs? Who could dare oppose that? While it is true, when writing on a subject as diversely theoretical as this, it is hard not to sound authoritarian. The main theme throughout this work has been constant: There can be no authority, from a human perspective, other than the person searching, and their guides.

This book is to give the reader a series of options, or platforms, to use for their own research, learning, and questioning. Of course, in so doing, it will unsettle those who prefer to follow the belief of others rather than define a belief for themselves. I hope the book is provocative and causes questions, challenges and unsettles the apathetic belief of those who would be this kind of follower.

And for those motivated into attempting to prove the theories, opinions and statements in this book wrong, or incorrect in any way, it will have achieved another purpose. That person will now look more closely at their own personal beliefs, something unlikely to have happened before, and if necessary, give them cause to shore up their own beliefs against any opposing point of view.

All the tools, knowledge and remedies given to me by my wonderful guidance team, I have put on these pages as an offer of assist you, the reader: The very same tools that I use, and will use, for the rest of my mortal life here on this tiny fragile planet.

On the Light Path — Peter Lyons

Not that this is the end of what I will receive. No doubt they will have much more for me to ponder on those long, and possibly breathless, night walks by the sea. I hope you found it as interesting to read as I did to write and truly hope there is at least one small part of this work you will find helpful, as you, with the wisdom of your guides, journey on your own particular Light Path.

Chapter XIV

Colophon

Title Font: Bitstream Vera Sans Mono
Text Font: Book Antiqua
Formatted in Adobe InDesign
Digitally Printed

Portland, Oregon

Contact One Spirit Press at

onespritpress@gmail.com

www.onespiritpress.com

You may reach the author at

petesyc@gmail.com

www.ingramcontent.com/pod-product-compliance
Lightning Source LLC
Chambersburg PA
CBHW071652160426
43195CB00012B/1440